Christ and Trauma

New Studies in Theology and Trauma

SERIES EDITORS:

Joshua Cockayne
Scott Harrower
Preston McDaniel Hill

AND

Chelle Stearns

PREVIOUSLY PUBLISHED BOOKS IN THE SERIES:

Sarah Travis, *Unspeakable: Preaching and Trauma-Informed Theology*

Joshua Cockayne, Scott Harrower, and Preston Hill,
Dawn of Sunday: The Trinity and Trauma-Safe Churches

Aimee Patterson, *Suffering Well and Suffering With:
Reclaiming Marks of Christian Identity*

Deborah van Deusen Hunsinger, *Spiritual Trauma Care:
Theology and Psychology in Dialogue*

Christ and Trauma

Theology East of Eden

EDITED BY
PRESTON McDANIEL HILL

CASCADE *Books* · Eugene, Oregon

CHRIST AND TRAUMA
Theology East of Eden

New Studies in Theology and Trauma

Cascade Books
An Imprint of Wipf and Stock Publishers
199 W. 8th Ave., Suite 3
Eugene, OR 97401

www.wipfandstock.com

PAPERBACK ISBN: 978-1-6667-0544-7
HARDCOVER ISBN: 978-1-6667-0545-4
EBOOK ISBN: 978-1-6667-0546-1

Cataloguing-in-Publication data:

Names: Hill, Preston McDaniel, editor.

Title: Christ and trauma : theology east of Eden / edited by Preston McDaniel Hill.

Description: Eugene, OR : Cascade Books, 2025 | Series: New Studies in Theology and Trauma | Includes bibliographical references.

Identifiers: ISBN 978-1-6667-0544-7 (paperback) | ISBN 978-1-6667-0545-4 (hardcover) | ISBN 978-1-6667-0546-1 (ebook)

Subjects: LCSH: Suffering—Religious aspects—Christianity. | Psychic trauma—Religious aspects—Christianity. | Psychic trauma—Patients—Pastoral counseling of. | Post-traumatic stress disorder—Religious aspects—Christianity. | Post-traumatic stress disorder—Patients—Religious life. | Spiritual healing. | Psychology, Religious.

Classification: BV4012.2 .C515 2025 (paperback) | BV4012.2 (ebook)

09/18/25

Contents

Contents

Introduction

East of Eden

Preston McDaniel Hill

In the summer of 2019 a group of theologians, philosophers, therapists, and practitioners gathered in St Andrews to discuss trauma. The goal of the "Theology and Trauma Conference" was to bear witness to the reality of trauma in our world and to explore the implications this reality may have upon the task of theology. The conference was marked by an ambition to transcend the narrower concerns of practical care in order to engage a rigorous theological consideration of how trauma as a theoretical framework for understanding the human condition may both challenge and enrich basic affirmations of Christian faith. Notwithstanding this broader scope, vigilant attention was paid to the concrete stories of trauma survivors in our communities to ensure that our theological discussion would remain clinically informed and robustly relevant to real trauma care. As a result, constant reference was made to the cultural moment which motivated many of our discussions. As an invaluable spotlight continues to be shed upon rampant abuse throughout multiple religious denominations it becomes increasingly clear that theologians and philosophers of religion cannot avoid confronting insidious violence and the aftermath of abuse that is tragically manifesting within our own spiritual communities. The ambitions of the conference seemed to strike a cultural nerve.

While the rise of movements such as #metoo and #timesup have raised awareness of overwhelming violence and its aftermath, these movements also pose fundamental challenges to traditional theological assumptions. For example: How are we to understand the theological relationship between justice and forgiveness in the aftermath of trauma? How is our ecclesiology affected by the fact of religious trauma and clergy abuse? How are we to make sense of atonement narratives, Christology, and doctrines of God in the light of traumatic abuse? What are the limits and prospects of legitimate forms of engaging with God in the aftermath of violence? Both as a concrete experience of suffering and as a theoretical framework, the reality of trauma raises the stakes on these theological questions. And these questions raised by trauma extend to central spheres of systematic theology, including anthropology, ecclesiology, Christology, theology proper, and eschatology.

Although "trauma theory" has been employed in philosophical scholarship and biblical studies, one can count on a single hand the few theologians to date who have mined the riches of trauma studies and the stories of trauma survivors as legitimate and important dialogue partners for theology today.[1] Given the growing awareness that traumas like sexual abuse are rampant in churches, it is incumbent upon theologians and philosophers to reflect deeply upon how the stories of survivors and an understanding of the dynamics of trauma may stand to enrich traditional articulations of the nature of God and all things in relation to God. A failure to think theologically in the light of trauma (what I will call "trauma theology" below) threatens not only to undermine the witness of trauma's survivors but also the theological commitments of their spiritual communities.

Below, I will introduce this collection of essays by giving a brief history and description of trauma studies and then providing a working definition of trauma theology. I will then refine the scope of the volume by describing its methodological parameters and intent. I will then give a synopsis of the chapters to lead into the volume's content.

TRAUMA STUDIES

Although trauma is a phenomenon as old as human violence itself, the study of trauma is relatively new. Studying trauma as a unique form of suffering has become a distinct manner of inquiry only in the past one hundred years. Judith Herman recounts the recent history of attention to traumatic suffering in both medical care and political action in her pathbreaking study *Trauma and Recovery*.[2] In a remarkable coalescence of survivor testimony

1. See, for example Beste, *God and the Victim*; Rambo, *Spirit and Trauma*; Jones, *Trauma and Grace*; Hunsinger, *Bearing the Unbearable*.

2. Herman, *Trauma and Recovery*.

and psychological diagnosis, Herman was one of the first authors to open up the enigma of trauma to a wider audience of nonspecialists by describing basic contours of overwhelming suffering. From the investigation of "hysteria" in the early twentieth century and the subsequent insights of Sigmund Freud and Pierre Janet on "traumatic neuroses" and "dissociation" to the medical treatment of combat trauma, domestic violence, childhood sexual abuse, and political captivity, Herman introduced a profound schema for practitioners of various disciplines to begin understanding the complexities of violence in individuals and societies. Her work is now recognized as a standard textbook for understanding trauma.

It was not until 1980 that the American Psychiatric Association canonized traumatic stress under the heading of "Post Traumatic Stress Disorder" (PTSD).[3] This title gathered the disparate diagnoses and terminologies that had accumulated across a spectrum of survivors' experiences, formally pulling together the uncanny commonalities which persons tend to share in the aftermath of violence. At first it was thought that traumatic events lie "outside the range of usual human experience."[4] However, we now know that 70 percent of adults experience a traumatic event at some point in their lives.[5] What makes trauma unusual therefore is not how rare it is but how degenerating are its unbearable effects on so many who have suffered. As Judith Herman states, "Traumatic events are extraordinary, not because they occur rarely, but rather because they overwhelm the ordinary human adaptations to life."[6]

"Trauma studies" was born in the mid-1990s as a multidisciplinary attempt from sympathetic literary theorists and clinicians to grapple with the challenges and promises that trauma presents to interpretation of texts, cultures, and history. What does overwhelming violence and its aftermath mean for human self-understanding? Literary scholar Cathy Caruth was particularly influential in describing trauma as a "missed" or "unclaimed" experience.[7] Drawing from Freud's interpretation of the tale of Tancred and Clorinda, Caruth states that "trauma seems to be much more than a

---

3. American Psychiatric Association, *Diagnostic and Statistical Manual.*

4. *DSM-III* cited in Hunsinger, "Bearing the Unbearable," 11.

5. Benjet et al., "Epidemiology"; van der Kolk et al., *Traumatic Stress,* 135.

6. Herman, *Trauma and Recovery,* 33.

7. Caruth's description exemplifies the claim of "trauma theory" that trauma is distinguishable from general suffering and valuable as a theoretical framework for interpretation due to its "unassimilable" character (Laub and Felman, *Testimony*).

pathology, or the simple illness of a wounded psyche: it is always the story of a wound that cries out, that addresses us in the attempt to tell us of a reality or truth that is not otherwise available."[8]

Caruth describes trauma very simply as a wound that results from an event of such terrifying magnitude that the event was too much to process in the moment. The terror was too great to be assimilated. As a result of surviving what was unbearable the memories of an "unclaimed" terror haunt the self and intrusively plague the mind of the survivor seeking resolution. Because the terror that was initially inflicted becomes embedded in the survivor's present consciousness, Caruth aptly calls trauma a "double wound." The original terror of the past continues to haunt in the present. This description of trauma as a continual haunting resonates deeply with persons and communities who have known a kind of suffering that incessantly prods the individual and collective psyche. Caruth states further that the very repetition of traumatic memory presents an ethical imperative for our contemporary communities to witness to traumatic wounds as survivors releases the "mute cry" of their unspeakable and unbearable testimony. The pressing question is whether space will be created to hear these open wounds.

Clinicians today define trauma as, "an inescapably stressful event that overwhelms one's coping mechanisms."[9] The exponential terror one feels during trauma means that the fears one undergoes do not cease after the event has ended. They return with a vengeance. Long after the threat is gone, the terror continues. The original fear evaporates only to condensate again in the mind and body in everyday living. Recent studies in neuroscience suggest that there is a neurological and somatic basis for the intrusion of traumatic memories. As Bessel van der Kolk consistently puts it, "the body keeps the score."[10] These studies suggest that traumatic memories become embedded in human persons not cognitively and linguistically, but somatically, within the visceral and "preverbal" sensations of the brain-body network.

The effect of this is significant because it means that "trauma is not stored as a narrative with an orderly beginning, middle, and end" but rather as "flashbacks that contain fragments of the experience, isolated images, sounds, and body sensations that initially have no context other than fear

---

8. Caruth, *Unclaimed Experience*, 4.

9. Van der Kolk et al., *Traumatic Stress*, 279.

10. Van der Kolk, *Body Keeps the Score*; for a helpful summary, see van der Kolk, "Body Keeps the Score."

and panic."[11] This means that traumatic memories are more than just the recollection of an unpleasant experience. When a survivor is triggered the original terror is physiologically felt *just as it was when they suffered the first time*. Recent advances in neuroscience show us that, during a trigger, the brain is literally "rekindled as if the trauma were actually occurring."[12] For survivors, the "double wound" is no mere theoretical description: it is a lived horror of repetitive fear.

Theologian Shelly Rambo puts simple and powerful words to the double-structured reality of trauma that distinguishes it from generic "suffering":

> Studies in trauma suggest that trauma has a double structure: the actual occurrence of a violent event(s) and a belated awakening to the event . . . an inability to fully process an event means that it returns. This return distinguishes trauma from suffering. Suffering is what, in time, can be integrated into one's understanding of the world. Trauma is what is not integrated in time; it is the difference between a closed and an open wound. Trauma is an open wound . . . death has not ended; instead it persists.[13]

Clinicians now recognize this repetition of devastating experience as the defining dissociative mechanism that constitutes traumatic rupture.[14] Theologian Serene Jones describes this phenomenon in terms of "recycled violence":

> For trauma survivors it is as if the mind becomes stuck in a playback loop. The mind keeps going over the scene of violence, again and again, often unconsciously, in an attempt to process it, but it is not able to do so. The mind's meaning-making structures have collapsed, so it simply repeats and recycles . . . the information rushes in too fast and furiously to be marked . . . because it simply cannot be processed and stored, [it] simply wanders and consistently replays itself.[15]

The immense magnitude of terror in a traumatic event overwhelms the person such that what was unbearable in the first wounding is necessarily borne out in secondary hauntings. The excess of the original terror remains

11. Van der Kolk, *Body Keeps the Score*, 135.

12. Van der Kolk, *Body Keeps the Score*, 44.

13. Rambo, *Spirit and Trauma*, 7.

14. Dissociation has been formally identified as the primary pathogenic mechanism involved in posttraumatic stress (van der Kolk and Fisler, "Dissociation").

15. Jones, *Trauma and Grace*, 29–30.

throughout one's everyday life. As a result of traumatic memory's persistence within present consciousness, in the words of Freud, the terror is continually felt "as contemporary experience, instead of . . . remembering it as something belonging to the past."[16] Freud memorably stated that "the patient is, one might say, fixated to the trauma. . . . This astonishes us far too little."[17] A contemporary of Freud named Pierre Janet made the stark assertion that inasmuch as the reminiscence, fixation (*idée fixe*), and intrusion of memories spontaneously arrest the traumatized mind, these experiences cannot properly be called "memory" because they remain unintegrated. "Strictly speaking, then, one who retains a fixed idea of a happening cannot be said to have a 'memory' . . . it is only for convenience that we speak of it as a 'traumatic memory.'"[18]

Both in clinical study and theoretical abstraction the reality of trauma complexifies our understanding of human suffering by pointing to the ways in which the effects of violence persist long after the violence has concluded.

TRAUMA THEOLOGY

Contemporary theology has only nascently begun the task of assimilating the deliverances of trauma studies and the stories of trauma survivors into its methodology.[19] A substantial effort toward thinking theologically in the light of trauma is found in the work of Shelly Rambo. In her book, *Spirit and Trauma*, Rambo proposes the concept of "remaining" to account for trauma theologically.[20] By considering "what remains" in the aftermath of violence Rambo proposes that Christian theology can expand its discourse to account not only for experiences of violence but for the persistence of the effects of violence beyond an initial event (this corresponds to the description of trauma as a double wound). The intuition in this proposal is that contemporary articulations of the relationship between God and humanity will be better able to accommodate for the reality of trauma if they can include an understanding of the persistence involved in traumatic harm.

16. Freud, *Beyond the Pleasure Principle*, quoted in van der Kolk, "Posttraumatic Stress Disorder," 12, and see 7–22.

17. Freud, *Beyond the Pleasure Principle*, quoted in Herman, *Trauma and Recovery*, 37.

18. Janet, *Psychological Healing*, quoted in Herman, *Trauma and Recovery*, 37.

19. See the following examples: Beste, *God and the Victim*; Shooter, *Survivors of Abuse*; O'Donnell, *Broken Bodies*; Harrower, *God of All Comfort*.

20. Rambo, *Spirit and Trauma*.

Thinking theologically about this phenomenon of the double wound is not only helpful as a theoretical framework for approaching overwhelming violence (as in "trauma theory"); it also pays respects to the real-world scars which survivors carry. For most survivors, life is no longer the same after trauma. Holocaust scholar Lawrence Langer makes this point well:

> The survivor does not travel a road from the normal to the bizarre back to the normal again . . . but from the normal to the bizarre back to a normalcy so permeated by the bizarre encounter with atrocity that it can never be purified again. The two worlds haunt each other.[21]

The haunting nature of trauma in survivor experience and the structure of trauma as a double wound in theory raises a series of questions for Christian theology. One of the most pertinent questions for faith communities might be whether or not the persistence of suffering involved in trauma runs counter to theological claims tending toward triumphalism or redemptive closure. Does the reality of trauma diminish the reality of redemption; or might a robust understanding of trauma enhance our understanding of redemption? Do theological affirmations stand to be threatened by the reality of traumatic suffering, or enriched by it?

It is the conviction of the essays in this volume that the reality of trauma stands to enrich contemporary discussions of theology and Christology in particular. If the claims of theology upon reality are as true as those who believe them affirm then those claims must be able to account for the totality of catastrophic experiences which humans endure in the real world. For this reason, theology stands to be enriched as a discipline by examining its claims in the light of the reality of trauma. In doing so its assertions will correspond more precisely to God's benevolent disposition revealed in Jesus Christ toward the concrete experiences of overwhelming human suffering found in the real world. Practicing "trauma theology" will thereby yield affirmations which correspond all the more accurately to reality (both divine and human) and are therefore all the more relevant for ecclesial communities today.

Though the term "trauma theology" risks sounding grandiose or novel, it is a helpful semantic marker that captures the conviction that characterizes it.[22] The contributions of this volume cohere around the simple

21. Langer, *Versions of Survival,* 88.

22. This conference and the contributions in it took place prior to the methodological explorations outlined in O'Donnell and Cross, *Feminist Trauma Theologies,* and their

conviction that trauma is a reality which deserves to be witnessed in theological discourse, not myopically as a practical problem to be solved but as a human devastation that exceeds a kind of sanguine optimism which often hinders theology's task more than it helps it. Doing theology in the light of trauma can therefore expand traditional Christian claims to more fully encompass the totality of devastations that occur in human experience. To do "trauma theology" therefore is not to enter an elite or exclusive club specializing in a restrictive methodology: it simply involves the willingness and urgency to examine basic affirmations of Christian faith in the light of overwhelming violence and its aftermath with a curiosity for how the aftermath may illuminate theology's task.

The practice of "trauma theology" will usually (though not exclusively) involve either (1) the employment of the conceptual tools of "trauma theory" (born within trauma studies described briefly above), or (2) the integration of survivor stories as a benchmark against which to test one's theological assertions. These two practices represent trauma theology's basic ambition of assessing theological claims in the light of the reality of trauma. However, either of these practices could be emphasized to a degree that proceeds beyond the scope of trauma theology as intended in this volume.

PARAMETERS: AVOIDING REDUCTIONISM
AND OBSCURANTISM

Though focused on the interplay between theology and trauma, this volume is not primarily an exercise in practical theology or pastoral care. No doubt, the irreducible particularity that trauma demands will require certain forms of concrete address which stories of harm deserve. Witnessing to trauma will always call for public action and political movement.[23] However, rather than merely advocating for best ecclesial practices in light of the unique care trauma survivors require, this volume instead attempts to examine traditional Christian theology through the lens of trauma. As

---

follow-up volume *Bearing Witness*. I regret those insights could not be included in this edited volume but gladly point readers to the excellent work of O'Donnell and Cross and the relevant contributors.

23. This sentiment is shared by leading psychiatric voices in the study of trauma. Judith Herman states, "Without the context of a political movement, it has never been possible to advance the study of psychological trauma." Studying trauma is "an inherently political enterprise because it calls attention to the experience of oppressed people" (*Trauma and Recovery*, 32, 237). See also van der Kolk, *Body Keeps the Score*, 349–58.

Cathy Caruth states, we are seeking "how we can listen to trauma beyond its pathology to the truth that it tells us."[24] What truth does trauma tell with respect to basic theological assertions? With trauma as a prodding lens this book aims to explore how the complexities of an enigmatic form of suffering might inform, reshape, and challenge basic theological affirmations. At one level, this book explores Christian theology through trauma theory.

Although attempting to think through Christian theology with trauma as a lens, this book does not thereby set out to theorize trauma into an abstract hermeneutical lens that is so malleable it can be absolutized into a haphazard literary principle. Recent trauma theorists have noted the dual dangers in the study of trauma of either "reductionism" or "obscurantism."[25] On the one hand, purely clinical approaches to trauma as a pathology can run the risk of operationalizing traumatic stress with tidy definitions and treatments that "reduce" the sheer messiness of suffering into false manageability. On the other hand, the more philosophical approaches to the enigmatic dimensions of trauma are in an opposite danger of "obscuring" the very concept of trauma by theorizing its effects so far above the testimony of actual survivors that it loses all resemblance to real instances of suffering. It is important that the study of trauma remain attentive to the persons who have suffered trauma. As Eric Boynton and Peter Capretto say,

> Wherever the future of trauma studies is headed, these person-centered claims must be taken seriously to ensure its discourse remains closely tied to the concrete and material context of traumatic encounter. . . . Personal suffering can be co-opted by a surreptitiously metaphysical defense of trauma.[26]

For this reason, while this book employs trauma as a lens for theological inquiry it does so with a constant and vigilant eye toward the lived, tangible, embodied testimonies that such theological inquiry seeks to witness.

Trauma theology, as I have sketched within these parameters, is caught between the constraints of practical application and theoretical abstraction. Somewhere between the purely pragmatic and the utterly hypothetical, trauma theology remains open both to trauma survivors and trauma theory but cannot be reduced to either alone, since this reduction would either rob trauma theology of its relevance for real-world survivors or eclipse its fruitfulness as a conceptual tool.

24. Caruth, *Trauma*, vii–viii.
25. Boynton and Capretto, "Introduction."
26. Boynton and Capretto, "Introduction," 3.

INTENT: TESTIMONY AND WITNESS

Given the above parameters, the intent of this trauma theology volume can best be seen as an extrapolation of Shelly Rambo's proposition that theology thrives in relation to extreme suffering when its posture is one of *witness*. Drawing from trauma theorists and Holocaust literature, Rambo states that

> surviving is not a state in which one gets beyond death; instead, death remains. . . . Persons who experience trauma live in the suspended middle territory, between death and life. . . . The possibility of trauma healing lies in the capacity to witness to this complex relationship between death and life, to the persistence of the storm even after the literal storm has ended. . . . How can theologians witness to the reality that the "after the storm is 'always here?'"[27]

How can theologians witness the reality of trauma and allow the testimony of survivors to constructively inform their discipline? Testimony and witness are concepts germane to the study of both trauma and theology. Testifying to an experience and bearing witness to it are both elements of basic human rhythms that bestow meaning to life in community. Testimony and witness also operate profoundly as a balm in the context of severe suffering. To be able to tell one's story and to have one's story faithfully heard is a dynamic at the very heart of valuing the dignity of personhood both in its flourishing and in its brokenness. Testimony and witness are also the bedrock of Christian self-understanding and ecclesial succession. As faith in Jesus Christ has been handed down from generation to generation it has consistently taken to codified forms of testament, witness, and remembrance in which these holy testimonies do not merely report bygone experiences but themselves repeatedly enact an encounter with the divine presence to which they bear witness. Testimony and witness constitute an interpersonal dynamic that occurs at the deepest levels of both divine and human relations.

What would it mean then for Christian theology to bear witness to categorically unbearable testimonies of violence? How might the most basic categories of theological discourse stand to be enriched by being intentionally cast in the light violence and its aftermath? In addition to bearing witness to the suffering that remains, how might Christian theology also faithfully testify afresh to the promise of healing in an east of Eden world?

---

27. Rambo, *Spirit and Trauma*, 25–26.

CHAPTER SYNOPSIS

This book attempts to ask basic theological questions in the light of the reality of trauma. As many contributions to the volume reveal, reference to the crucifixion narrative and the person of Christ are both natural (though not exclusive) starting points within Christian theology for speaking to the depths of traumatic suffering and its aftermath. Regardless of the specific *loci* that are explored, each contribution seeks to engage trauma as a substantial reality relevant for the analysis and articulation of basic theological questions.

Chapters 1–3 open the book by viewing Jesus as a trauma survivor. The first chapter, coauthored by Jacob and Rachael Denhollander, discusses the significant issue of abuse within evangelical churches, noting the challenge of addressing such abuse due to decentralized structures and inadequate theological schemas. It critiques the concept of Penal Substitutionary Atonement (PSA), often viewed as abusive, and argues that a proper Trinitarian understanding refutes this perception. The chapter emphasizes the necessity of affirming justice and the victim's experience, contending that true justice and forgiveness, as exemplified by the cross, must coexist in addressing abuse effectively and supporting victims within Christian communities. Continuing the theme of the cross as divine justice for victims, chapter 2 by David Tombs proposes Jesus as a victim of sexual abuse, arguing that crucifixion was a form of state terror that included sexual humiliation. It discusses the theological and pastoral significance of recognizing Jesus' experience of sexual abuse, suggesting it can provide solace to contemporary survivors and challenge stigma within the church. The chapter also addresses the importance of a Trinitarian understanding of Jesus' suffering and the potential for contextual Bible studies to foster deeper engagement with these issues. Chapter 3 by Preston McDaniel Hill further explores the psychology of Jesus during the crucifixion. Drawing on the author's personal experiences as a survivor of childhood sexual abuse, the chapter integrates theology and trauma recovery to explore Jesus' experience on the cross as a form of traumatic spirituality. It discusses the clinical understanding of PTSD, highlighting how trauma disrupts relationships with others and with God. Using Calvin's theology, the chapter suggests that Jesus' feelings of abandonment on the cross demonstrate that doubt and despair are valid responses to suffering and that faith can coexist with feelings of alienation from God.

Chapter 4 turns from the phenomenology of Christ to contemporary forms of social crucifixion. In this chapter, Adam Tietje examines the intersections of trauma experienced by women, particularly Black women, and veterans, arguing that their wounds call out to one another. The concept of moral injury is explored as a way to name the agentic aspects of war trauma, resonating with feminist critiques of the sexual trauma of women. The chapter contends that the political theologies of sacrifice underpin both the sexual trauma of women and the war trauma of soldiers, suggesting a deep connection between these forms of trauma and sacrificial agency within social and political structures. The fifth chapter by Samuel Youngs continues the line of war trauma specifically with application to the experience and theology of Jürgen Moltmann. The chapter explores how Moltmann's traumatic experiences during World War II influenced his theological perspectives, particularly his universalism. It argues that Moltmann's rhetoric of universal salvation is deeply colored by his trauma, noting that his personal history of suffering and guilt during the war shaped his theological assertions. The chapter emphasizes the reciprocal relationship between biography and theology, highlighting the significance of trauma-informed analysis in understanding theological developments.

Chapters 6–9 conclude the book with constructive approaches to Christology and atonement in the light of trauma. Chapter 6 by Michelle Panchuk explores how certain atonement theories, specifically PSA and Anselm's satisfaction theory, can contribute to religious trauma. It details the author's personal experiences of abuse and the problematic ways these theories can justify and perpetuate abuse. Panchuk argues that these doctrines often paint a picture of a wrathful God who relishes suffering, which can harm victims' spiritual and emotional well-being. The chapter highlights the need to rethink these theological concepts to prevent further harm. Chapter 7 by Roger P. Abbott investigates the complex relationship between forgiveness and trauma within a Christian context. It discusses the theological, psychological, and pastoral dimensions of forgiveness, emphasizing that while forgiveness is central to Christian doctrine, it often poses significant challenges for trauma survivors. The chapter proposes a model combining forgiveness and lament, following Jesus' example on the cross, to help believers navigate the struggle of forgiving traumatic offenses while maintaining their faith and relationship with God. Turning to a Catholic perspective, chapter 8 by Emilie Grosvenor examines the life of Mary through the lens of trauma and recovery, emphasizing the intertwined experiences of joy and sorrow. It critiques the traditional separation of joyful and sorrowful mysteries, arguing that this division fails to capture the complex emotions women often experience. The chapter presents seven trauma-informed mysteries reflecting on Mary's life, suggesting that her experiences offer valuable insights for understanding trauma, recovery, and discipleship in a contemporary context. Finally, Chelle Stearns offers a succinct and clear Christology of trauma in chapter 9. Stearns shares her journey of addressing theological questions about the resurrection's relevance for survivors of trauma, emphasizing the importance of the body in theological inquiry. By examining the embodied experiences of Jesus, the chapter argues for a theology that acknowledges and addresses trauma, offering hope and healing through a deeper engagement with the physical and emotional realities of Christ's humanity.

Each chapter represents an attempt to examine Christian theology in the light of trauma theory and trauma survivors. The contributions of this volume cohere around a conviction that the ubiquity and horror of trauma in our world calls for a decisive theological articulation of the divine-human relationship in the aftermath of overwhelming violence. This complex task requires a sympathetic posture toward the stories of survivors and conceptual rigor to wrestle with basic accounts of how God and humanity relate in the light of unbearable suffering. Refusing to shy away from these difficult questions will yield theological responses to the reality of trauma that are not only challenging but also profoundly rewarding for our ecclesial communities today.[28]

BIBLIOGRAPHY

American Psychiatric Association. *Diagnostic and Statistical Manual of Mental Disorders.* 3rd ed. Washington, DC: The American Psychiatric Association, 1980.

Benjet C., et al. "The Epidemiology of Traumatic Event Exposure Worldwide: Results from the World Mental Health Consortium." *Psychological Medicine* 46:2 (2016) 327–43.

Beste, Jennifer Erin. *God and the Victim: Traumatic Intrusions on Grace and Freedom.* New York: Oxford University Press, 2007.

Boynton, Eric, and Peter Capretto. "Introduction." In *Trauma and Transcendence: Suffering and the Limits of Theory,* edited by Eric Boynton and Peter Capretto, 1–12. New York: Fordham University Press, 2018.

Caruth, Cathy. *Unclaimed Experience: Trauma, Narrative, and History.* Baltimore: Johns Hopkins University Press, 1996.

———, ed. *Trauma: Explorations in Memory.* Baltimore: Johns Hopkins University Press, 1995.

28. This work could not have been complete without the generous support of a grant from the John Templeton Foundation (ID 62952). I give special thanks to the foundation for their ongoing support of my research program.

Harrower, Scott. *God of All Comfort: A Trinitarian Response to the Horrors of This World.* Bellingham, WA: Lexham, 2019.

Herman, Judith. *Trauma and Recovery: The Aftermath of Violence — From Domestic Abuse to Political Terror.* New York: Basic, 1992.

Hunsinger, Deborah van Deusen. "Bearing the Unbearable: Trauma, Gospel, and Pastoral Care." *Theology Today* 68 (2011) 8–25.

———. *Bearing the Unbearable: Trauma, Gospel, and Pastoral Care.* Grand Rapids: Eerdmans, 2015.

Jones, Serene. *Trauma and Grace: Theology in a Ruptured World.* Louisville: Westminster John Knox Press, 2009.

Langer, Lawrence. *Versions of Survival: The Holocaust and the Human Spirit.* Albany: State University of New York Press, 1982.

Laub, Dori, and Shoshana Felman. *Testimony: Crises in Witnessing in Literature, Psychoanalysis, and History.* New York: Routledge, 1991.

O'Donnell, Karen. *Broken Bodies: The Eucharist, Mary, and the Body in Trauma Theology.* London: SCM Research, 2019.

O'Donnell, Karen, and Katie Cross, eds. *Bearing Witness: Intersectional Perspectives on Trauma Theology.* London: SCM Press, 2022.

———. *Feminist Trauma Theologies: Body, Scripture, and Church in Critical Perspective.* London: SCM Press, 2020.

Rambo, Shelly. *Spirit and Trauma: A Theology of Remaining.* Louisville: Westminster John Knox Press, 2010.

Shooter, Susan. *How Survivors of Abuse Relate to God: The Authentic Spirituality of the Annihilated Soul.* New York: Routledge, 2016.

van der Kolk, Bessel. "The Body Keeps the Score: Memory and the Evolving Psychobiology of Posttraumatic Stress." *Harvard Review of Psychiatry* 1:5 (1994) 253–65.

———. *The Body Keeps the Score: Mind, Brain and Body in the Transformation of Trauma.* New York: Penguin, 2014.

———. "Posttraumatic Stress Disorder and the Nature of Trauma." *Dialogues in Clinical Neuroscience* 2:1 (2000) 7–22.

van der Kolk, Bessel, and Rita Fisler. "Dissociation and the Fragmentary Nature of Traumatic Memories: Overview and Exploratory Study." *Journal of Traumatic Stress* 8:4 (1995) 505–25.

van der Kolk, Bessel, et al., eds. *Traumatic Stress: The Effects of Overwhelming Experience on Mind, Body, and Society.* New York: Guilford, 2007.

Justice

The Foundation of a Christian Approach to Abuse

Jacob and Rachael Denhollander

While the numerous cover-ups of child sexual abuse in the Roman Catholic Church are notorious and well publicized, evangelical churches are beginning to come to terms with the fact that they, too, have a #MeToo problem. While the decentralized nature of evangelical churches and denominations makes it harder to precisely quantify how widespread sexual and domestic abuse is within evangelical communities, there is growing data and increased awareness within churches that there is a serious problem. In his 2018 dissertation, Wade Mullen documents 179 cases of sexual abuse by pastors in the United States from 2016–2017.[1] Stories of sexual abuse in Christian communities are all too often accompanied by equally distressing tales of how those communities themselves sided with the abuser, protecting them, returning them to positions of leadership and respect quickly and quietly, shielding them from consequences and traumatizing their victims in the process. This sometimes results from good old-fashioned cronyism and outright corruption—however, in many cases, abuse within the church is mishandled as a result of poor theology and misinformation about the dynamics of abuse. A poorly developed understanding of forgiveness can lead to victims being shamed for being "bitter" or "vindictive"—or pressured into premature forgiveness as a key to their healing. In this chapter we intend to explore how a doctrine that has historically been central to evangelical theology—namely, Penal Substitutionary Atonement (PSA)—points to an understanding of God and his justice

---

1. Mullen, "Impression Management Strategies," 183–224.

that provides both comfort and vindication for victims of abuse and serves as an overarching guiding principle for Christian communities as they seek to grapple with acting righteously in the face of abuse. Accordingly, this paper is arranged into two sections. First, we will examine the claim that PSA is itself a picture of abuse and demonstrate that, properly understood and articulated, PSA is instead a repudiation of the sinful power dynamics that enable abuse and an affirmation of the victim's longing for justice. In the second section, we will examine four ways in which this understanding of justice informs the ways in which Christian communities understand abuse and how they treat victims of sexual abuse.

PENAL SUBSTITUTIONARY ATONEMENT: ABUSE OR CONTRA ABUSE?

The idea that Jesus Christ offered himself as a substitute to suffer the penal consequences of sin in place of sinners has come under sustained theological criticism as being the product of unhealthy and abusive patriarchal perspectives on women and minorities. In the late 1980s, Rita Nakashima Brock labeled any model of atonement in which Jesus is subjected to punishment to satisfy God as "cosmic child abuse"[2]—an evocative description that has embedded itself into contemporary discussions about the atonement. Elizabeth Johnson claims that an understanding of Jesus as being punished on behalf of sinners is "virtually inseparable from the underlying image of God as an angry, bloodthirsty, sadistic father, reflecting the very worst kind of male behavior."[3] Delores Williams writes that to glorify the idea of Jesus as the helpless surrogate for sinners on the cross is to "glorify suffering" and unacceptably render the exploitation of black women as "sacred."[4] This critique of PSA has been accepted by many theologians as necessitating a careful reformulation—if not outright rejection—of penal, substitutionary views of atonement.[5] Clearly, any attempts to ground a Christian response to abuse in the justice of God as seen at the cross must at a bare minimum avoid grounding that in an abusive paradigm. Is PSA such a paradigm?

The answer to that question is, "It depends." What separates an abusive view of substitutionary atonement from a biblical view of substitutionary

2. Brock, *Journeys by Heart*, 56; Brock, "Little Child," 52.

3. Johnson, "Redeeming the Name," 124.

4. Williams, *Sisters in the Wilderness*, 148.

5. Crisp and Sanders, *Locating Atonement*, 13–14.

atonement is the status of the Son. In an abusive paradigm the Father acts against or on the Son, to bring about an end that accomplishes the Father's will for Father's own distinct purposes. The need for justice is seen as something that resides in the Father, a need that is satisfied by the death of another. In this scenario, the Son is an innocent third party inserted between the Father and humanity, upon whom the Father may pour out his anger and so be reconciled to humankind.[6] The problem with such a portrayal is that it considers PSA in isolation from orthodox Trinitarian theology that stresses the complete equality and unity of the Godhead, in which no one member dominates or controls the others, and in which the actions of each member is inseparably connected to the others. As Margo Houts observes, "We can expect abusive imagery to run rampant when the controls which Trinitarian doctrine places on atonement imagery are removed."[7] This is not to say that this version of PSA exists only in the imagination of feminist theologians—we have personally heard sermons in evangelical churches that dramatically describe the atonement in precisely these subordinationist terms. An evangelistic billboard advertising a church on the interstate near where we live portrays a bleeding man on a cross accompanied by the text, "He was placed into a human body by his Father to be killed in our place."

However, when the "Trinitarian controls" are in place, PSA goes from a picture of abuse to its precise opposite: God setting aside his own divine prerogatives to bring about justice. PSA looks like child abuse if the Son is a passive object of his Father's intention—specifically, the Father's intention that the Son should suffer and die on the cross as the substitute for sins. However, this simply cannot be the case if—as the church has long taught—Father, Son, and Spirit share a single divine nature and, therefore,

6. This view of penal substitution as setting the Father against Son is not unique to feminist theologians, and appears in many different nuanced versions. It is also a very popular argument among Anabaptist-influenced theologians committed to nonviolent theories of atonement. For instance, Vee Chandler writes that "a division in the Godhead is just what the penal-substitution theory creates causing it to stand in direct and open contradiction to a fundamental understanding of the Christian faith, that Christ is one with God, one in character, purpose, and disposition toward humankind. The theory places a gulf between God and Christ, representing God as a judge who insists on punishment, and Christ as the volunteer who endures God's wrath." Chandler, *Victorious Substitution*, 54. The accusation is clear: penal substitution teaches us to think of God the Father acting against God the Son for the benefit of the Father. Thus, both feminist and nonviolence theologians reject penal substitutionary atonement, the latter because they see PSA as violating the unity of the Trinity, the former because they see it as consistent with a patriarchal "Trinity."

7. Houts, "Atonement and Abuse," 30.

the same will. The incarnate Son of God dies on the cross not because he was coerced into it by his Father, but because that was the way God chose to forgive sinners and uphold justice. This was not a decision imposed by the Father on the Son, but a decision of the Triune God to accomplish salvation in this way. There is no innocent third party inserted or coerced into assuming the guilt of another. The atonement represents God's own action to bring salvation to his people.

A further "Trinitarian control" deriving from the unity of God's will is the fact that, unlike human persons, the three divine persons do not act separately but are each involved in whatever God does.[8] As Adonis Vidu summarizes, "The actions of the Father, Son, and Spirit must be mutually involved in each other, such that the common action of the Trinity cannot be broken into simpler constituent actions."[9] Any articulation of PSA that is explicitly based upon such an understanding of the inseparability of the divine operations cannot resemble child abuse, for this requires an understanding of the Father and Son acting separately, one against one the other—an impossibility according to this doctrine. Rather, at the cross, the Father, Son, and Spirit work to do *the same* work.

Finally, and most importantly for the purposes of this paper, a proper Trinitarian understanding also puts the wrath of God into context, revealing it to be of a completely different nature from the anger of an abuser. If all three persons of the Godhead share one divine nature, it is impossible for one of the members of the Trinity to possess an attribute that is not also possessed by the other persons. If the wrath of God is grounded in his righteous and loving nature—the response of a good and holy being to all that is wrong and evil in the world—then it is wrong to think of the Son

8. Gregory of Nyssa wrote that when men work together to accomplish a common goal their actions are still properly called "many," because they are distinguished by the differing character of the individual actors. It is not so within the divine nature, however: "But in the case of the Divine nature we do not similarly learn that the Father does anything by himself in which the Son does not work conjointly, or again that the Son has any special operation apart from the Holy Spirit; but every operation which extends from God to the Creation, and is named according to our variable conceptions of it, has its origin from the Father, and proceeds through the Son, and is perfected in the Holy Spirit. For this reason the name derived from the operation is not divided with regard to the number of those who fulfil it, because the action of each concerning anything is not separate and peculiar, but whatever comes to pass, in reference either to the acts of His providence for us, or to the government and constitution of the universe, comes to pass by the action of the Three, yet what does come to pass is not three things." Gregory of Nyssa, "On 'Not Three Gods,'" 334.

9. Vidu, "Place of the Cross," 24.

as satisfying the wrath of the Father. Indeed, the Bible itself speaks of the "wrath of God" rather than the "wrath of the Father."[10] At the cross, then, it is not the wrath of the *Father* that is satisfied by the Son, but rather, it is the justice of *God* which is satisfied. The atonement does not represent the Father giving vent to deeply personal emotion; rather, the atonement is the Triune God's fulfillment of his commitment to upholding righteousness and punishing sin while simultaneously upholding his love for humans.

It is precisely at this point that the difference between the motivation of an abusive father and the motivation of God in the atonement can be seen. Abuse often happens because of the cool, calm, and calculated coercion of the abuser, who uses circumstances and the disparity of power to illegitimately satisfy his or her personal desires. As has already been discussed, the atonement is not an instance of the Father coercing or compelling the Son to suffer violence for his own personal purposes, because the Father does not have distinct purposes apart from or over against his Son, nor do the persons of the Trinity act apart from or against one another. However, abuse can also occur when an abuser goes into an "uncontrollable" rage (or is "overcome" with sexual desire) and "takes it out" on their victim—and it seems to be this idea of abuse that critics have in mind when they speak of "cosmic child abuse." A Trinitarian atonement cannot be a picture of a Father having so much pent up frustration and anger that he was bound to take it out on someone, and the Son lovingly inserting himself into the situation so that the blow would fall on him rather than defenseless humanity—for any anger toward sin and desire for justice must be equally predicated of each person of the Trinity. It is not, as Darrin Belousek asserts, a "violent intra-Trinitarian transaction: The first person of the Trinity, God the Father, punishes the second person of the Trinity, God the Son, to satisfy the first person."[11] It is not the personal anger and frustration of the Father that is satisfied at the cross, but God's justice. The wrath of God is a declaration of God's hatred for all unrighteousness, not a mandate for the powerful to take out anger against those who frustrate them. Rather than an abusive God demanding that an innocent subordinate sacrifice himself in order to accomplish his will, we have instead a picture of God himself sacrificing himself to accomplish his loving purpose for his people. In this way, PSA is not a picture of abuse of authority and power, but of the

10. See, e.g., Ps 7:11; Ezek 25:17; John 3:36; Rom 1:18, 12:18.

11. Belousek, *Atonement, Justice, and Peace,* 293.

surrender of its prerogatives.[12] In short, the wrath of God vindicates the victim of abuse and stands against the unrighteous, self-centered abuser.

While at first glance the preceding discussion may seem to be a primarily academic point with little bearing on how evangelicals approach abuse, it is in fact highly relevant. As evangelical Christians begin to grapple with the reality of abuse in their own communities, the charge that such abuse is enabled and mirrored in penal substitutionary atonement takes on new urgency. Does addressing abuse also entail a rejection of a doctrine considered foundational by many evangelicals? The reality is that if conservative evangelicals perceive addressing abuse as tied to accepting what they perceive as "liberal" or "feminist" theology, efforts to confront these issues in evangelical communities will flounder. Of course, holding on to PSA ought not be a pragmatic move to retain evangelical "bona fides"—being convinced from Scripture that the atonement has penal, substitutionary dimensions is enough to warrant its defense. However, it is our contention that the theological resources needed for confronting abusive paradigms are present in evangelical theology, obscured though they may be under layers of bad application and the conceptual detritus of syncretistic cultural-religious systems. As Donald MacLeod writes, while defending penal substitutionary atonement, we must "at once concede the justice of the feminist protest against the patriarchy."[13] It is not incorrect to identify and root out the dynamics that allow abuse to flourish; rather, it incorrect to identify the cross as an instantiation of these dynamics.

JUSTICE AND ABUSE

Thus, not only do we deny that PSA is necessarily a model of abuse, we instead perceive that a sacrificial model of penal substitutionary atonement allows us to make at least four observations relevant to the issue of justice and abuse:

---

12. Here, we find ourselves sympathetic with Elizabeth Johnson's description of the cross as the "kenosis of patriarchy." Johnson, *She Who Is*, 160–61.

13. MacLeod, *Christ Crucified*, 62.

1. A victim's sense of injustice and desire for vindication is upheld at the cross—injustice and unrighteousness is real, and God hates it.

Research has shown that one of the greatest needs for a survivor of abuse is to have their pain and experience validated—affirmed as real. According to a study of sexual abuse victims by Sarah Ullman, "the only social reactions related to better adjustment by the victims were being believed and listened to by others."[14] A survivor of abuse longs for those around them to affirm that their experience was legitimate, and that it matters. While society and even often the church downplay the evil of abuse, the righteous anger of God validates the cries of the for justice. As Fleming Rutledge writes, "It makes many people queasy nowadays to talk about the wrath of God, but there can be no turning away from this prominent biblical theme. Oppressed peoples around the world have been empowered by the scriptural picture of a God who is angered by injustice and unrighteousness."[15] It is at the cross where we see that sin and evil are no trivial thing.

Survivors of abuse desperately need our response to reflect this aspect of biblical truth. As survivors of abuse are seeking to know if the evil they experienced is seen and believed, desiring to know that it matters, evangelicals can answer with a resounding "Yes!"—pointing to the cross, where God incarnate suffered, and saying, "This is how much it matters."

2. An affirmation of justice is necessary to accurately reflect God's own righteousness.

C. S. Lewis famously wrote, "My argument against God was that the universe seemed so cruel and unjust. But how had I got this idea of *just* and *unjust*? A man does not call a line crooked unless he has some idea of a straight line. What was I comparing this universe with when I called it unjust?"[16] Justice, in its most basic Christian definition, is conformity to what is right, conformity to the "straight line," conformity to the moral measuring stick which is itself measured against the Creator. God's own pursuit of justice reflects his utter holiness and separation from sin.

When our response to victims denies the need for justice, or pits justice against forgiveness as though the two were incompatible or dichotomous,

14. Ullman, "Social Reactions," 524.

15. Rutledge, *Crucifixion*, 129.

16. Lewis, *Mere Christianity*, 38.

we fail to affirm the holiness of God. God himself does not deny the need for justice, but couples his forgiveness with the satisfaction of the requirements of justice. As Lewis aptly put the matter, we know the crooked line because we first know the straight. But the converse of this is that, if one denies the crookedness, they have minimized the value and reality of that which is straight. Christian responses which minimize the evil of abuse have in turn minimized the righteousness and holiness of God.

3. The example of God at the cross inverts power dynamics at play in oppression and abuse.

Out of every crime committed on a victim who survives, sexual assault causes more severe and long-lasting harmful effects than any other crime.[17] Research has additionally found that, compared to survivors of nonsexual assault trauma, sexual abuse victims are:

- three times more likely to suffer from depression;
- six times more likely to suffer from post-traumatic stress disorder;
- thirteen times more likely to abuse alcohol;
- twenty-six times more likely to abuse drugs;
- four times more likely to contemplate suicide.[18]

The devastating impact of abuse, in large part, is due to the fact that abuse upends the concepts necessary to function as a relational person. Abusers frequently use grooming techniques, utilizing gifts, innocent touch, or manifestations of kindness to condition a victim and prepare them for abuse. More often than not, perpetrators are individuals who are perceived as safe and trustworthy, or even believed to be sacrificially caring for the victim. Concepts of trust, safety, security, love, compassion, and care are all twisted by a perpetrator and wielded like weapons to facilitate violation at the deepest level. Every concept we as humans rely on to have healthy relationships with each other becomes distorted and unsafe—redefined to be tools used to facilitate harm. Perhaps most tragically, in many cases a survivor does not even realize how warped his or her perception

17. See, e.g., Kilpatrick et al., "Victim and Crime Factors," 199–214.

18. National Victim Center and Crime Victims Research and Treatment Center, "Rape in America," 7–8.

of these concepts has become. The twisting and redefining of these values has taken place for so long and has so encompassed the survivor's world, they have no framework by which they can properly understand and define these concepts.

In cases of violent abuse, power, strength, and cunning intelligence are utilized to overpower and subdue for the abuser's own pleasure. In fact, the reason most abusers engage in sexual abuse is not simply about sexual release; they enjoy the imbalance in power and control the they are able to demonstrate. It is critical that survivors are able to define, understand, and relearn these foundational concepts. Failure to recognize harmful abuse and manipulation of power can lead to survivors continually reentering abusive relationships, at times becoming abusers themselves, and nearly always being unable to interact relationally with the world around them.

The cross stands in stark opposition to the behavior of an abuser, providing the ultimate example of each of these concepts that abuse destroys. In the incarnation, at the cross, the Son sets aside his divine prerogatives—the strong becomes weak. God himself enters into human brokenness and accomplishes on behalf of humankind what humans neither deserve nor can accomplish by themselves. The one who is owed obedience as creator enters into creation to render that which is due him. At the cross, God acts for others—to overcome evil, uphold justice, free the enslaved, and restore creation. God himself perfectly identifies with the victim because he himself has willingly subjected himself to injustice. The cross is the ultimate repudiation of the idea that power is to be wielded for the benefit and pleasure of those who possess it. In the cross, victims have the framework and foundation for beginning to properly define and understand concepts which were twisted, subverted, and manipulated during their abuse, and begin to heal the damage which was done.

4. Forgiveness does not undermine the demands of justice, but is consistent with them.

Evangelicalism is fraught with examples of pastors and Christian leaders covering up abuse, instructing abuse victims to not pursue criminal charges, asking courts for leniency for a convicted abuser, or refusing to enforce boundaries and restrictions on an abuser, all done under the notion that any other action is necessarily a sign of being unforgiving, bitter, or vengeful. Frequently, victims report that leaders, parents, and even the abusers themselves appeal to forgiveness as a reason why everyone should simply move on. Hand-waving toward forgiveness is sometimes used by Christians to excuse themselves from getting involved in the messes created by abuse. If the victim has forgiven, everyone can just move on and the problem has disappeared. This point is made with brutal clarity by Sister Dianna Ortiz, a nun who was kidnapped and raped in 1989 by Guatemalan forces under the command of Americans:

> I was asked by others, friends as well as strangers, not whether I was receiving any justice from my government but whether I had forgiven my torturers. I wanted the truth. I wanted justice. They wanted me to forgive, so that they could move on. I suppose, once I forgave, all would be well—for them. Christianity, it seemed, was concerned with individual forgiveness, not social justice.

This left her feeling helpless, hopeless, abandoned:

> I lived in a world created by my torturers. They had told me, as so many other tortured persons have been told, "Even if you survive what we have done to you and tell the world, no one will believe you. No one will care." That is the world I lived in: No one cared. No law, no God, no justice, no peace, no hope.[19]

When forgiveness is seen as the opposite of justice, despair ensues. In this way, forgiveness becomes another means of abuse—shutting the victim out, denying the rightness of their cry for justice, and heaping further shame. However, a proper understanding of God's forgiveness recognizes that ignoring evil, minimizing its impact, and granting evildoers impunity is not the same thing as forgiveness. As Miraslov Volf writes, forgiveness is not a substitute for justice:

> Forgiveness is no mere discharge of a victim's angry resentment and no mere assuaging of a perpetrator's remorseful anguish, one that demands no change of the perpetrator and no righting of wrongs. On the contrary: every act of forgiveness enthrones justice; it draws attention to its violation precisely by offering to forego its claims.[20]

We would modify this and say that forgiveness is not the foregoing of the claims of justice, but a recognition that in Christ, through the cross, the ultimate claims of justice have been fulfilled. Forgiveness is made possible

19. Ortiz, "Theology," 346.
20. Volf, *Exclusion and Embrace*, 123.

because the very real debt which did exist, was *paid*. In every possible scenario in Christian theology, the reality of evil and need for justice is upheld. Either divine punishment will be meted out on the individual who has done the wrong, or it is taken up by God upon himself, but even perfect, divine forgiveness rightly seeks and upholds the need for justice.

Nicholas Wolterstorff objects to this, arguing that under such a satisfaction model, "it's not forgiveness that is taking place but vicarious punishment."[21] However, the fact that God takes punishment upon himself, not foisting it onto a third party, entwines vicarious punishment and forgiveness together. A banker cannot be said to have forgiven a loan when a third party pays the loan on behalf of another; however, when the banker himself pays the loan on behalf of another, this is both satisfaction of the debt and forgiveness. As Augustine wondered, "Thou payest debts while owing nothing; and when Thou forgivest debts, losest nothing."[22]

And yet, Biblical justice compels us to see ourselves on both sides of God's justice: we must move to uphold righteousness and see that sin is condemned, crime punished, and victims restored, while at the same time refraining from viewing criminals and abusers as "other" or fundamentally different from ourselves—for evil lies within our hearts as well. Alexander Solzhenitsyn, himself a victim of great injustice at the hand of the Soviets, poignantly reflected this thought when he penned,

> If only it were all so simple! If only there were evil people somewhere insidiously committing evil deeds, and it were necessary only to separate them from the rest of us and destroy them. But the line dividing good and evil cuts through the heart of every human being. And who is willing to destroy a piece of his own heart?[23]

In upholding the justice of God's condemnation of our abuser, we come face to face with the justice of God's condemnation of our own sin. Deanna Thompson notes that "privilege and oppression often go hand-in-hand. Even victims may participate wittingly or unwittingly in the oppression of others."[24] Not only do we harm one another to varying degrees, but "all have sinned and fall short of the glory of God." In claiming God's free offer of forgiveness for ourselves, we recognize that the same offer is held out to every person, even those who have greater sins.

21. Wolterstorff, *Justice in Love*, 192.

22. Augustine, "Confessions," I.IV.4.

23. Solzhenitsyn, *Gulag Archipelago*, 1:168.

24. Thompson, *Crossing the Divide*, 114.

An attitude of justice longs for wrongs to be made right and for wrong-doing to be punished; an attitude of forgiveness longs for the inclusion and restoration even of our enemies—for them to cross over from death to life. These two are compatible with one another; what is excluded is an attitude of hatred, vengeance, and revenge, which longs for the destruction and ex-clusion of those who have harmed us.

How then does this understanding of forgiveness and justice translate to how a victim of abuse pursues human justice, and how does the church walk alongside him or her? Does the fact that God will ultimately bring justice preclude making use of the criminal or civil court system? Does the fact that God offers everyone eternal life mean that a victim should offer their abuser the opportunity to escape criminal or civil penalties? The short answer to this is a resounding, "No!" The character of God as revealed at the cross demonstrates that justice is good and right. And insofar as human justice reflects God's justice, human justice is good. Thus, in broad terms, the commands to show love for enemy and to not repay evil for evil do not impinge on the pursuit of human justice, but rather, regulate *how* and *why* we pursue justice. Human justice is not (or at least ought not to be) an instrument of individual vicarious revenge. Instead, it is a communal declaration of siding with both the victim and God in condemning the evil that was done, punishing the wrongdoer, and defending the rights of the innocent. The decision to punish or not punish a rapist or a child molester does not lie with the victims; instead, it is the duty of police and prosecutors to defend and prosecute. Thus, a victim can have both an attitude of for-giveness—renouncing hatred and bitterness and their claim to vengeance, desiring what is best for their abuser—while simultaneously participating in criminal proceedings.

In the case of abuse, and in particular where children are involved, there is the additional incentive of protecting both current and possible future victims. The nature of abuse is such that those who are abused rarely have anything to offer in response to being believed and advocated for, while those who abuse have much to offer the community. To come along-side the victim in such situations is to self-consciously follow the model of Christ and sacrificially pursue justice because it is right, not because there are immediate pragmatic or material benefits. To minimize or hide abuse out of concern for reputations, money, influence, or mere apathy and a de-sire to not get involved is to utterly repudiate the witness of Christ.

Furthermore, seeking to undermine the validity of human justice is no mercy to the abuser, especially an unrepentant one. The temporal nature of human justice serves as a picture of God's final justice. It presents the abuser an opportunity to come face to face with the reality and severity of his sin. It is a call to the abuser to repent, to side with both God and their victim and condemn the evil they have perpetrated. It is only in this scenario that the possibility of reconstructing a relationship is possible. So long as an abuser denies the evil they have done and the harm they have perpetrated, they have cut themselves off from the possibility of true love and experiencing the joy of forgiveness. Truly repentant abusers who have come to side with God and their victims do not use their repentance as an excuse to escape human justice or make demands of their victims; true repentance involves acknowledging the harm they have done and the rightness of punishment. God has provided himself as a substitute to justly suffer the eternal consequences of our sins; no such substitute exists to take up the temporal punishment. It is the tactic of an abuser to claim repentance in order to escape consequences and attempt to exert control over their victims.

However, the courtroom often fails to bring justice. Under the worst circumstances, courts are even an instrument of perpetrating injustice. And even under the best outcomes, it fails to achieve the restoration of what was damaged or broken. Thus, a Christian understanding of justice both acknowledges the good of societally administered justice and also its inadequacies. While evangelicals ignore the importance of the justice system to their peril, they similarly misplace their trust if they look to it as the final arbiter of how they should judge wickedness. Nor should victims of abuse place their hope and ability to heal in the uncertain determinations of the justice system—rather, their confidence must rest in the perfect justice of God.

CONCLUSION

In this paper, we have established that evangelicals possess the theological truths needed to bring comfort and hope and truth to survivors of abuse, predicated on a proper understanding of justice as seen in the atonement and character of the Triune God.

BIBLIOGRAPHY

Augsburger, David W. *The Freedom of Forgiveness*. Chicago: Moody, 1988.

Augustine. "The Confessions of St. Augustin." In *The Confessions and Letters of Augustin*. Nicene and Post-Nicene Fathers. Series 1, vol. 1. Edited by Philip Schaff. Peabody, MA: Hendrickson, 2004.

Balboni, Jennifer M., and Donna M. Bishop. "Transformative Justice: Survivor Perspectives on Clergy Sexual Abuse Litigation." *Contemporary Justice Review* 13.2 (2010) 133–54.

Bash, Anthony. *Forgiveness and Christian Ethics*. New Studies in Christian Ethics 29. Cambridge: Cambridge University Press, 2007.

Belousek, Darrin W. Snyder. *Atonement, Justice, and Peace: The Message of the Cross and the Mission of the Church*. Grand Rapids: Eerdmans, 2012.

Benatar, May. "A Qualitative Study of the Effect of a History of Childhood Sexual Abuse on Therapists Who Treat Survivors of Sexual Abuse." *Journal of Trauma and Dissociation* 1:3 (2000) 9–28.

Brock, Rita Nakashima. "And a Little Child Will Lead Us." In *Christianity, Patriarchy, and Abuse: A Feminist Critique*, edited by Joanne Carlson Brown and Carol R. Bohn, 42–61. New York: Pilgrim, 1989.

———. *Journeys by Heart: A Christology of Erotic Power*. New York: Crossroad, 1988.

Brock, Rita Nakashima, and Rebecca Ann Parker. *Proverbs of Ashes: Violence, Redemptive Suffering, and the Search for What Saves Us*. Boston: Beacon, 2001.

Brown, Christa. *This Little Light: Beyond a Baptist Preacher Predator and His Gang*. Cedarburg, WI: Foremost Press, 2009.

Brown, Joanne Carlson. "Divine Child Abuse?" *Daughters of Sarah* 18:3 (1992) 22–28.

Brown, Joanne Carlson, and Carole R. Bohn, eds. *Christianity, Patriarchy, and Abuse: A Feminist Critique*. New York: Pilgrim, 1989.

Butner, D. Glenn. *The Son Who Learned Obedience: A Theological Case Against the Eternal Submission of the Son*. Eugene, OR: Pickwick, 2018.

Cantón-Cortés, David, et al. "The Effects of Perpetrator Age and Abuse Disclosure on the Relationship Between Feelings Provoked by Child Sexual Abuse and Posttraumatic Stress." *Anxiety, Stress and Coping* 24:4 (2011) 451–61.

Chandler, Vee. *Victorious Substitution: A Theory of the Atonement*. Newburgh, IN: Trinity Press, 2012.

Cossins, Anne, et al. "Uncertainty and Misconceptions About Child Sexual Abuse: Implications for the Criminal Justice System." *Psychiatry, Psychology and Law* 16:3 (2009) 435–52.

Coutts, Jon. *A Shared Mercy: Karl Barth on Forgiveness and the Church*. New Explorations in Theology. Downers Grove, IL: InterVarsity Academic, 2016.

Crisp, Oliver D., and Fred Sanders, eds. *Locating Atonement: Explorations in Constructive Dogmatics*. Grand Rapids: Zondervan, 2015.

Gavrielides, T. "Clergy Child Sexual Abuse and the Restorative Justice Dialogue." *Journal of Church and State* 55:4 (2013) 617–39.

Green, Lorraine. "An Overwhelming Sense of Injustice? An Exploration of Child Sexual Abuse in Relation to the Concept of Justice." *Critical Social Policy* 26:1 (2006) 74–100.

Gregory of Nyssa. "On 'Not Three Gods.'" In *Gregory of Nyssa: Dogmatic Treatises, Etc.* Nicene and Post-Nicene Fathers. Series 2, vol. 5. Edited by Philip Schaff and Henry Wace. Peabody, MA: Hendrickson, 2004.

Guðmundsdóttir, Arnfríður. "Crucified—So What? Feminist Rereadings of the Cross-Event." In *T&T Clark Companion to Atonement*, edited by Adam J. Johnson, 335–54. Bloomsbury Companions 5. London; New York: T&T Clark, 2017.

Hedges-Goettl, Len, and Daniel G. Bagby. *Sexual Abuse: Pastoral Responses*. Nashville: Abingdon, 2004.

Helm, Herbert W., et al. "The Implications of Conjunctive and Disjunctive Forgiveness for Sexual Abuse." *Pastoral Psychology* 54:1 (2005) 23–34.

Holmgren, Margaret R. *Forgiveness and Retribution: Responding to Wrongdoing*. Cambridge: Cambridge University Press, 2012.

Houts, Margo. "Atonement and Abuse: An Alternate View." *Daughters of Sarah* 18:3 (1992) 29–32.

Jeffery, Steve, et al. *Pierced for Our Transgressions: Rediscovering the Glory of Penal Substitution*. Wheaton, IL: Crossway, 2007.

Johnson, Adam J., ed. *T&T Clark Companion to Atonement*. Bloomsbury Companions 5. London: T&T Clark, 2017.

Johnson, Elizabeth A. "Redeeming the Name of Christ." In *Freeing Theology: The Essentials of Theology in Feminist Perspective*, edited by Catherine Mowry LaCugna, 115–38. New York: Harper Collins, 1993.

———. *She Who Is: The Mystery of God in Feminist Theological Discourse*. New York: Crossroad, 1992.

Jülich, Shirley. "Views of Justice Among Survivors of Historical Child Sexual Abuse: Implications for Restorative Justice in New Zealand." In "Gender, Race, and Restorative Justice." Edited by Kimberly J. Cook et al. Special issue, *Theoretical Criminology* 10:1 (2006) 125–38.

Ketring, Scott, and Leslie Feinauer. "Perpetrator-Victim Relationship: Long-Term Effects of Sexual Abuse for Men and Women." *The American Journal of Family Therapy* 27:2 (1999) 109–20.

Kilpatrick, Dean G., et al. "Victim and Crime Factors Associated with the Development of Crime-Related Post-Traumatic Stress Disorder." *Behavior Therapy* 20:2 (1989) 199–214.

Kraybill, Donald B., et al. *Amish Grace: How Forgiveness Transcended Tragedy*. San Francisco: Jossey-Bass, 2007.

Kroeger, Catherine Clark, and Nancy Nason-Clark. *No Place for Abuse: Biblical and Practical Resources to Counteract Domestic Violence*. 2nd ed. Downers Grove, IL: InterVarsity, 2010.

LaCugna, Catherine Mowry, ed. *Freeing Theology: The Essentials of Theology in Feminist Perspective*. New York: Harper Collins, 1993.

Lamb, Sharon. "Women, Abuse, and Forgiveness: A Special Case." In *Before Forgiving: Cautionary Views of Forgiveness in Psychotherapy*, edited by Sharon Lamb and Jeffrie G. Murphy, 155–71. Oxford: Oxford University Press, 2002.

Lamb, Sharon, and Jeffrie G. Murphy, eds. *Before Forgiving: Cautionary Views of Forgiveness in Psychotherapy*. Oxford: Oxford University Press, 2002.

Lampman, Lisa Barnes, and Michelle D. Shattuck, eds. *God and the Victim: Theological Reflections on Evil, Victimization, Justice, and Forgiveness*. Grand Rapids: Eerdmans, 1999.

Lewis, C. S. *Mere Christianity*. San Francisco: HarperCollins, 2001.

MacLeod, Donald. *Christ Crucified: Understanding the Atonement*. Downers Grove, IL: InterVarsity Academic, 2014.

Maier, Bryan. *Forgiveness and Justice: A Christian Approach*. Grand Rapids: Kregel Ministry, 2017.

Marshall, Christopher D. *Beyond Retribution: A New Testament Vision for Justice, Crime, and Punishment*. Grand Rapids: Eerdmans, 2001.

————. *The Little Book of Biblical Justice: A Fresh Approach to the Bible's Teachings on Justice*. Little Books of Justice & Peacebuilding. Intercourse, PA: Good Books, 2005.

McGee, Robert S., and Donald W. Sapaugh. *The Search for Peace: Release from the Torments of Toxic Unforgiveness*. Ann Arbor: Servant Publications, 1996.

Miller, Debra K. "The Effects of Childhood Physical Abuse or Childhood Sexual Abuse in Battered Women's Coping Mechanisms: Obsessive-Compulsive Tendencies and Severe Depression." *Journal of Family Violence* 21:3 (2006) 185–95.

Mullen, Wade. "Impression Management Strategies Used by Evangelical Organizations in the Wake of an Image-Threatening Event." PhD diss., Capital Seminary and Graduate School, 2018.

Murphy, Jeffrie G., and Jean Hampton. *Forgiveness and Mercy*. Cambridge Studies in Philosophy and Law. Cambridge: Cambridge University Press, 2012.

National Victim Center, and Crime Victims Research and Treatment Center. "Rape in America: A Report to the Nation." April 23, 1992.

Ortiz, Dianna. "Theology, International Law, and Torture: A Survivor's View." *Theology Today* 63:3 (2006) 344–48.

Poling, James N. *The Abuse of Power: A Theological Problem*. Nashville: Abingdon, 1991.

Ransley, Cynthia, and Terri Spy, eds. *Forgiveness and the Healing Process: A Central Therapeutic Concern*. New York: Brunner-Routledge, 2004.

Rawls, John. *Justice as Fairness: A Restatement*. Edited by Erin Kelly. Cambridge: The Belknap Press of Harvard University Press, 2001.

Rutledge, Fleming. *The Crucifixion: Understanding the Death of Jesus Christ*. Grand Rapids: Eerdmans, 2017.

Schmidt, Karen L. *Transforming Abuse: Nonviolent Resistance and Recovery*. Gabriola Island, BC: New Society Publishers, 1995.

Shea, Diane J. "Effects of Sexual Abuse by Catholic Priests on Adults Victimized as Children." *Sexual Addiction and Compulsivity* 15:3 (2008) 250–68.

Solzhenitsyn, Aleksandr I. *The Gulag Archipelago, 1918–1956: An Experiment in Literary Investigation*. Vol. 1. New York: Harper & Row, 1973.

Tchividjian, Basyle, and Shira M. Berkovits. *The Child Safeguarding Policy Guide for Churches and Ministries*. Greensboro, NC: New Growth, 2017.

Thompson, Deanna A. *Crossing the Divide: Luther, Feminism, and the Cross*. Minneapolis: Fortress, 2004.

Tracy, Stephen. "Sexual Abuse and Forgiveness." *Journal of Psychology and Theology* 27:3 (1999) 219–29.

Ullman, Sarah E. "Social Reactions, Coping Strategies, and Self-Blame Attributions in Adjustment to Sexual Assault." *Psychology of Women Quarterly* 20:4 (1996) 505–26.

Vidu, Adonis. "The Place of the Cross Among the Inseparable Operations of the Trinity." In *Locating Atonement: Explorations in Constructive Dogmatics*, edited by Oliver D. Crisp and Fred Sanders, 21–42. Grand Rapids: Zondervan, 2015.

Volf, Miroslav. *Exclusion and Embrace: A Theological Exploration of Identity, Otherness, and Reconciliation*. Nashville: Abingdon, 1996.

————. *Free of Charge: Giving and Forgiving in a Culture Stripped of Grace*. Grand Rapids: Zondervan, 2005. Kindle.

Walzer, Michael. *Spheres of Justice: A Defense of Pluralism and Equality.* New York: Basic, 1983.

Williams, Delores S. *Sisters in the Wilderness: The Challenge of Womanist God-Talk.* Maryknoll, NY: Orbis, 2013.

Wolterstorff, Nicholas. *Justice in Love.* Edited by John Witte Jr. Emory University Studies in Law and Religion. Grand Rapids: Eerdmans, 2011.

Woznicki, Christopher, and Jesse Gentile. "Refocusing the Image: Domestic Violence, Refugees, and the Imago Dei in John Calvin's Pastoral Theology." *McMaster Journal of Theology and Ministry* 19 (2017–2018) 81–111.

Wright, N. T. *Evil and the Justice of God.* Downers Grove, IL: InterVarsity, 2006.

Jesus as a Victim of Sexual Abuse

David Tombs

In July 1998 I presented a paper at the Society of Biblical Literature International Meeting on "Biblical Interpretation in Latin America: Crucifixion, State Terror, and Sexual Abuse."[1] This argued that crucifixion should be seen as a form of first-century state terror, and part of its message of terror was the threat of sexual abuse as a form of punitive humiliation. It concluded that in addition to the sexual abuse that is revealed in the text there might have been further sexual assault in the *praetorium* and this possibility should be considered even though it is unlikely there will ever be sufficient direct evidence to answer this with certainty. To support this claim, the paper looked at reports on torture in Latin America in the 1970s and 1980s to give a better understanding of crucifixion as a form of torture. It highlighted the prevalence of sexual violence in torture practices past and present. Drawing on approaches to contemporary social context pioneered in Latin American liberation theology, it argued that using twentieth-century torture reports can help identify elements of sexual abuse in the text. Recognizing sexual violence in first-century crucifixion in this way should not be seen as "reading sexual abuse into the text"; rather torture reports can provide a reader with a context to recognize what is genuinely in the text, but which had remained unacknowledged for too long. The paper was well received and subsequently published in 1999 as a journal article in *Union Seminary Quarterly Review*.[2]

1. I am grateful to Fernando Segovia and Jeremy Punt (the SBL Biblical Hermeneutics session chairs) for their gracious response to the change in direction. The original proposal had been for "Biblical Interpretation in Latin America: From 1968 to the Present."

2. Tombs, "Crucifixion."

In 2001, I moved from London to live and work in Belfast for the Irish School of Ecumenics, Trinity College Dublin (2001–14), teaching a new postgraduate program on reconciliation in the aftermath of conflict. My experience in Northern Ireland deepened my understanding of different forms of violence and encouraged me to learn more about the challenges of conflict transformation in various contexts and conflicts. This deepened my appreciation of how religion could contribute towards violence in some contexts but could also act as a powerful agent for peace and reconciliation in other contexts. Alongside this learning, the clerical abuse crisis in the Irish Catholic church also demonstrated the ongoing relevance of Jesus' experience as a victim of sexual abuse to current public issues, even though Jesus' own experience of secular violence was not an issue that the churches wished to take up. In addition, the time in Ireland also provided opportunities to learn more from scholars in South Africa, especially those working on biblical and theological issues related to violence and reconciliation.

Since 2015 I have been at the University of Otago, Aotearoa New Zealand, working on theology and public issues.[3] This position has provided opportunities to revisit the challenging questions around crucifixion and develop new collaborations to explore these further. In this I have been fortunate to work with various colleagues in South Africa, especially biblical scholar Gerald West and sociologist Elisabet le Roux.[4]

The first section of this chapter provides a brief overview of why Jesus' experience should be seen as a victim of sexual abuse in the stripping in the *praetorium* and enforced nudity on the cross. It summarizes the main argument from my article "Crucifixion, State Terror, and Sexual Abuse" and discusses how a collaboration with Gerald West and Ujamaa colleagues in 2019 developed insights from this article into a contextual Bible study to explore Jesus' experience.

The second section turns to why these issues are important pastorally and theologically, and why recognizing Jesus as a victim of sexual abuse may be helpful for both survivors and the wider church. To illustrate this, it discusses the suggestion made by Hilary Scarsella, a US scholar and activist, who identifies the combination of both certainty and uncertainty in relation to Jesus' experience in the *praetorium*. Scarsella argues that the

3. I took up my current post as Director of the Centre for Theology and Public Issues at the University of Otago (Aotearoa New Zealand) in January 2015.

4. I have also learned much from Louise du Toit and her work on sexual and gender-based violence; see Du Toit, *Philosophical Investigation*; Du Toit and Le Roux, "Feminist Reflection."

uncertainty should be seen as having value, since it is relevant to contested accounts around many contemporary sexual assaults. Then, to understand why some critics are reluctant to consider this reading of Jesus' experience, I turn to insights offered by Le Roux on the destructive role of stigma in responses to survivors of sexual violence. Le Roux argues that stigmatizing responses to survivors are significant in many of the negative responses to seeing Jesus as a survivor of sexual abuse.[5] Finally, to illustrate some of these stigma dynamics, I look at Michelle Bolsonaro's response to a Palm Sunday 2022 article in the Brazilian newspaper *Folha de Sao Paulo* in which I discussed this research with journalist Marvio dos Anjos.[6] Bolsonaro's view that seeing Jesus as a victim of sexual abuse is an example of 'Christophobia' illustrates Le Roux's argument on stigma towards survivors. It shows how much work still needs to be done to improve responses to sexual violence and abuse within the church.

JESUS' EXPERIENCE OF AND SEXUAL ABUSE

The crucifixion of Jesus is one of the most often told stories in history. It is so well known, and the details are so firmly established, that it is easy to read the biblical texts without noticing some disturbing details which deserve notice. There are indications of sexual abuse which are explicitly referenced but rarely given any attention or properly acknowledged. The mockery in the *praetorium* (governor's headquarters) may initially appear as a side issue to the main action that will follow in the crucifixion. When it is read in this way, for most Christians there is little need to dwell on the mockery. It is treated like a mere precursor to the important events to follow after Jesus is led away. The mocking itself is rarely seen as having much significance. The warning signs of sexual abuse that sit just beneath the surface of the text are not noticed. It takes a careful reading and a concern for disturbing details to notice these. However, a more careful reading makes a compelling case for recognizing this as a dense narrative of sexual abuse. As noted when the argument on Jesus as a victim of sexual abuse was first presented:

> Based on what the Gospel texts themselves indicate, the sexual element in the abuse is unavoidable. An adult man was stripped

5. Le Roux prefers the term "survivor" of sexual abuse, whereas I usually refer to Jesus as a "victim" of sexual abuse.

6. Dos Anjos, "Corpo, cruz e abuso."

naked for flogging, then dressed in an insulting way to be mocked, struck and spat at by a multitude of soldiers before being stripped again (at least in Mark 15:20 and Matt. 27:31) and reclothed for his journey through the city—already too weak to carry his own cross—only to be stripped again (a third time) and displayed to die whilst naked to a mocking crowd. When the textual presentation is stated like this, the sexual element of the abuse becomes clear; the assertion is controversial only in so far as it seems startling in view of usual presentations. The sexual element to the torture is downplayed in artistic representations of the crucifixion that show Jesus wearing a loincloth. These images distance us from the biblical text, perhaps because the sexual element has been too disturbing to confront.[7]

In 2018, the Centre for Theology and Public Issues at the University of Otago were privileged to host Gerald West and Beverley Haddad from the University of KwaZulu-Natal (South Africa).[8] West is well known for his contextual Bible study work at the Ujamaa Centre at the University KwaZulu-Natal.[9] The Ujamaa approach to contextual Bible study involves open-ended questions that guide participants through a "slow reading" of a text that includes attention to details that are otherwise easily missed. It allows participants to bring their own context, offer their own thoughts, hear from each other, and explore the issues through conversation, dialogue, and group reflection.

West's time at Otago provided the opportunity to start working collaboratively on a crucifixion Bible study.[10] In March 2018, I presented a Lent lecture at St. Paul's Anglican Cathedral, Wellington, on reading of Mark 15:16–24 with attention to the stripping as a form of sexual abuse.[11]

---

7. Tombs, "Crucifixion," 104.

8. West was invited as the De Carle Distinguished Lecturer for a lecture series on the Bible as a site of struggle (February-April 2022), and Haddad as Visiting Research Fellow at the Centre for Theology and Public Issues.

9. The Ujamaa Centre, previously known as the Institute for the Study of the Bible, was founded in 1989 and they have been pioneers on contextual Bible studies in South Africa; see especially, West, *Contextual Bible Study*. Their work has included their especially well-known study on Tamar, which they started in 1996. See West and Phumzile Zondi-Mabizela, "Bible Story."

10. West was one of the first biblical scholars to draw on the article in his own work; see West, "Indigenous Exegesis."

11. The lecture incorporated some work I had done more recently with Jayme R. Reaves; see Reaves and Tombs, "#MeToo Jesus."

West was present for the lecture, and the Ujamaa workshop on Tamar at the Cathedral the next day. He saw the potential in the stripping of Jesus for the work that the Ujamaa Centre were already doing on masculinity and on male sexual violence against men.[12]

This became the basis for our collaboration. In 2019 I made two trips to the Ujamaa Centre at Pietermaritzburg to work with West and other colleagues.[13] In the first visit, in June, I presented a public lecture titled "The Stripping of Jesus: Sexual Violence: Hidden in Plain Sight."[14] The next day West, Charlene van der Walt, and Sithembiso Zwane led an Ujamaa workshop for activists, students, and staff on "Constructing Contextual Bible Study Resources to Engage with Sexual Violence against Men." The workshop invited participants to explore how the passages on the stripping in the *praetorium* in Mark 15:16–20 and Matt 27:26–31 might be developed into a contextual Bible study. The workshop participants worked in four small groups to create questions that would generate discussions to address key issues in the text.

Three groups at the workshop choose to focus on Matthew and the other group chose Mark. Turning attention to the strippings in Matt 27:26–31 helped to bring out the disturbing details even more clearly. There are two explicit strippings recorded, in v. 28 and v. 31. There is a third stripping implied in v. 26, since it was standard practice to scourge a victim while naked. There is a further stripping referenced in v. 31, when Jesus is led away to be crucified because it was Roman custom to strip a prisoner for crucifixion, and the shame and humiliation of the exposure added to extreme pain and suffering of the cross. These details usually remain hidden in plain sight but a careful reading shows that they are part of the text and not projected onto the text from the outside.

> [26] So he released Barabbas for them; and after *flogging* Jesus, he handed him over to be crucified. [27] Then the soldiers of the governor took Jesus into the governor's headquarters, and *they gathered the whole cohort around him.* [28] They *stripped* him and

12. Ujamaa Centre, "Redemptive Masculinity."

13. In addition to West, I am grateful to Beverley Haddad, Charlene van der Walt, Sithembiso Zwane, and Maarman Samuel Tshehla, and to all those connected with the Ujamaa Centre. The project was funded through a University of Otago Research Grant. In describing this collaboration, I draw especially on West, "Jesus, Joseph, and Tamar Stripped," 110–128, and West, "Contextual Bible Study."

14. Some of the material presented was later published as Tombs, "Hidden in Plain Sight."

put a scarlet robe on him, [29] and after twisting some thorns into a crown, they put it on his head. They put a reed in his right hand and knelt before him and mocked him, saying, "Hail, King of the Jews!" [30] They spat on him, and took the reed and struck him on the head. [31] After mocking him, they *stripped* him of the robe and put his own clothes on him. Then they led him away to *crucify* him. (Emphasis added)

The four studies were shared with everyone present in the afternoon. After discussion of the insights and wisdom in different approaches it was agreed that the Matthew passage offered a better basis for further work and ongoing development because it offered additional detail on the stripping. As West points out: "Matthew, it would seem, foregrounds the embodied sexual violence against Jesus."[15] Furthermore, because the author of Matthew probably drew on Mark's account, the additions that Matthew introduces are especially important because they are intentional.

West and colleagues gathered the outcomes from the four groups together and wove them into a shared version to take forward to the next stage. During the semester, students in the MA program in Religion and Gender were given the task of facilitating a group Bible study based on the workshop for a community group of their choice as part of their course assignment. At the end of semester, in October, the students presented their experience back to the class and discussed how it had been received. These presentations at the end of the semester provided the opportunity for me to return to Pietermartizburg and hear about their experiences.

One of the most memorable moments in the first workshop had been when the participants were asked how many soldiers were involved in the strippings in the *praetorium* in v. 28 and v. 31. This is a detail that is often missed even though it is explicitly recorded and even emphasized in the text. A careful reading indicates that v. 27 says, "They gathered the whole cohort around him." So, although it is impossible to say exactly how many soldiers directly put their hands on Jesus, the number of soldiers involved in the event is very high. Most estimates of a first-century cohort (*speira*) put the number at about five hundred soldiers.[16] If the statement in the text

15. West, "Jesus, Joseph, and Tamar Stripped," 121.

16. See Zeichmann, *Roman Army*. A cohort was one-tenth of a legion and numbered six centuries. In the first century a cohort usually comprised eighty legionaries. It is possible that the term *speira* may be used more loosely in John 18:3 when the temple guard go to arrest Jesus. It is not clear in John 18:3 how many of the temple guards were involved but most translators avoid the word cohort here. Since the temple guard were not Roman

that the whole cohort was gathered is correct it is a disturbingly high number of soldiers and also indicates the role of direction and organization. The stripping is not a spontaneous humiliation by just a few, but an intentional spectacle which is orchestrated and with a purpose. With these details in mind, the text can be reread in a new perspective. Furthermore, ahead of the first workshop, West had investigated further into the Mark and Matthew passages. He points out that, among other things, "both accounts use the same Greek word for the stripping of Jesus, *ekduo*, which is also used by the Septuagint to translate the Hebrew word *pashat* in the story of the stripping of Joseph (Gen. 37.23)."[17] West therefore identifies what he calls a "trans-textual" connection between the stripping of Tamar and the stripping of Joseph.[18] This in turn points to a trans-textual connection between the stripping of Joseph and the stripping of Jesus. West therefore argues that there a trans-textual connection from Tamar to Joseph to Jesus.[19]

The disturbing elements of Jesus' stripping in the *praetorium* are often missed completely or given minimal attention. One of the reasons for this is that the image of Jesus' stripping that most Christians are familiar with is the final stripping at the cross, referenced in v. 31 and recorded in v. 35. Verse 35 states, "And when they had crucified him, they divided his clothes among themselves by casting lots." John 19:23 states that the clothes were divided into four and gave one part to each soldier. This implies that there were only four soldiers directly involved in the stripping at the cross, although there may have been more present in other roles. It is this stripping at the cross which is recalled as the Tenth Station of the Cross, and this is a much more common image in art than the stripping in the *praetorium*. In most images of the Tenth Station of the Cross, Jesus is shown as being undressed by just two or three people, and sometimes by a single

---

soldiers this might allow John to use the term more loosely without necessarily showing that it could also be used loosely when referring to Roman soldiers. By contrast, cohort is commonly used by translators in Mark 15: and Matt 27:27, and also Acts 10:1, 21:31, and 27:1. Furthermore, Mark 15:16 and Matt 27:27 state "the whole cohort" and it would be very strange to indicate "the whole cohort" if they only meant cohort quite loosely.

17. West, "Jesus, Joseph, and Tamar Stripped," 114.

18. West explains, "The three texts discussed here are brought into dialogue because of the emancipatory potential we as socially engaged biblical scholars see in crossing over, back and forth, between them, even if this requires transgressing the boundaries that biblical scholarship constructs between them, perhaps through forging and finding unrecognized intertextual resonances." West, "Jesus, Joseph, and Tamar Stripped," 115–16. See also West, "Tamar Summons Jesus."

19. West, "Jesus, Joseph, and Tamar Stripped," 116–22.

person. There is rarely much aggression or violence in these images, and those around Jesus are not always depicted as soldiers. It is often more like a genteel disrobing, in which the dignity of Jesus would have been maintained. Even so, John 19:23 indicates that it was not only Jesus' clothes but also his tunic (or undergarment) that were taken from him, which suggests that he was fully naked on the cross. Early Christian writers assumed full nudity. There is no mention of a loincloth in any of the canonical gospels, but a loincloth has been a standard feature in Christian art from the fifth century onwards. This offers some dignity in response to such humiliation but there is a risk that those who view these images fail to see crucifixion for the scandal that it was.

A student report on responses to the stripping when the Bible study was shared in the wider community provided a memorable detail from the second workshop. The students had been encouraged to use different translations of the text depending on what would be familiar to the group. A student who had facilitated the workshop with a group of men who spoke isi-Zulu reported the strong reaction that the men had had when reading in isiZulu that Jesus was stripped. They felt the word "Amhlubula" (they stripped him) conveyed the offensiveness and emotional intensity of the experience much more strongly than the English version. The confronting nature of the text became much more obvious when the isiZulu term was used.

Following the second workshop, West and colleagues wrote up a revised version of the Bible study to take on board the practical experiences of the different pilot projects and the feedback received.[20] As is their practice, they worked with other groups, to share and refine the Bible study further. West notes: "CBS are constantly being changed as we learn from doing them."[21] This included work with a group in Nairobi who offered further insights from their context. This led to some further refinements:

A BIBLE STUDY ON THE CRUCIFIXION OF JESUS

1. Listen to a "slow" reading of Matt 27:26–31 in a number of different translations and languages. What have you heard from this slow reading of a well-known story that disturbs you?

20. See Ujamaa Centre, "Contextual Bible Study."
21. See West, "Contextual Bible Study."

2. Who are the characters in this story, and what do we know about each of them?

3. What forms of violence are used against Jesus?

4. How many times is Jesus stripped? Matthew makes it clear that Jesus was stripped more than once. Reread the text carefully and identify how many times Jesus is stripped.

5. Is stripping a form of violence? Why do the soldiers strip Jesus?

6. Matthew also makes it clear that Jesus was stripped in front of a whole "cohort" of about five hundred soldiers. What other forms of sexual abuse might have taken place when so many men were involved in the repeated stripping and beating of Jesus?

7. In what situations in your context are men sexually abused by other men?

8. Are there resources in your community to address male sexual violence against men?

9. What can we do to address the issue of male sexual violence against men? Devise a specific "action plan" of an action that you can participate in.[22]

One of the sensitive questions raised in the Bible study in question 6 is whether Jesus might have been subjected to additional violence and abuse in the *praetorium* beyond the stripping recorded in the text. Given what happens in detention with disturbing regularity, torture reports raise questions about a possible silence in the biblical text. We cannot answer this further question with certainty, but we can do more to acknowledge that this question exists and cannot be dismissed as unimportant. In Latin American torture reports stripping and nudity are sometimes recorded as a degrading abuse in their own right, but they are also very often mentioned as preparation for additional sexualized abuses. A study of Sri Lankan detainees conducted by the Medical Foundation for the Care of Victims of Torture (London) notes,

> Sexual abuse in detention starts with forced nudity, which many of the Sri Lankan detainees described. This is usually associated with

22. See West, "Contextual Bible Study."

26

verbal sexual threats and mocking, which adds to the humiliation and degradation of being tortured.[23]

It was therefore important, and remains important, to make a distinction between what the biblical passage revealed and what the passage might conceal, and to be attentive to both. The fact that Jesus was a victim of sexual abuse (in terms of the stripping and forced nudity) is clear and incontrovertible. It is also clear that stripping and forced nudity often lead to additional sexual assaults: a proper assessment of this requires further evidence. In the case of Jesus, it is fair to say that additional abuse is a reasonable possibility, even though there is insufficient evidence to conclude this with certainty.[24]

PASTORAL AND THEOLOGICAL PERSPECTIVES

The theologian Serene Jones has described Jesus' experience as a "seriously undertapped resource" that pastors might use to address sexual assault and sexual abuse.[25] Jones writes, "Imagine how different our national debate might be if sexual abuse of Christ was a commonly understood part of the passion narrative, and used to underscore the severity and horror of contemporary sexual assaults."[26] In recent years valuable work has been done on Jesus' experience of sexual abuse, including work by Michael Trainor, Christopher Greenough, Jayme Reaves, Hilary Scarsella, Susannah Larry, Erin Heim, and others.[27] These works offer further perspectives on the significance of the stripping, how it is presented in the biblical texts, and what other abuses may have been involved.

23. Peel et al., "Sexual Abuse."

24. For discussion of a possible clue on the additional sexual violence suggested by the language in Matt 27, see Tombs, "Reading Crucifixion Narratives."

25. "One seriously undertapped resource for this is speaking of Jesus' own experience of sexual abuse. Please, take a moment to read this wonderful paper by @TombsDavid." @SereneJones, Twitter, Oct. 5, 2018, 9:51 a.m.

26. "Imagine how different our national debate might be if sexual abuse of Christ was a commonly understood part of the passion narrative, and used to underscore the severity and horror of contemporary sexual assaults," @SereneJones, Twitter, Oct. 5, 2018, 9:51 a.m.

27. Trainor, *Body of Jesus*; Scarsella, "Bearing Witness to Jesus"; Heim and Johnson, "Resurrection"; Greenough, *Bible and Sexual Violence*; Larry, *Leaving Silence*, 183–212. An overview of work on the theme by Trainor, Elaine Heath, and Wil Gafney is offered in Reaves and Tombs, "#MeToo Jesus," 401–7.

As noted above, with regard to further abuses beyond the stripping, the biblical text does not allow for certainty. The full details of what happened in the *praetorium* will never be known but even so there is enough biblical evidence to acknowledge that Matt 27:26–31 presents Jesus a victim of sexual violence. Hilary Scarsella provides a concise summary on both what is known and what is not known. She identifies the stripping and enforced nudity as the basis on which "we can say confidently, then, that Jesus's crucifixion was sexually violent. Jesus was a victim of sexual violence."[28] Then, turning to the possibility of further sexual assault, Scarsella recognizes that this is a reasonable possibility but not a certain fact; she writes,

> Thus, given (1) what we know about the general frequency with which military dominance is asserted through sexual means, (2) that soldiers apparently did sexually assault men in the ancient world to degrade, dehumanize, and humiliate, (3) that there was a period during Jesus's crucifixion in which he was behind closed doors in the company of assailants who stripped him of his clothes and forced his nakedness, it is eminently reasonable to hold open the possibility that Jesus may have been sexually assaulted in the praetorium.

Jesus' experience of sexual violence and abuse can therefore be seen as an example of both certainty (related to the stripping in the *praetorium* and nudity on the cross) and uncertainty (on whatever further might have happened in the *praetorium*, and perhaps on the cross) in relation to sexual violence. Scarsella's depiction of certainty and uncertainty about Jesus' experience offers a significant resource to consider the pastoral and theological issues raised by his experience.[29]

For readers who want to know for sure what exactly happened in the *praetorium* the evidence gap may be frustrating. However, Scarsella suggests

28. Scarsella, "Bearing Witness," 156. Likewise, Caroline Mackie notes, "The Gospel writers tell us that Jesus was stripped naked publicly, a form of sexual abuse by any standards." Mackie, review of *When Did We See You* (Reaves et al.), para. 2.

29. To preserve this distinction, in "Crucifixion," I referred to these two different elements as "sexual humiliation" (for the stripping and enforced nudity which are revealed) and "sexual assault" (for the further sexual violence that might be concealed). Conversations with West have helped me see that even though the article names the sexual humiliation (not just the sexual assault) as sexual abuse, the use of the term sexual humiliation not sexual assault for the stripping risks understating the element of sexual assault within the stripping and enforced nudity. It might therefore be more precise to distinguish between the sexual assault of the stripping and enforced nudity revealed in the text, and the possibility of further sexual assault that might be concealed in the text.

that this "epistemological limitation" over whether or not there was further sexual assault might offer a valuable opportunity to help churches grapple with reports of sexual assaults. She explains,

> If it happened, it is likely to have happened out of view of any of Jesus's loved ones who went on to tell the story of what he was made to endure. If Jesus was sexually assaulted, in other words, it happened the way sexual assault often does—without leaving the kind of evidence that can be called on to secure knowledge of its historical circumstances for those who were not present in the moment of its occurrence.[30]

Scarsella points out that in many cases, accounts of sexual assault do not have additional witnesses who can corroborate disputed accounts. Reports often come down to the different versions offered by the two people involved.[31] So while the uncertainty is frustrating for those who want certainty, it may be more useful than it first appears for addressing the realities of sexual assault. Scarsella suggests, "It is precisely our lack of access to evidence-based certainty in one direction or the other that becomes significant for considering the relationship of sexual assault in Jesus's story to contemporary engagement with the crisis of sexual violence."[32]

Over the years, many people have written to me from Latin America and elsewhere to say what this reading of Jesus as a victim of sexual abuse means to them at a personal level. It is deeply gratifying to receive thanks and encouragement like this. Some of those who write are survivors and they speak very directly about what the work means to them personally, and why they see it as helpful and important, even though it is painful. Some say it helps them know that Jesus understands their suffering and was present with them when they faced abuse. Others speak of their sense of reassurance that even though Jesus was in no way to blame for what happened he was still subjected to abuse. His experience demonstrates that no blame or shame should attach to the victim because of what they have been subjected to by others. In many cases survivors say they already know this at a rational level but have sometimes found it hard to fully embrace this at an emotional level. Focussing on Jesus' experience is therefore an

---

30. Scarsella, "Bearing Witness," 161.

31. Scarsella gives the examples of Christine Blasey Ford and Deborah Ramirez, who came forward with testimony against US Supreme Court Justice Brett Kavanaugh during his confirmation process in 2018. Scarsella, "Bearing Witness," 161.

32. Scarsella, "Bearing Witness," 161.

important reassurance that they should resist any temptation to self-blame and take comfort when faced with prejudice and negative attitudes from others. Some have even described it as helping them to maintain their faith when they have faced discouragement and disillusionment.

Hearing survivors speak of the positive outcomes they see in this reading of crucifixion is important affirmation for the work. However, it would be wrong to think that this part of Jesus suffering is only relevant to survivors. One important contribution that it might make for the wider church is reinforcing the need to take all reports of sexual abuse seriously—even those that initially might seem implausible or unlikely—so that they are investigated properly and not just dismissed out of hand.

Many people find the idea of an abused Jesus disturbing and confronting. This is especially common if people hear a misrepresentations or sensationalized version or if they make negative assumptions about what they think the motives must be behind it. Without a sense of why Jesus is said to be a victim of sexual abuse many people are simply bewildered, or dismissive, that such a reading could be imagined. Some put it down to a misguided attempt at relevance, or "wokeness," or a #MeToo bandwagon.

In a few cases there is even stronger criticism. It has been said that it is "offensive," "outrageous," "blasphemous" and even "Satanic." Critics readily assume that the only possible motivation for someone to write on this subject is to insult or mock Jesus.[33] To understand why this so common I have learned a lot from collaboration with another South African scholar, Elisabet le Roux, a specialist in religion and development at Stellenbosch University.

Le Roux has completed a number of projects on sexual violence in different settings in the Global South and the responses that churches make to this. Her research is often commissioned by faith-based relief and development agencies like Tearfund, the Anglican Episcopal Relief Development Agency, and Worldvision. They seek robust research with the hope that it will not just offer better understanding but this will then help towards a better practical response. In a chapter by Le Roux that draws on a decade of work in the Democratic Republic of Congo, Liberia, Burundi, Rwanda, South African and Colombia, she discusses heartbreaking stories of women who experienced sexual violence. In many cases, the women interviewed feared that if their husbands discovered what happened, they would be divorced and abandoned. In Colombia, Le Roux interviewed

---

33. See Reaves and Tombs, *When Did We See*, 1–11.

women survivors of sexual violence who described the stigma they carried, and feared that even their own their own mothers might reject them. Le Roux shows how deep the prejudice against survivors can go. She opens her chapter with the words of a male church member in Sake, DRC:

> For me, I do not think I can consider a woman who has been sexually violated. For me, she is no longer a perfect woman, because she has now been violated, she just lost her value. From my point of view I can no longer even go to her family, to look for a wife, because I know that family is already cursed, she is no longer valuable once sexually violated. I know she can be treated, but that is just in terms of letting her forget what happened to her, but she is no longer valuable in the society.[34]

Le Roux explains: "These words . . . are a typical example of the stigma and discrimination that survivors of sexual violence face."[35] These negative responses towards survivors are referred to as the "secondary victimization" that they experience from family, their community, and even their churches. In the eyes of the man she cites, the stigma is so strong that it attaches not only to the woman herself, but even to others in her family. It is for this reason that stigma is sometimes described as metaphorically "contagious." The friends and family of a stigmatized victim become stigmatized because of their relationship to the victim. This vicarious stigmatization increases the damage done by secondary victimization. It extends the stigma beyond the immediate victim and also makes it much more likely that the victim will be abandoned or rejected by family and friends. The result is that in many cases survivors report that the way others in the community respond to them impacts them more than the original victimization. Secondary victimization is often longer lasting and more widespread than the original violence.

The Tearfund report *To Make Our Voices Heard* provides further evidence in support of Le Roux's claims. Drawing on research by Patricia Bongi Zengele with survivors in the Central African Republic, it describes "the heartbreakingly common theme of rejection and abandonment by husbands and family of rape survivors."[36] For example, it cites one woman who reported: "It is difficult to talk about these experiences because it is shameful and dehumanises you as a human being. In the beginning I did

34. Le Roux, "Jesus Is a Survivor," 178.

35. Le Roux, "Jesus Is a Survivor," 178.

36. Tearfund, *To Make Our Voices Heard*, 6.

not want to talk about this but finally I disclosed it to my husband who became very angry and left me."[37]

Le Roux reports that many survivors point to the church as the institution that is best placed to support them as they face the aftermath of sexual violence. However, instead of offering active support and care, many survivors told her that church leaders remained silent. Sexual violence was treated as taboo within the church. Churches do not see sexual violence as an appropriate topic to talk about in churches. This contributed to survivors' feelings of stigma, isolation, and negative judgment from their faith communities.

Alongside the unhelpful silence, some survivors also experienced more direct stigma and discrimination. Many spoke of the painful stigmatizing treatment they experienced at the hands of church leaders and members. Le Roux says, "Often the stigma and discrimination they experience from fellow church members and religious leaders are the most hurtful."[38] In addition, Le Roux says that many survivors also self-stigmatize and internalize these harsh judgments. Recognizing the level of perceived stigma from the community, from the churches, and even within themselves, Le Roux therefore speaks of the "comprehensiveness of stigma" and asks, "If this is the reality of stigma, how does one address it?"[39]

Based on her work with survivors of sexual violence, and aware of the significance that survivors see in the potential of faith-communities, Le Roux recognizes the importance of initiatives by churches and Christian-based NGOs to address sexual violence more proactively and more constructively.[40] Sometimes critics of these initiatives try to dismiss concern for sexual violence as falling outside of the core work of the church. Le Roux explains that an effective response to this is to show that concern for sexual violence is in keeping with the church's own core beliefs and values. Compassion and concern are Christian values that should motivate churches to respond. Far from being alien to the churches, these core values require churches to do more. This message can be supported and reinforced through attention to biblical texts because churches already identify biblical teaching as authoritative.

---

37. Tearfund, *To Make Our Voices Heard*, 17–19.
38. Le Roux, "Jesus Is a Survivor," 182.
39. Le Roux, "Jesus Is a Survivor," 182.
40. Le Roux et al., "Getting Dirty."

For this reason, Le Roux advocates strongly for an approach that makes use of scriptural resources when working with faith leaders and faith communities in the Global South. Churches that recognize a Scriptural mandate for action are far more likely to make meaningful and sustained changes to their policy and practice, especially when the biblical material connects with their local experience. Thus contextual bible studies along the lines pioneered by the Ujamaa Centre are so valuable.

Understanding Jesus as a victim of sexual violence has great potential for this work on stigma for at least three reasons. First, Jesus and the cross are so central to Christian faith that it is impossible to dismiss or deny the importance of his experience. What happened to Jesus is unlikely to be dismissed as unimportant to the church. Nor can Jesus be blamed for what was done to him. The common victim-blaming response is not readily available. Jesus cannot be faulted for provoking the sexual violence. He is in many ways the "ideal victim" who is innocent of blame.[41] Likewise, Jesus is also protected from being stigmatized in the eyes of believers in the aftermath of what happened. While other survivors might be seen as lessened or damaged in some way, and while this might be an instinctive first reaction in relation to Jesus, the obvious problems that follow from seeing Jesus as lessened by something that was done to him are too obvious for Christians to accept this. It might initially be asked whether or not Jesus is still a perfect savior despite what happened to him, but this question is quickly dropped because it is clear that Jesus should not be seen as spoiled or lessened because of something done to him. The same recognition can—and should—be granted for all survivors, and it is important that churches make this further step. Churches should not need to think of Jesus in order to think more clearly about the innocence of survivors. Nonetheless, the experience of Jesus is important because experience shows it can prompt churches to interrogate and reexamine their negative thinking about survivors.[42]

Second, attention to the stigma associated with sexual violence offers opportunities to go beyond care and compassion for survivors—important

---

41. Christie uses the term "ideal victim" for a stereotypical victim who, "when hit by crime—are most readily given the complete and legitimate status of being a victim." Christie, "Perfect Victim," 18. That is to say, they are least likely to be blamed for their victimhood. Two characteristics which differ between Jesus and the stereotypical ideal are the maleness of Jesus (Christie notes that most ideal victims are female) and his failure to fight back.

42. Tombs, "Confronting the Stigma."

as these are—and open up conversations on complicity with secondary victimization within churches. Le Roux argues,

> Scriptural engagement with the concept of Jesus as a survivor of sexual abuse is an effective intervention because it has the ability to serve both the stigmatizer (in as far as it responds to public stigma, institutional stigma and stigma by association) and the stigmatized (in as far as it responds to self-stigma).[43]

When Jesus' experience of sexual violence is mentioned a common first reaction within churches is incredulity or negative judgment. However, these first reactions are often revised if the conversation around the reasons for seeing Jesus as a victim can be sustained. In the process of discussing Jesus' experience people often become more aware of the negative reactions which are common responses to this, and some may also recognize negative reactions they themselves have felt or expressed. This process can help towards an understanding of secondary victimization of survivors within the churches. The negative responses that are initially expressed against Jesus being seen as a victim of sexual violence can be questioned and examined. They invite the further question: "Are the negative attitudes to this understanding of Jesus indicative of negative attitudes towards survivors within the church?" Very often people in churches are not fully aware that they have these attitudes. Most in the churches would see themselves as loving and compassionate rather than hostile and judgmental. They do not mean to act in harmful ways but they have never been encouraged to reflect on the secondary victimization they support. Discussions of first responses to Jesus experiences, and a greater understanding of what is behind these, can be one of the most effective ways of surfacing latent stigma against survivors and secondary victimization within churches.

Third, opportunities for this learning within churches can be supported by participatory bible study. Participatory bible study has the advantage that participants can learn for themselves through a facilitated engagement with the text. This is a much deeper approach to learning than simple instruction and just being told. For this reason, Le Roux recommends the contextual Bible study on the stripping and crucifixion of Jesus developed by the Ujamaa Centre discussed above.

Thus, in terms of exploring stigma, Le Roux sees huge potential in the acknowledgment of Jesus as a survivor. Attention to his experience

---

43. Le Roux, "Jesus Is a Survivor," 186.

debunks beliefs in the sinfulness of survivors, that they have lesser value, are not to be trusted, and are deserving of what happened. It provides a powerful illustration that people should not be blamed or stigmatized for the sexual violence to which they are subjected, and sexual violence does not lessen or reduce a person's value and worth. In recent years, a Peruvian colleague, Rocío Figueroa, and I have completed two interview-based projects on understandings of Jesus experience among survivors of sexual abuse. We have interviewed seven adult male survivors and five adult female survivors.[44] Each survivor has spoken of the value and importance to the wider church—not just survivors—of seeing Jesus as a victim of sexual abuse because it addresses victim-blaming and stigmatizing so powerfully. For example, one participant said to us: "Seeing his innocence, I see my innocence."[45] A number of them told us quite emphatically that the issue is more applicable to the wider church than it is to survivors themselves, because it is the wider church that most needs to hear this and to change.

An example of the dynamics discussed by Le Roux was offered when the Brazilian newspaper *Folha de São Paulo* published a lengthy article on Jesus as a victim of sexual abuse in their illustrated supplement for Palm Sunday (April 10, 2022).[46] In response, First Lady Michelle Bolsonaro and others tweeted strong objection to the article. Bolsonaro described it as an example of Christophobia, and cited a warning from Gal 6:7:

> Insanity, Christophobia and lack of scruples. Do not be deceived: God is not mocked. For whatever a man sows, that he will also reap. GALATIANS 6.[47]

A number of more positive respondents pointed out that this sounded like Bolsonaro had not read the *Folha* article (at least not beyond the headline) and certainly not read the research it discussed.[48] At one point the *Folha* article discussed why some of those who claimed to love Jesus were

44. Figueroa and Tombs, "Recognising Jesus"; Figueroa and Tombs, "Seeing His Innocence."

45. Figueroa and Tombs, "Seeing His Innocence," 296.

46. Dos Anjos, "Corpo, cruz e abuso."

47. Twitter autotranslation of Michelle Bolsonaro, "Insanidade, cristofobia e falta de escrúpulos. Não se deixem enganar: de Deus não se zomba. Pois o que o homem semear isso também colherá." Twitter, @MiBolsonaro, April 11, 2022, 2:59 a.m. See also Bolsonaro, "Michelle critica teólogo que disse que Jesus sofreu abuso."

48. The *Folha* article had a more provocative title than the printed paper version, so those who responded to just the title may have had little sense of the discussion in the article itself.

often especially dismissive of reading Jesus as a victim of sexual abuse and why this suggested a negative view of survivors and a shallow understanding of what it means to love someone. Bolsonaro's tweet implies that Jesus would be severely lessened or reduced if he was abused in this way. As if he could no longer be loved, or perhaps no longer be respected, or viewed as a savior figure. The *Folha* article explained that this attitude amounts to victim-blaming and stigmatizing Jesus in ways that need to be challenged and changed. Most Christians would not express these negative attitudes openly but the suggestion that the identification of Jesus as victim of abuse is "Christophobia" is very revealing. Recognizing that stripping and enforced nudity were used as an intentional way to mock Jesus, and identifying this as an issue of concern for the church, is not hating or mocking Jesus. On the contrary, it is a way of taking Jesus' experience seriously and compassionately and being open to how this could be meaningful for survivors and the wider church.

Church leaders have so far been remarkably slow to show leadership in this discussion. One reason for the church's reticence to speak of Jesus as a victim of sexual abuse is probably because wider theological concerns impede a constructive response. Thinking of Jesus' experience in this way can be theologically challenging and deeper theological concerns need to be identified and discussed more carefully. For example, how might this perspective make a difference to how the atonement is understood? Surely sexual abuse could not be seen as part of God's salvific plan? What difference does this understanding of crucifixion make to a Christian understanding of resurrection?[49]

There needs to be a wider discussion of these questions, especially because Christ's suffering has often been used for misguided and dangerous pastoral advice to survivors in some churches. Detailed discussion of these theological challenges are beyond the scope of this chapter. There is a danger that the confronting nature of the research encourages people to move too hastily to easy answers that avoid the true extent of the theological challenge. Suffice it to say, however, that the principle in liberation theology of grounding theological reflection on concrete experience offers important direction. There will be questions that may not yet have answers, and that need careful thought. At this stage, it may be easier to indicate what should not be said, rather than say how these questions can be resolved. To this end, I would argue that nothing in Jesus' experience suggests he consented

49. On this, see especially Heim and Johnson, "Resurrection."

to sexual abuse, or voluntarily embraced sexual abuse, in any way. Likewise, the abuse was not divinely ordained, nor was it any way providential. What happened to Jesus should not be seen as excusing abuse, nor should it ever be suggested that someone's abuse was part of God's plan, or that they should be willing to submit themselves to abuse in imitation of Christ. For those seeking a more meaningful message in relation to the suffering of the cross, an excellent starting point is offered in the insight of liberation theologian Jon Sobrino, that the challenge of faith is not to venerate the cross, but to take the suffering down from their respective crosses.

CONCLUSION

My initial writing on Jesus as victim of sexual violence was shaped by a wish to take a story of extreme sexual violence during torture seriously and to reflect on it in the light of the gospel narratives and Roman writings on crucifixion. In the years since first publishing on this subject the recognition of Jesus as a victim of sexual abuse has grown slowly but still not yet been embraced by the churches. At a personal level I have found the collaborations and connections with different scholars in South Africa particularly helpful for thinking more deeply about the issues raised by Jesus' experience. The contextual Bible study developed by the Ujamaa Centre provides a practical way of exploring these themes in an accessible way that has been enriched by biblical insights from Gerald West and his colleagues. It allows for discussion of both what is revealed and what might be concealed in the text. It also makes a safe space for considering the victim-blaming and stigmatizing of survivors of sexual violence. Recognizing Jesus as a victim of sexual abuse is not reducing Jesus' suffering—or the meaning of the cross—only to this. Nor is it to suggest that Jesus shares the experiences of other victims of sexual abuse in every way. Rather, recognizing Jesus as a victim of abuse acknowledges an aspect of his experience that is often ignored and marginalized and which can be meaningful and transformative if it is addressed honestly and compassionately.

BIBLIOGRAPHY

Albrecht, Elizbeth Soto, and Darryl W. Stephens, eds. *Liberating the Politics of Jesus: Renewing Peace Theology through the Wisdom of Women*. London: T&T Clark, 2020.

Bolsonaro, Michelle. "Michelle Critica Teólogo Que Disse Que Jesus Sofreu Abuso: 'Insanidade.'" UOL, April 11, 2022. https://noticias.uol.com.br/politica/ultimas-noticias/2022/04/11/michelle-critica-teologo-que-disse-que-jesus-sofreu-abuso-insanidade.htm.

Christie, Nils. "The Perfect Victim." In *From Crime Policy to Victim Policy*, edited by Ezzat A. Fattah, 17–30. New York: Palgrave Macmillan, 1986.

Claassens, Juliana, et al., eds. *Transgression and Transformation: Feminist, Postcolonial and Queer Biblical Interpretation as Creative Interventions*. London: T&T Clark, 2021.

Dos Anjos, Márvio. "Corpo, cruz e abuso." *Folha de S.Paulo*, April 10, 2022. C8–C9.

Du Toit, Louise. *A Philosophical Investigation of Rape: The Making and Unmaking of the Feminine Self*. New York: Routledge, 2009.

Du Toit, Louise, and Elisabet le Roux. "Feminist Reflection on Male Victims of Conflict Related Sexual Violence." *European Journal of Women's Studies* 28:2 (2020) 115–28.

Fattah, Ezzat A., ed. *From Crime Policy to Victim Policy: Reorienting the Justice System*. New York: Palgrave Macmillan, 1986.

Figueroa, Rocío, and David Tombs. "Recognising Jesus as a Victim of Sexual Abuse: Responses from Sodalicio Survivors in Peru." *Religion and Gender* 10:1 (June 2020) 55–75.

———. "Seeing His Innocence, I See My Innocence." In *When Did We See You Naked? Jesus as a Victim of Sexual Abuse*, edited by Jayme R. Reaves et al., 287–312. London: SCM Press, 2021.

Greenough, Christopher. *The Bible and Sexual Violence Against Men*. London: Routledge, 2021.

Heim, Erin, with Dru Johnson. "Resurrection and the #metoo Movement: Parts 1–2." *OnScript Podcast*, June 16, 2020 (https://onscript.study/podcast/erin-heim-with-dru-johnson-resurrection-and-the-metoo-movement-part-1/) and Oct. 6, 2020 (https://onscript.study/podcast/erin-heim-resurrection-and-the-metoo-movement-part-ii/).

Larry, Sussanah. *Leaving Silence: Sexualized Violence, the Bible, and Standing with Survivors*. Harrisonburg, VA: Herald, 2021.

Le Roux, Elisabet. "Jesus Is a Survivor." In *When Did We See You Naked? Jesus as a Victim of Sexual Abuse*, edited by Jayme R. Reaves et al., 178–94. London: SCM Press, 2021.

Le Roux, Elisabet, et al. "Getting Dirty: Working with Faith Leaders to Prevent and Respond to Gender-Based Violence." *The Review of Faith and International Affairs* 14:3 (2016) 22–35.

Mackie, Carolyn. Review of *When Did We See You Naked? Jesus as a Victim of Sexual Abuse* by Jayme R. Reaves et al. *Women in Theology*, Aug. 4, 2021. https://womenintheology.org/2021/08/03/review-when-did-we-see-you-naked/.

Melanchthon, Monica, and Robyn Whitaker, eds. *Terror in the Bible: Rhetoric, Gender, and Violence*. Atlanta: SBL, 2021.

Pearson, Clive, ed. *Enacting a Public Theology*. Stellenbosch, South Africa: Stellenbosch University Press, 2019.

Peel, Michael, et al. "The Sexual Abuse of Men in Detention in Sri Lanka." *The Lancet* 355:9220 (2000) 2069–70.

Reaves, Jayme R., et al., eds. *When Did We See You Naked? Jesus as a Victim of Sexual Abuse*. London: SCM Press, 2021. https://scmpress.hymnsam.co.uk/media/75409/when-did-we-see-you-naked-pdf.pdf.

Reaves, Jayme R., and David Tombs. "#MeToo Jesus: Naming Jesus as a Victim of Sexual Abuse." *International Journal of Public Theology* 13:4 (2019) 387–412.

Scarsella, Hilary. "Bearing Witness to Jesus, Resurrected Survivor of Sexual Violence." In *Liberating the Politics of Jesus*, edited by Elizbeth Soto Albrecht and Darryl W. Stephens, 151–66. London: T&T Clark, 2020.

Tearfund. *To Make Our Voices Heard: Listening to Survivors of Sexual Violence in Central African Republic*. Teddington, UK: Tearfund, 2015.

Tombs, David. "Confronting the Stigma of Naming Jesus as a Victim of Sexual Violence." In *Enacting a Public Theology*, edited by Clive Pearson, 71–86. Stellenbosch: SUNMedia, 2019. https://doi.org/10.18820/9781928314684/07.

———. "Crucifixion, State Terror, and Sexual Abuse." *Union Seminary Quarterly Review* 53 (1999) 89–109.

———. "Hidden in Plain Sight: Seeing the Stripping of Jesus as Sexual Violence." *Journal for Interdisciplinary Biblical Studies* 2:1 (2020). https://jibs.hcommons.org/2022/07/20/tombs-hidden-in-plain-sight/.

———. "Reading Crucifixion Narratives as Texts of Terror." In *Terror in the Bible: Rhetoric, Gender, and Violence*, edited by Monica Melanchton and Robyn Whitaker, 139–60. Atlanta: SBL, 2021.

Trainor, Michael. *The Body of Jesus and Sexual Abuse: How the Gospel Passion Narrative Informs a Pastoral Approach*. Eugene, OR: Wipf & Stock, 2014.

West, Gerald O. *Contextual Bible Study*. Pietermaritzburg, South Africa: Cluster Publications, 1993.

———. "Contextual Bible Study Work with Matthew's Gospel in South Africa." *Currents in Theology and Mission*. Dubuque, IA: Wartburg Theological Seminary, forthcoming.

———. "Jesus, Joseph, and Tamar Stripped: Trans-Textual and Intertextual Resources for Engaging Sexual Violence Against Men." In *When Did We See You Naked? Jesus as a Victim of Sexual Abuse*, edited by Jayme R. Reaves et al., 110–28. London: SCM Press, 2021.

———. "Indigenous Exegesis: Exploring the Interface Between Missionary Methods and Rhetorical Rhythms—Locating Local Reading Resources in the Academy." *Neotestamentica* 36 (2002) 147–62.

———. "Tamar Summons Jesus: A Trans-Textual (2 Samuel 13:1–22; Mark 5:22–43; Matthew 20:17–34) Search for Sectorial Solidarity with Respect to Gender and Masculinity." In *Transgression and Transformation: Feminist, Postcolonial and Queer Biblical Interpretation as Creative Interventions*, edited by Juliana Claassens et al., 184–203. London: Bloomsbury, 2021.

West, Gerald O., and Phumzile Zondi-Mabizela. "The Bible Story That Became a Campaign: The Tamar Campaign in South Africa (and Beyond)." *Ministerial Formation* (July 2004) 4–12.

Ujamaa Centre. "Redemptive Masculinity: A Series of Ujamaa Centre Contextual Bible Studies That Proclaim Life for Men and Women." Pietermaritzburg, South Africa: Ujamaa Centre, 2009. https://wptest173.ukzn.ac.za/wp-content/uploads/2022/12/Redemptive_masculinity_A_series_of_Ujam.pdf.

———. "A Contextual Bible Study on the Crucifixion of Jesus: Engaging the Issue of Male Violence Against Men." Pietermaritzburg, South Africa: Ujamaa Centre, 2019. https://hdl.handle.net/10523/10233.

Zeichmann, Christopher B. *The Roman Army and the New Testament*. Lanham, MD: Fortress Academic, 2018.

When Jesus Doubted God

Perspectives from Calvin on Post-Traumatic Faith

PRESTON MCDANIEL HILL

WITNESSING TRAUMA

THE WILLINGNESS TO WITNESS trauma is often autobiographical. This is true of me in my role as a professor of theology and practicing therapist specializing in trauma. During my postgraduate education, I tried to stay in one lane and focus solely on Reformation theology and history. That would have been clean and tidy—theology in the academy, and trauma in the real world. But trauma and recovery has pursued me and refused to let go.

No one starts from nowhere. We all carry stories that frame our daily professions and relationships. So how did I end up teaching integration of theology and psychology to trauma therapists after completing postgraduate research on John Calvin? I am still not sure. But I do know that these thought worlds, separate as they might seem, are deeply integrated in me, the person; that we cannot help but be who we are; and that there is a clear reward to integrating our professional lives with our lived experiences. A person-centered, holistic approach to life may just be what the world, divided as it is today by endless abstract classifications, is hungry for. What we may need is to encounter reality fresh and face-to-face, whether that reality is violent or beautiful.

As a professor of theology and pastoral counselor, I have had the privilege of witnessing countless students and friends share stories of surviving violence. I have also had the privilege of sharing my story with them. As a survivor of childhood sexual abuse, I live daily with symptoms of complex post-traumatic stress disorder (C-PTSD) that affect every aspect of my life. Recovery has been slow and steady. The journey is long, but the friends on the road are more numerous than I had assumed, even in the academy. Indeed, it has been a privilege to research trauma with fellow survivors and witnesses who are keen to explore how theology can be reimagined in our "east of Eden" world.

Stories like mine and my students are not uncommon. Recent studies report that 70 to 90 percent of adults experience a traumatic event at some point in their lives.[1] As a result, some psychiatrists have concluded that "trauma is now our most urgent public health issue."[2] The COVID-19 pandemic and political unrest of 2020 and 2021 make such an assessment hard to deny. Scholars in the last thirty years have also proposed that traumatic violence is a global public health issue best approached through interdisciplinary collaboration, but theologians have only just begun to join this conversation. We are just beginning to ask how theology can contribute to our understanding of trauma and possibilities for recovery.

But there's a more specific question that I hear repeated often by students, friends, and colleagues, and it's a question that has been important to my journey as well—how are we to understand the experience people often have after trauma that they are angry at God and feel alienated from God by their suffering? Put differently, what can theology contribute to our understanding of human persons who feel forsaken by God after trauma, and how might theology offer insight in trauma recovery?[3]

A BASIC SKETCH OF PTSD

But before mining theological resources to assist in recovery, we must first understand trauma.

What is the story of trauma? Where did it come from? The clinical study of trauma waxed and waned throughout the 1900s, and it was not until 1980 that the treatment of outspoken Vietnam veterans led the American Psychiatric Association to canonize traumatic stress with the diagnosis

1. Benjet et al., "Epidemiology."

2. Van der Kolk, *Body Keeps the Score*, 358.

3. See these questions raised in Sartor and Hill, "Attachment Theory"; Stump, *Atonement*, 339–77; Rea, *Hiddenness of God*, 157–59, 177–79; Rea, "Ill-Made Knight"; Panchuk, "Shattered Spiritual Self."

PTSD.[4] The medical treatment of combat trauma in the late 1900s opened up doors for parallel diagnoses related to such atrocities as domestic violence, childhood sexual abuse, and political captivity.

Trauma has come to be defined as "an inescapably stressful event that overwhelms one's coping mechanisms."[5] During a highly stressful event of overwhelming violence in which one is powerless to fight or flee, human persons are able to survive the psychic stress of the event by undergoing a complex process of hyperarousal and alterations of consciousness that protect the person from fully experiencing the threat. In clinical terms, this process is a "freeze" response called "dissociation" that has been formally identified as the central pathogenic mechanism involved in PTSD.[6] During dissociation, a traumatized person who is threatened with violence undergoes an extreme narrowing of perception as a defense mechanism, and this numbs the person's consciousness against the brutality being experienced.

Survivors frequently report dissociation as a kind of out-of-body experience in which they have the perception of floating above their own bodies, as if they were watching the trauma happen to someone else.[7] Through such experiences "the helpless person escapes from [their] situation not by action in the real world but rather by altering [their] state of consciousness. . . . This altered state of consciousness might be regarded as one of nature's small mercies, a protection against unbearable pain."[8]

However, clinicians and neuroscientists agree that while dissociation is adaptive in trauma, it is maladaptive for recovery.[9] Because the traumatic experience is walled off from ordinary consciousness, the memories of the trauma are not recalled in an integrated fashion in the post-traumatic context. Instead, they may be experienced as intrusive and sporadic flashbacks of sensory overload. Freud was essentially correct, then, when he noted that traumatized persons "suffer mainly from reminiscences" because "the patient is, one might say, fixated to the trauma." Traumatized persons suffer from unintegrated memories of terror that interrupt their present consciousness. Serene Jones writes that in PTSD "the mind's meaning-making

---

4. See American Psychiatric Association, "PTSD."

5. Van der Kolk, "Trauma and Memory," in *Traumatic Stress*, 279; Van der Kolk, *Body Keeps the Score*, 66.

6. Van der Kolk and Fisler, "Dissociation."

7. E.g., Herman, *Trauma and Recovery*, 87–88.

8. Herman, *Trauma and Recovery*, 42–43.

9. Van der Kolk, *Body Keeps the Score*, 92.

structures have collapsed" and that "because [information] cannot be processed and stored, [it] simply wanders and consistently replays itself." This ongoing repetition results in what Babette Rothschild describes as a "misperception—in mind and body—that past trauma is still happening."[10] The experience of having one's present mental state constantly interrupted by the fear of an overwhelming threat of the past is at the very heart of the PTSD syndrome.

In the last thirty years, the study of trauma has moved off the psycho-analytic couch, making its way into the humanities. Trauma theory began in the mid-1990s as an interdisciplinary attempt to explore how trauma affects human self-understanding. Literary scholar Cathy Caruth was particularly influential in summarizing a traumatic event as a "missed" or "unclaimed" experience. She describes trauma as the wound that results from an event of such terrifying magnitude that the event is too much to process as it happens—the terror is too great to comprehend. As a result, the memories of the past violence haunt the human psyche seeking to be processed or "claimed."[11] When traumatic memories are unclaimed in this way, it creates the experience of a "double-wound": the initial traumatic event and the stress that follows. Even though the traumatic events are over, the terror continues to wound the mind in the present, creating a double-wound.

From these conceptualizations of trauma, literary theorists have developed a framework that is now called trauma theory through which hermeneutical possibilities are opened in the important differences between suffering (which has ended and is in the past) and trauma (which persists so that suffering continues in the present). As Freud puts it, the threat of trauma is continually felt by survivors "as contemporary experience, instead of . . . remembering it as something belonging to the past." This sense of continual experience is what theologian Shelly Rambo gets at when she asserts that trauma is radically different from general suffering. Suffering is what one can recover from, what one can heal from. Trauma, however, is what is unbearable, what one cannot handle, what overwhelms. Rambo says that "this is the difference between a closed and an open wound . . .

---

10. Freud, *Beyond the Pleasure Principle*, 7–8; Jones, *Trauma and Grace*, 29–30; Rothschild, *Eight Keys*, 27.

11. For more on this, see Caruth, *Trauma* and *Listening to Trauma*.

trauma is the suffering that does not go away. The study of trauma is the study of what remains."[12]

POST-TRAUMATIC RELATING TO GOD

Given the way that psychological trauma *remains* even after the events are over, survivors experience negative effects on their relationships with other human persons in the present. However, recent philosophers and theologians have also pointed out that traumatic events do not only disrupt our relationship with other humans; they also disrupt our relationship with God. Some scholars have called this post-traumatic disruption of the divine-human relationship a "stain on the soul," as if it were a kind of moral leftover or residue from adverse experiences.[13]

Surviving violence can cause one to live with a deep suspicion toward any previously held notions of the goodness or trustworthiness of God. One psychiatrist puts it this way: "The traumatic event challenges an ordinary person to become a theologian, a philosopher, and a jurist. The survivor is called upon to articulate the values and beliefs that she once held and that the trauma destroyed. She stands before the emptiness of evil. . . . All questions are reduced to one. . . . Why? . . . Why me?"[14] Asking the question *why?* is a natural and legitimate response to horrendous evils because trauma has negative effects on human persons' perceptions of their relationships with God.

Trauma can cause persons with post-traumatic stress to doubt God's goodness or to see God as "a cruel judge" who is either powerless to help, unwilling to help, or altogether indifferent.[15] For example, consider the story of Holocaust survivor Elie Wiesel as told by Judith Herman:

> There are people with strong and secure belief systems who can endure the ordeals of imprisonment and emerge with their faith intact or strengthened. But these are the extraordinary few. The majority of people experience the bitterness of being forsaken by God. The Holocaust survivor Wiesel gives voice to this bitterness: "Never shall I forget those flames which consumed my faith

---

12. Freud, *Beyond the Pleasure Principle*, 12; and Rambo, *Spirit and Trauma*, 7, 15.

13. See Sartor and Hill, "Attachment Theory"; Stump, *Atonement*, 372–76; and Rea, "Ill-Made Knight," 117–34.

14. Herman, *Trauma and Recovery*, 178.

15. Gostečnik et al., "Trauma and Religiousness," 690–701.

forever. Never shall I forget that nocturnal silence which deprived me, for all eternity, of the desire to live. Never shall I forget those moments which murdered my God and my soul and turned my dreams to dust. Never shall I forget those things, even if I am condemned to live as long as God Himself. Never."[16]

While stories like these are uncomfortable to hear, it is imperative that we listen. Many people assume that this kind of insecure connection with God is contrary to religious faith, that faith means feeling *only* that God is one's "safe haven" and source of comfort, protection, delight, and security.[17] What about those like Wiesel who feel forsaken by God? Is there room for faith in feeling forsaken?

Questions like these present a unique challenge to theologians and students in the religious disciplines today. It appears that psychological trauma creates a loss of connection with God and can cause persons to feel alienated from God and angry toward God. And because trauma is a double-wound, this sense of alienation from God is compounded and difficult to address. If theology is the discipline that addresses the relationship between God and human persons, what can theology contribute to our understanding of this experience of feeling forsaken by God? How can the religious disciplines facilitate recovery for these experiences?

FEELING FORSAKEN BY GOD: CALVIN'S TRAUMATIZED CHRIST

To answer these questions, I will draw from my doctoral research, which has focused on the Christian doctrine of Christ's descent into hell, particularly as the doctrine was articulated by the Reformer and theologian John Calvin, who makes hell sound strikingly similar to trauma.[18] In Calvin's theology, hell is rarely conceived of as a physical place—it "signifies not so much the locality as the condition of those whom God has condemned and doomed to destruction." Hell, then, is the "wretched" feeling of being "cut off from all fellowship with God." For Calvin "where there is guilt before God, there hell immediately shows itself," such that "we always find a hell within us."[19]

16. Herman, *Trauma and Recovery*, 94.

17. Granqvist and Kirkpatrick, "Attachment and Religious Representations," 919.

18. See Hill, "Feeling Forsaken," 188–96.

19. Calvin, "Psychopannychia," 480; Calvin, *Institutes* 3.25.12; Calvin, *Comm.* Heb

Scholars have noted that Calvin is able to pastorally apply this psychological understanding of hell not only to those who "entangled in sin, carry death and hell along with them" but also to those who suffer persecution and endure mental distress: "there is no condition more unhappy than to live in trouble of mind, and to have a continual warfare raging within one's self, or rather without ceasing to be tormented by a hell within" (*tormente dune gehenne interieure*).[20]

Calvin's psychological description of hell results in a certain kind of demythologized account of Christ's descent into hell. He suggests that the traditional story of Christ harrowing souls imprisoned in limbo is "childish" and is "nothing but a story," whereas Christ's actual descent into hell occurred when he "suffered in his soul the terrible torments of a condemned and forsaken man." Calvin calls this experience a kind of "death of the soul," a terrifying sense that one's relationship with God is in peril:[21]

> Would you know what the death of the soul is? It is to be without God—to be abandoned by God. . . . Full of terror and desolation, [it] drives those to despair who feel that it is inflicted on them by an angry and punishing God. The only thing which can temper the bitterness of its agonies is to know that God is our Father, and that we have Christ for our leader and companion.[22]

Hell in Calvin's theology is thus the condition of a soul that results when we are entirely bereft of the conviction that God is favorably disposed toward us because we perceive ourselves to be engaged in an adverse relation with God. To be in hell is to feel forsaken by God rather than loved by God.

Calvin indicates that this feeling of being forsaken by God is what Christ experienced in the garden of Gethsemane and during the crucifixion,

---

2:15; and Calvin, *Comm.* 1 John 3:2. Also, see these remarks by Calvin: "The grave is called *sheol* . . . these words, therefore, here denote not so much the place as the quality and condition of the place" (*Comm.* Ps 16:10); and: "Would you know what the death of the soul is? It is to be without God—to be abandoned by God, and left to itself" ("Psychopannychia," 454–55).

20. Calvin, "Psychopannychia," 455; and Calvin to Monsieur de Falais, Oct. 14, 1543, in *Letters of John Calvin*, 397. Calvin says that "hell has opened to receive him" when one feels the "protracted sorrow" and "mental distress" of a "terrorized conscience" (*Comm.* Ps 6:6–7). For more on Calvin's application of this hellish mental distress to persecution, see Jones, "Soul Anatomy: The Healing Acts of Calvin's Psalms," in *Trauma and Grace*, 43–67.

21. Calvin, *Institutes* 2.16.9 and 2.16.10.

22. Calvin, "Psychopannychia," 454–55 and 483.

two intense emotional struggles that caused severe psychological pain and stress on Christ's body. He pays profound attention to the embodied expression of Christ's fear: "Something commonly considered miraculous was related about him: from the fierceness of his torments, drops of blood flowed from his face."[23] And he employs Christ's bloody sweat as proof that his fear was extreme. This traumatic fear of death continued to the climax on the cross when Jesus cried out, "My God, my God, why have you forsaken me?"

There, Calvin points out a key paradox in the words of Jesus. First, Christ says "My God, my God." He is calling God his own and taking God to himself. This is a cry of faith and trust. Second, Christ cries "why have you forsaken me?" He is crying out against God. This is a cry of despair and fear. Calvin notes that this is a remarkable coincidence that seems paradoxical: Christ does not cease to call God his own and to put his trust in the Father even as he cries out against him. Even when Christ felt forsaken and "suffered beyond measure," Calvin notes that "he did not cease to call him his God, by whom he cried out that he had been forsaken.[24]

This raises an important question. Was Christ sinning when he cried out against God? If faith in God is a religious virtue and Christ is supposed to be morally perfect, how can Christ experience some kind of a loss of faith? Calvin responds that these emotions are apt given the violent events, and therefore "it in nowise detracts from his heavenly glory. . . . There is no reason why Christ's weakness should alarm us."[25] So even though Christ felt forsaken by God, Christ did so in the context of a relationship of lament with God. This demonstrates that it is possible to conceive of faith as a dynamic struggle that is not the opposite of doubt but is rather the very presupposition that legitimates doubt as an appropriate response toward surviving violence.

This means that for Calvin it is possible that doubt and despair are not sinful but are appropriate responses to extreme suffering. Christ has demonstrated by his descent into hell that it is possible for human persons to suffer unspeakable torments, to despair with imperfect faith, and to doubt God's

23. Calvin, *Institutes* 2.16.12.

24. Calvin, *Institutes* 2.16.12. Calvin calls this dialectic of faith and despair "a great paradox" (*repugnantiae*) which could also be translated "contradiction" or "incompatibility."

25. Calvin, *Institutes* 2.16.12.

goodness while still reaching toward that goodness. Feeling alienated from God does not mean we cannot be in a legitimate relationship with God.

FAITH AND DOUBT

The insecure dynamic that Calvin identifies between Christ and God is helpful, I think, when we consider our own relationships to God. That dynamic shows us that insecurity in terms of our attachment to God is not sinful *as such*. Even Jesus felt this way. Consider again the cry of dereliction, "My God, why have you forsaken me?" It seems that Jesus was experiencing an insecure attachment to God during an event of traumatic violence.

It may seem alarming at first to say that Jesus, the eternal and perfect divine Son of God, experienced an insecure attachment to God. But drawing from Calvin, I am arguing that Jesus' sinlessness and moral perfection are compatible with feeling alienated from God. I think this is why the book of Hebrews says that "we do not have a high priest who is unable to sympathize with our weaknesses, but we have one who in every respect has been tested as we are, yet without sin" (Heb. 4:15 NRSV). As Calvin says, Jesus is "bone of our bone and flesh of our flesh"; he is like humanity in every way, yet he has never sinned, and so an insecure attachment is not sinful as such.[26] Thus, I believe that Christ's cry of dereliction can be a helpful framework for those of us who have suffered the effects of trauma in relationship with God. It means that when traumatized persons such as myself feel a loss of safety in relationship with God, we are not sinning, and we are not alone. We are, in fact, in the *best* of company. We are having an experience that God has also experienced in a morally perfect way in the person of Christ. It is completely legitimate to lose a sense of safety in one's relationship to God after trauma, since even God's own sinless Son knows this experience. As those who are included in Christ by the power of the Spirit, we are likewise included in Christ's perfect life before God, which does not prohibit emotional expressions of doubt but includes them in the embrace of perfect faith.

---

26. Untangling sinfulness from normal responses to trauma is essential to post-traumatic growth. This involves being able "to *understand the response to trauma itself:* shattered beliefs about the self, others, the future. This is, I want to emphasize, the normal response to trauma; it is not a symptom of post-traumatic stress disorder, nor does it indicate a defect of character" (Seligman, *Flourish*, 162).

Moreover, as Calvin indicates, we may learn to lament with Christ by crying out "why have you forsaken me," and this lament is possible in the context of a committed relationship with God, where we can call God "my God." In other words, expressing feelings of alienation from God or anger toward God can be a completely legitimate mode of relating with God in the aftermath of trauma and can even be a cathartic or healing experience that is divinely sanctioned by the example of the person and work of Jesus Christ. That is good news for people who feel alienated from God. It is a paradox, but we can say that God knows what it feels like to be alienated from God, and God also knows how to find reconnection with God through such an experience.

Seeing that insecure attachment with God is not sinful is important for an effective response to trauma survivors that can facilitate recovery and healing. Consider the case of Diane, an adult survivor of childhood sexual abuse:

> My father abused me until I was four years old. He threatened to kill my mother or younger brother if I told. . . . Yet my mother continued to keep us in that environment. They eventually divorced. . . . After her divorce, my mother had affairs—the first one involved a priest; the other, a married man. The priest was sexually inappropriate with me. . . . [He] molested me when I was eighteen. . . . Growing up was also filled with constant health issues, nightmares about being chased and raped. . . . I have felt alone and unprotected most of my life. I knew God was there, but his promises were not for me. . . . Although I sought and served God with all of my strength, I still felt a wall and a distance between us.[27]

How can Diane be blamed for a lack of connection with God given the trauma she has survived? She recounts, "I was furious with God. I was also terrified of him, but longed to be close to and secure in him." When sharing these conflicting desires with one of her professors in college, the response she received from the professor startled her: "How could you *not* have trust issues with him?" There was no judgment, no chastisement. Instead, the response was empathetic, validating, and freeing. Diane says that this response freed her to take initial steps in trusting God again. Knowing that her insecure attachment was a legitimate response to trauma and was not sinful freed her to find secure attachment again.

---

27. "Diane's Story," in Schmutzer, *Long Journey Home*, 357–58.

CHRIST'S BODY KEEPS THE SCORE

How can one conclude a story about trauma? As Judith Herman says, always return to the body.[28] Along those lines, the psychiatrist Bessel van der Kolk has recently become popular for his studies in PTSD showing that "the body keeps the score" of the effects of trauma on persons. That is, trauma is not merely about emotional despair or feeling forsaken; it is about how these feelings manifest in unbearable sensations that people feel in their bodies.

Here, I think Calvin's theology can be of help as well. Recall that for Calvin, Christ's descent into hell was not just when he cried out to God on the cross but also when he feared violence and sweat blood in the garden of Gethsemane. We might say that Christ's body was keeping the score of trauma.[29] In this way, we can show not only that it is legitimate to feel alienated from God but also that it is legitimate to feel disabled in one's body as a result of trauma.

I end by recalling my story and the stories of my students and friends. Like many survivors, I live with daily triggers and reminders of the violent past that disrupts and disables. I am thankful for the recovery that has made it possible for me to walk again, even if with a limp. As Judith Herman (a hero of mine) says, recovery doesn't mean that the past is completely healed or that the memories are gone, just that they are losing their gripping and paralyzing force. With time and care, they become integrated into a larger story of grace, memories to befriend rather than avoid. I am comforted that there are theological riches that can be retrieved and reimagined to help in this befriending process. Unlikely as it may seem, Calvin has been a friend to me on that journey. And the Christ of whom he speaks remains the dearest friend of all. I still believe this Christ can teach us how to doubt with faith, how to relate to God after trauma, how to stay in the tension of death and resurrection, and how to hope for the dawn even while it is still dark.[30]

28. Herman, *Trauma and Recovery*, 266 and 269.

29. Hill, "Does God Need a Body."

30. My special thanks go to the team at The Other Journal who gave permissions to reproduce material originally published there February 2022.

BIBLIOGRAPHY

American Psychiatric Association. "PTSD." *Diagnostic and Statistical Manual of Mental Disorders: DSM-III.* 3rd ed. Washington, DC: The American Psychiatric Association, 1980.

Benjet, Corina, et al. "The Epidemiology of Traumatic Event Exposure Worldwide: Results from the World Mental Health Survey Consortium." *Psychological Medicine* 46:2 (2016) 327–43.

Calvin, John. *Calvin's Commentaries.* 22 vols. Edinburgh: Calvin Translation Society, 1843–56. Repr., Grand Rapids: Baker, 1998.

———. *Institutes of the Christian Religion.* Edited by J. T. McNeill and F. L. Battles. Philadelphia: Westminster John Knox, 1960.

———. *Letters of John Calvin.* Edited by Jules Bonnett. Philadelphia: Presbyterian Board of Publications, 1858.

———. "Psychopannychia." In *Tracts and Treatises*, edited by Henry Beveridge. 3 vols. Grand Rapids: Eerdmans, 1958.

———. *Tracts and Treatises in Defense of the Reformed Faith.* Grand Rapids: Eerdmans, 1958.

Caruth, Cathy. *Trauma: Explorations in Memory.* Baltimore: Johns Hopkins University Press, 1995.

———, ed. *Listening to Trauma: Conversations with Leaders in the Theory and Treatment of Catastrophic Experience.* Baltimore: Johns Hopkins University Press, 2014.

Cassidy, Jude, and Phillip Shaver, eds. *Handbook of Attachment: Theory, Research, and Clinical Applications.* 3d ed. New York: Guilford, 2016.

Freud, Sigmund. *Beyond the Pleasure Principle.* Translated by James Strachey. New York: Liveright, 1961.

Gostečnik, Christian, et al. "Trauma and Religiousness." *Journal of Religion and Health* 53:3 (2014) 690–701.

Granqvist, Pehr, and Lee A. Kirkpatrick. "Attachment and Religious Representations and Behavior." In *Handbook of Attachment: Theory, Research, and Clinical Applications*, edited by Jude Cassidy and Phillip R. Shaver, 3rd ed., 917–40. New York: Guilford, 2016.

Herman, Judith. *Trauma and Recovery: The Aftermath of Violence—From Domestic Abuse to Political Terror.* New York: Basic, 1992.

Hill, Preston. "Does God Need a Body to Keep the Score of Trauma?" *Theological Puzzles* 1 (2021). https://www.theo-puzzles.ac.uk/2021/04/20/phill/.

———. "Feeling Forsaken: Christ's Descent into Hell in the Theology of John Calvin." PhD diss., University of St Andrews, 2021.

———, ed. *Christ and Trauma: Theology East of Eden.* Eugene, OR: Pickwick, 2025.

Jones, Serene. *Trauma and Grace: Theology in a Ruptured World.* Louisville: Westminster John Knox, 2009.

Panchuk, Michelle. "The Shattered Spiritual Self: A Philosophical Exploration of Religious Trauma." *Res Philosophica* 95:3 (2018) 505–30.

Rambo, Shelly. *Spirit and Trauma: A Theology of Remaining.* Louisville: Westminster John Knox, 2010.

Rea, Michael. *The Hiddenness of God.* New York: Oxford University Press, 2018.

———. "The Ill-Made Knight and the Stain on the Soul." *European Journal for Philosophy of Religion* 11:1 (2019) 117–34.

Rothschild, Babette. *Eight Keys to Safe Trauma Recovery: Take-Charge Strategies to Empower Your Healing*. New York: Norton, 2010.

Sartor, Dan, and Preston Hill. "Attachment Theory and the Cry of Dereliction: A Science-Engaged Model of Atonement for Posttraumatic Stains on the Soul." *Theologica* (forthcoming).

Schmutzer, Andrew, ed. *The Long Journey Home: Understanding and Ministering to the Sexually Abused*. Eugene, OR: Wipf & Stock, 2011.

Seligman, Martin. *Flourish: A Visionary New Understanding of Happiness and Well-Being*. London: Atria, 2011.

Stump, Eleonore. *Atonement*. New York: Oxford University Press, 2018.

van der Kolk, Bessel. *The Body Keeps the Score: Brain, Mind, and Body in the Transformation of Trauma*. New York: Penguin, 2014.

van der Kolk, Bessel, and Rita Fisler. "Dissociation and the Fragmentary Nature of Traumatic Memories: Overview and Exploratory Study." *Journal of Traumatic Stress* 8:4 (1995) 505–25. van der Kolk, Bessel, et al. *Traumatic Stress: The Effects of Overwhelming Experience on Mind, Body, and Society*. New York: Guilford, 2007.

A Cruciform Trauma

War, Gender, Sacrifice, and Moral Injury

Adam Tietje

Shelly Rambo's latest contribution to the growing body of theology and trauma literature picks up where her theology of Saturday leaves off. In *Resurrecting Wounds*, Rambo invites us to once again read the Gospel of John with her.[1] She takes us through a series of close readings of texts and communities in conversation with the upper room encounter of Thomas with the wounds of Jesus. The risen Christ bears the wounds of the trauma of the cross. In the face of attempts to elide and erase the wounds of various traumatic histories (personal and collective), Rambo beckons us to find the emergence of new life at the very site of our wounds. Moreover, Rambo claims that Jesus' wounds

> provide a site of crossing, not by erasing the memory of crosses, but by bringing the memories together, not to erase them by folding them into one, but by making room for distinctive histories to be held. . . . Histories of suffering can come together to cancel each other out, or they could meet, to discover that they are, at some level, touching.[2]

There is in fact "a danger of not linking the wisdom and insight of each."[3] Powerful political interests profit from the disassociation of histories of suffering, as those seeking justice fight and compete for attention and

---

1. Rambo, *Resurrecting Wounds*.

2. Rambo, *Resurrecting Wounds*, 98.

3. Rambo, *Resurrecting Wounds*, 99.

resources.[4] She draws these conclusions in her chapter on racial trauma and the unique trauma of Black women. In the very next chapter, she examines the trauma of veterans. By placing these chapters side by side, Rambo invites us into the possibility that the distinct traumas of women and Black women in particular might in some way be brought together with the trauma of soldiers in war. Unfortunately, in her study, Rambo leaves us with no clear through line.

I want to pick up where Rambo leaves us. I want to examine together the trauma of women, and Black women particularly, and veterans and suggest that their wounds do indeed call out to one another as Rambo suggests. The meeting site is in the wounds of Christ and the way Christ's wounds have figured, in often deeply problematic ways, in the moral formation of women and soldiers. Specifically, I want to argue that the trauma of women and veterans are enacted in the context of similar political narratives of sacrifice that foster and enforce sacrificial agency.

Moral injury has become a way to name the agentic aspects of war trauma. Some feminists have resonated with the concept.[5] I contend that this resonance emerges precisely because the moral and political agency of soldiers and veteran is subject to similar, if not the very same, social and political forces as women and Black women particularly, namely, political theologies of sacrifice. Moral injury helps us name and locate the resonance of these experiences of guilt, shame, and betrayal in the context of sacrificial agency. In this chapter, then, I show the deep connections between the political theologies of sacrifice that fund the sexual trauma of women and Black women in particular and the political theologies of sacrifice that fund American war and the war trauma of soldiers and veterans. I argue that moral injury is a wound of the sacrificial agency of soldiers within the *polis* as *oikos*.

MORAL INJURY AND PTSD: SITES OF CROSSING?

Moral injury first emerged in the clinical world as a conceptual and therapeutic response to the ways in which the moral dimensions of the trauma of war veterans exceeded the bounds of the conceptualization of Post-Traumatic Stress Disorder (PTSD) in the *Diagnostic and Statistical Manual*

4. Rambo, *Resurrecting Wounds*, 95–97.
5. Guth, "Moral Injury."

of Mental Disorders (DSM) (even granting that *DSM-III* included guilt).[6] Jonathan Shay, a Veterans Affairs (VA) psychiatrist, first used the term moral injury to capture that excess in light of the experiences of betrayal the Vietnam veterans he worked with named.[7] Shay's conception focuses on the way that war corrupts character and how that corruption is linked to failures of leadership. Shay defines moral injury as "a betrayal of what's right, by a person who holds legitimate authority (e.g., in the military—a leader) in a high-stakes situation."[8] That betrayal could come at the hands of one's immediate leaders or be tied all the way back to the actions or inaction of those holding political power. Shay's account of moral injury built on the clear connections that Vietnam veterans made between their personal suffering and the politics and prosecution of the war itself.

More than a decade later, and many years into the wars in Iraq and Afghanistan, Brett Litz et al.[9] took up the concept of moral injury as a way to name and respond to the moral pain of veterans that is connected to their own agency or perceived failures and also results in some form of psychosocial impairment or maladaptive or destructive behaviors.[10] Moral injury, as Litz frames it, involves a perceived moral violation that leads to painful moral emotions and cognitions with a resulting inability to navigate that pain toward meaning and connection. These violations include violations in which the self is perpetrator (moral emotions of guilt and shame) and/or victim (moral emotions of anger and disgust). Litz shifts the focus of moral injury away from the wider institutional (or even national) context with which Shay is concerned and zooms in on the individual agency of soldiers and veterans.

Theological ethicists, notably Warren Kinghorn, Joseph Wiinikka-Lydon, and Karen Guth, have also begun to examine moral injury.[11] Kinghorn's work on moral injury is particularly helpful as he stands astride both the clinical and theological worlds and thinks through the disciplinary

---

6. *Diagnostic and Statistical Manual.*

7. Shay, *Achilles in Vietnam.*

8. Shay, "Moral Injury," 183.

9. The authors are also VA providers/researchers, with the exception of William Nash who, at the time, was a psychiatrist in the United States Marine Corps.

10. Litz et al., "Moral Injury."

11. Others key thinkers include Michael Yandell and Brian Powers. See Yandell, *War and Negative Revelation*; and Powers, *Full Darkness.*

limits of psychiatry theologically.[12] Kinghorn's deepest worry about the clinical framework is that therapeutic responses to moral injury are strictly directed to the reduction of moral pain and symptoms. Within this framework, then, clinicians have been more than happy to "prescribe" religious solutions. Kinghorn names this therapeutic instrumentalism.[13] If moral injury is a wound of moral agency, then addressing moral injury by necessity requires a larger account of the moral life as embedded within a community of meaning and virtue. While there are deep problems with the clinical responses to moral injury, the acknowledgment of moral injury itself presents hopeful possibilities. It represents a recognition of the importance of the moral agency of veterans in war and the need for veterans on the other side of war to situate their moral pain within a larger moral world such as the church. Kinghorn sees moral injury as an opening for churches to better understand the veterans in their midst and more seriously reckon with their relationship to American war.

Joseph Wiinikka-Lydon defines moral injury as a form of "burdensome knowledge" in the aftermath of violence.[14] He examines moral injury in the context of political violence more broadly than just war, and as applicable not just to soldiers and veterans, but to all those caught up in the fray. For Wiinikka-Lydon, moral injury in this broader context is a kind of "harm done to one's moral subjectivity and ability to imagine oneself as a morally capable person."[15] Moral injury is indicative of something gone deeply awry in the life of a political community. Thus, although burdensome, the experience of moral injury is also ripe for prophetic insight and includes an inherent prophetic critique.

Karen Guth, like Wiinikka-Lydon, broadens the aperture on moral injury and argues it is a useful concept for thinking through the tainted legacies of the Christian tradition around sexism and slavery. For Guth, moral injury helps illuminate the moral complexities of tainted legacies. Those tainted legacies can also be named as morally injurious. She argues that feminist and womanist theologies are, in part, "responses to wounds sustained from morally injurious forms of Christianity" and that the work

---

12. Kinghorn, "Moral Engagement."

13. Kinghorn, "Combat Trauma."

14. Wiinikka-Lydon, "Moral Injury," 220.

15. Wiinikka-Lydon, *Moral Injury*, 37.

of feminist and womanist theologians is helpful for navigating morally injurious legacies.[16]

Moral injury began as an acknowledgment of the moral dimension of war trauma. It became a way to acknowledge and address what PTSD alone fails to account for. Soldiers are not just bodies upon which trauma happens. Moral injury acknowledges that the ongoingness of war is bound up, not just with what happened, but with what soldiers themselves do or fail to do as both perpetrators and victims of violence. Soldiers are people with moral agency and moral injury is a wound intimately bound up with that agency. Even as clinicians now more fully attend to the agentic aspects of war trauma, the clinical framework conceptualizes and cares for moral injury as a "personal" wound. Theological ethicists such as Kinghorn and Wiinikka-Lydon contend that moral injury is a sign of something gone awry within a wider moral and political context. It is very much the political borne bodily. The work of Kinghorn and Wiinikka-Lydon together suggest that the care of moral injury must reckon with moral injury as a political problem. Guth's attention to the resonance of moral injury with the work of feminist and womanist theologians recalls a similar conjunction between the wounds of men and the wounds of women a generation earlier in the wake of Vietnam.

If moral injury is a sign of something gone deeply awry in the life of a political community, then what might the moral injury of American soldiers and veterans indicate about American political life? To answer this question, it is necessary to first contextualize the moral injury conversation within the wider trauma conversation out of which it grew. It was, in fact, born of distinct yet similarly directed political movements of both women and veterans, mostly men, in the 1970s that led to the inclusion of PTSD in *DSM-III*. It is widely known that PTSD emerged as a diagnosis in response to the efforts of Vietnam veterans who sought recognition and care through the VA. Often left out of the story is the role that feminists played as they, too, sought recognition, political rights, and access to care resources.[17] At the same time veterans demanded recognition, feminists brought to light the reality of domestic sexual trauma.

16. Guth, "Moral Injury," 182.

17. For example, Young's *Harmony of Illusions*. Fassin and Rechtman outline the role that veterans *and* feminists played in *Empire of Trauma*, 78–84.

Since World War I, the respective traumas of men and women have been linked through symptomology.[18] With this linkage in view—and in light of the intertwining histories of the study of war trauma and sexual trauma and their related political movements—Judith Herman concludes that the sexual trauma of women is "the combat neurosis of the sex war."[19] Women were struggling not only for liberation from subordination, but also from subordination "maintained and enforced by the hidden violence of men."[20] In the sexual trauma of women and the combat trauma of men,[21] Herman finds a kind of mirrored relationship between men and women, but inverted across the public/private divide. She writes,

> Fifty years ago, Virginia Woolf wrote that the "public and private worlds are inseparably connected. . . . The tyrannies and servilities of one are the tyrannies and servilities of the other." It is now apparent that the traumas of one are the traumas of the other. The hysteria of women and the combat neurosis of men are one. Recognizing the commonality of affliction may even make it possible at times to transcend the immense gulf that separates the public sphere of war and politics—the world of men—and the private sphere of domestic life—the sphere of women.[22]

Herman directly connects the sexual trauma of women to domestic tyrannies and servilities. The women's liberation movement specifically challenged the way domestic tyrannies and their attendant traumas were depoliticized and privatized as personal or family problems. The mantra, the personal is political, succinctly and aptly summarizes the feminist response. The subordination and abuse of women was and is a political problem that requires a political response.

The Vietnam veterans also saw the war and their suffering after the war as a political problem. On the surface, then, the inclusion of PTSD in *DSM-III* would seem like a great victory for veterans (and women) in their quest for recognition. Indeed, PTSD granted legitimacy to the claims of veterans and access to care and benefits through the VA. However, it also

18. See Herman, *Trauma and Recovery*, 20–32.

19. Herman, *Trauma and Recovery*, 32.

20. Herman, *Trauma and Recovery*, 32.

21. Of course, women are not the only ones who experience sexual trauma. Likewise, men are not the only ones who experience combat trauma. Even so, Herman's gender analysis (and my own that follows) still applies and I argue helps illuminate the trauma of women in the military, especially in the context of military sexual trauma.

22. Herman, *Trauma and Recovery*, 32.

foreclosed further political reckoning around the Vietnam War.[23] As Fassin and Rechtman put it,

> [DSM-III] allowed the nation to confront its defeat in Vietnam. Instead of facing up to the impossible choice of either condemning some of its soldiers for their actions or itself assuming responsibility for their crimes, the nation could rest easy in the psychiatrists' comforting conclusion: these were ordinary men placed in extraordinary conditions who needed to be cared for rather than judged and perhaps condemned. Trauma, and particularly PTSD, which included them in the same diagnostic category as victims, provided a comprehensive solution. It gave all veterans, including the perpetrators of atrocities, a status that conferred the right to compensation. Moreover, it allowed the latter the benefit of the doubt with the aim of rehabilitating them, crediting them with a residue of humanity evidenced by the traumatic memory they retained of their actions.[24]

The recognition of veterans via *DSM-III* was a real recognition that allowed for their reincorporation into America's social body. However, this reinclusion was accomplished at the expense of any reckoning with the moral and political failure of the war. The clinical recognition of the trauma of war veterans allowed them to be heard just to the extent that it affirmed that war was horrible and that neither they, nor anyone in particular, had to bear the full weight of responsibility.

On the surface, then, it would seem rather pedestrian to say the experiences and suffering of veterans is political. Working as they do to defend the *polis*, of course the work of soldiers and veterans is political. In reality though, America's stories about its war making serve to depoliticize and then to privatize the trauma of veterans.[25] They grant meaning to the experiences and suffering of soldiers to the extent that they conform to a certain civil religious orthodoxy. They mask the reality of the moral suffering of soldiers behind the veil of personal sacrifice. America's stories about war can affirm that war is horrible and that soldiers suffer because they do so *pro nobis*. Soldiers are sacrificial agents who willingly endure even unto death.

Of note, the very same theologies of sacrifice that justify and mask the trauma of women in the private sphere serve to privatize and depoliticize

---

23. Fassin and Rechtman, *Empire of Trauma*, 92–95.

24. Fassin and Rechtman, *Empire of Trauma*, 94–95.

25. Ebel, *GI Messiahs*, 18.

war trauma. Following Herman, I argue that the afflictions of men at war and women at home are intimately related. Herman argues that this relationship is more than just symptomological, but related—as she says via her quote of Woolf—through tyrannies and servilities. Herman suspects that it is the violence of war that comes home to haunt women and concludes that the abolition of war and the liberation of women are "inseparably connected." But, what are the tyrannies and servilities of women and soldiers and how are they inseparably connected? To answer that question, we need to examine the relationship between gender and war.

THE *POLIS* AS *OIKOS*

Feminists have long argued that war and gender are co-constitutive. The politics of gender and its representations inform the prosecution of war and the politics of war inform the representation of traditional gender roles and their socialization among children.[26] Gender provides a seemingly stable set of "natural" distinctions around which political life can be organized and ordered. Masculine virtues are those virtues that prepare boys to fight, virtues that entail representations of that which needs protecting. Feminine virtues are those virtues that prepare girls to eventually maintain households and social structures while men fight for them and the homeland as that which is to be protected. In this way, gender codes the relationship between soldiers and the home front.

It is against this backdrop that the inclusion of women and openly LG-BTQ soldiers in the American military has been an ongoing source of turmoil in both the wider culture and within the military, in particular.[27] The presence of women in the military is destabilizing precisely because gender is so intimately bound up with war on every level, both in the way it shapes the stories we tell about war on a grand scale and the way individual soldiers understand themselves within that story. For straight men in the military, to be a soldier is to be a "real" man. When women remained excluded from combat and special operations military occupational specialties (MOS), a certain gendered stability persisted. Women serving in support roles within the military recapitulated their support roles on the home front and kept

26. See Goldstein, *War and Gender*, esp. 410–14.

27. For an entry into the debates, one could watch Fox News since its inception or see van Creveld, "Less Than We Can Be."

their identity as "protected" intact.[28] The "masculinity" of the military and soldiers (i.e., their readiness for war) is called into question by the inclusion of the excluded (women, openly LGBTQ soldiers), those who are supposed to be outside, the protected. The foment around the "feminization" of the military as an emasculating threat reveals how the identity of the military and soldiers is both fundamentally gendered and unstable.

What the critics of the "feminization" of the military fail to realize is that even apart from the inclusion of women, soldiers are already "feminized."[29] The analogy between women and soldiers has long been made clear in feminist political theory, in which the good soldier/good wife (or good mother) analogy highlights both the co-constitutive relationship between gender and war *and* its fundamental instability. The analogy first shows up in Mary Wollstonecraft's *A Vindication of the Rights of Woman*. Wollstonecraft argues that differences in virtue between men and women are a result of differences in education and moral formation. To make her case, she compares women and soldiers:

> As a proof that education gives this appearance of weakness to females, we may instance the example of military men, who are, like them, sent into the world before their minds have been stored with knowledge, or fortified by principles. The consequences are similar. . . . Soldiers, as well as women, practice the minor virtues with punctilious politeness. . . . Like the fair sex, the business of their lives is gallantry; they were taught to please, and they only live to please. . . . The great misfortune is this, that they both acquire manners before morals.[30]

Both women and soldiers undergo a kind of superficial moral formation of manners before morals, as both are formed for lives of obedience.

Jean Bethke Elshtain, in her book *Women and War*, builds on Wollstonecraft's analogy, but rather than women generally, she homes in on good mothers and good soldiers.[31] She finds the good soldier/good mother binary emblematic of the gendering of the public/private distinction, which she traces back to the Greek distinction between the *oikos* and the *polis*.[32]

---

28. This myth was upended during the wars in Iraq and Afghanistan as the distinction between combat and support MOSs was shown to be flimsy when bullets start flying.

29. Pin-Fat and Stern, "Private Jessica Lynch," 40.

30. Wollstonecraft, *Vindication*, 105–6.

31. Elshtain, *Women and War*, 225.

32. Elshtain, *Public Man*.

The *oikos* is the realm of biological necessity (*bios*), a sphere of production and reproduction. Out of this realm of necessity (and upon it), men enter a world of free action and speech, the *polis* (*zoon politikon*). The *oikos/polis* distinction names two distinct forms of association, one which constitutes the family or household and the other which encompasses political life.

For feminist political theorists, this also names a distinction through which patriarchal gender norms enforce the gender binary across the public/private divide. Women are confined to life in the private realm of the *oikos*, to the rearing of children, the realm of necessity. Men are free for life in the *polis*, the public world of political freedom and action. Mothers sacrifice for their children within the private world of the household, while men sacrifice for the *polis*.

In order to escape confinement to the *oikos*, some feminists embraced contract theory. Challenging this embrace, Carole Pateman argues in *The Sexual Contract* that the social contract upholds patriarchy all the way down. The free "individual" is gendered masculine and created through the maintenance of natural subordination in the private sphere through the marriage contract. Pateman writes,

> Women are incorporated into a sphere that both is and is not in civil society. . . . The antinomy private/public is another expression of natural/civil and women/men. The private, womanly sphere (natural) and the public masculine sphere (civil) are opposed but gain their meaning from each other. . . . What it means to be an "individual" . . . is revealed by the subjection of women in the private sphere.[33]

Traditionally, women are "incorporated" or included within the *polis* precisely by their exclusion and relegation to the *oikos* through the marriage contract. The marriage contract, then, is foundational to both the creation of the public civil sphere and the sexual difference it establishes and enforces.

Political philosopher Graham Parsons, too, argues that the social contract is gendered all the way down. While Pateman traces this through the marriage contract, Parsons finds it in the enlistment contract and the civil-military distinction.[34] The military, long perceived as the domain of men and masculinity, is not quite the paragon of manly agency it is supposed. Rather, in an analogous way to the binding of a woman to her husband in

33. Pateman, *Sexual Contract*, 11.

34. See Parsons, "Contract." I explore his argument in a more extended way in Tietje, "Ambiguity of Care."

a marriage contract, the enlistment contract binds soldiers to the state. The legal relationship between soldiers and the state mirrors the private, domestic sphere of eighteenth and nineteenth century women.[35] For soldiers, the *polis* becomes an *oikos*. He writes, "Within traditional political society (i.e., prior to the mid-nineteenth century), we have then two spheres that deny full status of citizenship to people and two contracts that solidify that subordinate status. The two spheres are the family and the military. The two contracts are the marriage contract and the enlistment contract [and we should also add the slave contract]." Parsons concludes that "the civil/ military distinction is the masculine counterpart to the patriarchal public/ private distinction."[36] Just as traditional political society denied full citizenship to women and relegated them to a subordinate status within the private domestic sphere on the basis of the marriage contract, so too are soldiers denied full citizenship and relegated to a subordinate status on the basis of the enlistment contract. Soldiers, too, are included within the *polis* through their exclusion.

For feminist thinkers like Bonnie Mann and others, gender is not epiphenomenal, but at the very heart of the way that sovereignty and the state of exception are both imagined and practiced. Mann concludes,

> The state of exception which substitutes force for law, in which force becomes law, echoes and repeats the structure of sovereign masculinity, in which the will of the manly man is the only source of meaning. The sovereign man, in essence, declares his own state of exception, in which he fantasizes that he is no longer subject to human vulnerability and intersubjective dependency (i.e., to the human condition). Since *force* is what is left when the normative power of the law is suspended, the state of exception also echoes and repeats the hyperbolic displays of agency that characterize sovereign masculinity, through which the sovereign man performatively constitutes his manhood. The state in a state of exception performatively constitutes its own manhood through hyperbolic displays of force.[37]

35. When the Supreme Court reaches for an analogy to understand the new status of a soldier, they find only one, marriage. The marriage contract is the lens through which the Court articulates the enlistment contract. See *In re Grimley*, 137 U.S. 147 (1890).

36. Parsons, "Contract." These quotes are from an unpublished draft of Parson's article. Any success of his conclusions are owed to him and any failure is mine.

37. Mann, *Sovereign Masculinity*, 212.

If, as Schmitt argues, "concepts of the modern theory of the state are secularized theological concepts,"[38] Mann's "sovereign man" is a kind of immanent frame icon (independent and invulnerable) through which sovereignty (and, of course, its theological concepts) is shown to be bound up with a kind of masculinity in what she calls sovereign masculinity. To make explicit what is already hinted at above, masculinity stands in a "relation of exception" to femininity.

There certainly remain many relevant distinctions to be made between the military and household. My argument is not that the military *is* the *oikos*. Neither am I arguing that soldiers *are* women. However, following Parsons, I have argued that the good soldier (like the good wife/mother) is not a public and political exemplar. The *oikos* and the military are both tied to the state of nature and outside the *polis* proper (fig. 1). The military and the *oikos* are both spaces of inclusion through exclusion by which the outside/state of nature is taken into the *polis* itself. The American military is a standing army that exists within a permanent state of exception. While the political situations of soldiers and women are not exactly the same, I am arguing that soldiers, like women in the *oikos*, are included through their exclusion and subject to the precarity of the state of nature. The military stands in relation to the rest of society as the place in which the state of nature is taken into the heart of the *polis* (fig. 2) *and* it has become a space of permanent exception unto itself, a place in which the collapse of *oikos* and *polis* into one another is made manifest (*polis* as *oikos*, fig. 3). Like the camps, within the military, too, the "city and house [read: *oikos* and *polis*] [become] indistinguishable."[39]

Figure 4

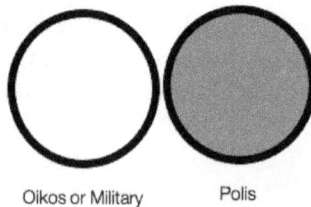

Oikos or Military   Polis

38. Schmitt, *Political Theology*, 5.
39. Agamben, *Homo Sacer*, 188.

Figure 5

Military in relation to
Society

Figure 6

Polis as Oikos (Military as
permanent state of
exception)

We are now in a position to show both why the inclusion and now full inclusion of women remains so contested. The presence of women reveals the military as a zone of indistinction in which, upon enlistment, soldiers are included in the *polis* through their very exclusion. Yet to the extent that soldiers are instruments of sovereign masculinity, the military and soldiers show up at the very center of the mythos of the nation, as the quintessential "insiders" at the very heart of the nation. The masculinity of soldiers is central to both this story and its lived reality. The inclusion of women, however, gives the lie to this inclusion. At first, it would seem that it simply gives the lie to notion that martial sacrifice is inherently masculine. This is certainly true on one level and represents a real victory for liberal feminists in the context of the military. I would take it step further and suggest, with feminists like Pin-Fat and Stern, that because military masculinity is already outside, excluded, instrumentalized, and subordinated, the concerns over the "feminization" of the military fail to recognize that the military and soldiers are already structurally "feminized."

Soldiers intuitively know this and code relationships of subordination and domination in gendered language[40] because like women in the context

40. As Goldstein shows: "Within armies, by the same principle, subordinates are coded as feminine." Goldstein, *War and Gender*, 356. Gender also codes the relationship between soldiers and the enemy. Goldstein writes on the same page: "Male soldiers use gender to represent domination. Psychologically, they assume a masculine and dominant position relative to a feminine and subordinate enemy."

of the *oikos* they are dominated legally, politically, and socially within the military as a permanent state of exception. Soldiers are formed to conform to this subordinate and feminine posture, formed to submit, obey, and sacrifice their freedom and bodily autonomy even unto death. *And*, as feminists have well argued, soldiers are also formed to dominate, emasculate, and kill a feminized enemy. This puts soldiers in quite the bind socially and psychologically.[41]

For soldiers, then, the performance of masculinity is doubly intensified. First, this is because, as noted, the formation for killing in war is itself the distillation and inculcation of the masculine virtues. Masculine virtues are the virtues required for the use of force in the fighting of war. And secondly, the performance of masculinity for male soldiers is further intensified because these men are feminized in the *polis* as *oikos*. Hypermasculinity, an exaggerated performance of masculinity, is well summarized as "the belief that in order to be a man you must in no way resemble a woman."[42] Soldiers intuitively know that they do. This is just the sexualized and gendered lens through which they understand their experience as soldiers and how they narrate their positionality among themselves. They are continually being "fucked." Thus, hypermasculinity among soldiers is exaggerated and overcompensated masculinity performed in an attempt to overcome their structural feminization. In addition to the intensification of masculinity that is part and parcel to war itself, the hyper or toxic performances of masculinity among soldiers can also be read as attempts to deny or escape the reality that they are legally, politically, and socially gendered as feminine.

I contend that this is actually the most salient fact for the daily existence of soldiers in combat or garrison. It is this fact that codes and intensifies other relationships fraught with the potential gendered dynamics of domination and subordination, whether with their own subordinates, with spouses/wives and children in their homes, or with the enemy (or potential/perceived enemy) on the battlefield. In each of these domains,

---

41. The binds, of course, differ for men, women, and LGBTQ soldiers. In what follows, I primarily outline the bind of men. Women are doubly feminized and thus must work even harder to ensure their soldierly *bona fides* through masculine gender performance or face the threat of a double feminization. The bind for LGBTQ soldiers typically lands in one direction or the other depending on whether they conform to masculine or feminine gender performance. The case of those who refuse either is understudied or unstudied as far as I'm aware, but potentially very illuminating.

42. Michael, "Hypermasculinity Is a Plague."

soldiers' experience of feminization can lead to an intensification of the performance of a masculine gender role. It is not surprising, then, that the threat of violence is the backdrop for this performance. Violence, aggression, and lethality are the means by which soldiers have been formed to establish their masculinity vis-à-vis a feminized enemy.[43] In the context of military training and war, the violence of soldiers is *disciplined* violence (or, at least, that is the intent). Soldiers are the instruments (read: dominated and feminized instruments) of the violence of the state. Thus, the dangers of the intensification of soldiers' performance of their masculinity are heightened in contexts where soldiers are not disciplined and soldiers may overcompensate to prove precisely that they are "not women" even though they sometimes put on a uniform and play one. Though this is not my primary line of argumentation, these effects—of the gendering of the *polis* as *oikos*—are present in any number of contexts, whether that be in thinking about military sexual trauma, domestic violence in military families, soldier and veteran suicide rates.

Soldiers, like women, serve in the *oikos*, the *polis* as *oikos*. Wollstonecraft argues that good wives/women are like good soldiers. The inverse is also true, good soldiers are like good wives. At just the point where it seems the sacrificial paths for men and women diverge, the civil-military distinction genders soldiers as feminine vis-à-vis the state within the *polis* as *oikos*. This move renders soldiers' bodies and sacrifices public and political, while simultaneously attenuating their political agency and relegating them, like women, to agency within the *oikos*, the *polis* as *oikos*.

THE *OIKOS*, THE *POLIS* AS *OIKOS*, AND SACRIFICE

For women within the traditional *oikos*, subordination is inculcated in the context of the overarching political fact of their existence that *as women* they stand under the authority of and in service to the men in their lives, i.e., husbands and fathers. This relationship of subordination is not an end in itself. It is subordination as a form of sacrifice for some other good. Women sacrifice for the sake of the household. They put their bodies on the line in order to conceive, gestate, birth, and rear children. They are formed for a kind of sacrificial love that subordinates their own needs and desires for the good of their family, their children, and their husband.

---

43. This aspect of masculinity in relation to war is at the center of Stan Goff's *Borderline*.

The attenuation, abrogation, or constraint of agency of women in the traditional household is a form of sacrifice for the *oikos*. While it is disciplined in the context of relations of domination and subordination, women in the *oikos* are formed from childhood to embody these sacrificial roles. I name the agency that women embody within these sacrificial roles as sacrificial agency. While sacrificial agency is certainly a sacrifice of agency (i.e., the abrogation of agency in the context of patriarchal relations), by sacrificial agency I am also naming the broader reality, the entire moral ecology in which women are formed not just to sacrifice themselves and to accept their social and political exclusion and subordination, but to endure willing and out of love for and duty to their family.[44]

While feminist political theorists have critiqued the political dynamics that foster and sustain women in relations of domination and subordination (which I examined, in brief, above), feminist theologians have critiqued the underlying theology. The twentieth-century debate in Christian ethics around agape primarily defined as self-sacrifice is exemplary.[45] Anders Nygren sets the terms of this debate in *Agape and Eros*.[46] Nygren sees agape and eros in opposition to one another. Eros is self-love, and while natural, it bends us toward selfishness and is thus always morally negative.[47] In contrast to eros, agape is disinterested love[48] and self-sacrifice is the chief end. Agape love "gives itself away . . . sacrifices itself, even to the uttermost."[49] At the heart of Nygren's agape ethics lies the Christian doctrine of atonement and God's own self-sacrificial love exemplified by Jesus on the cross.

Of course, if Christian love, agape, is the rejection of one's own power and interests, it is an unrealistic foundation for politics. At least, this is Reinhold Niebuhr's conclusion. Politics involves the negotiation of interests and power. While individuals might exemplify agape, social bodies

---

44. On the surface, these sacrifices would not seem to be political. Yet, the labor and sacrifice of women in the *oikos* are essential to the survival and flourishing of their political community. Thus, while not political agents themselves, the sacrifices of women are nonetheless sacrifices for the political community.

45. This is precisely what Barbara Hilkert Andolsen does. Thus, the brief sketch I offer here draws primarily from her account in "Agape in Feminist Ethics."

46. Nygren, *Agape and Eros*.

47. Nygren, *Agape and Eros*, 217.

48. A Christian love of neighbor is not grounded in anything inherent in the neighbor, but wholly in God's love. Because human love bends inward it can only be grounded in divine agape.

49. Andolsen, "Agape in Feminist Ethics," 70.

can only be characterized by selfish pursuit of their interests. Thus, for Niebuhr, individuals might pursue self-sacrificial love in their interpersonal relationships, but in politics and public life, the best we might hope for is justice negotiated among the competing interests of various groups. Niebuhr exemplifies the apotheosis of Christian ethics in the wake of the growing social distinction between private life (agapic love) and public life (justice).[50] Feminist theologians like Mary Daly and Margaret Farley argue that Nygren's account of agape and eros and Niebuhr's distinction between love and justice reinscribe the distinction between public and private virtue and reinforce the subordination of women and concomitant sacrificial roles.

Womanist theologians have critiqued the theology underlying the sacrificial roles of Black women at the intersection of gender and race.[51] In *Sisters in the Wilderness*, Delores Williams names the unique oppression of Black women in America as "social-role surrogacy."[52] Williams finds surrogacy to be an apt description for the roles Black women occupied during and after slavery. Black women were forced to fill the roles of others as substitutes for the presence, labor, care, intellect, and sexuality of white men and women. All of these roles emerged, of course, under the constant terror and threat of violence and death.[53]

Williams argues that the social legacy of the surrogacy roles of Black women problematizes Christian images of redemption.[54] Doctrines of atonement that understand Jesus to have taken human sin upon himself

50. Niebuhr, *Love and Justice*, 27–29.

51. I say theologically similar because womanist critiques of self-sacrifice also home in on the reinscription of oppression via atonement theology. I say historically parallel because while the oppression of women in the context of industrialization also presses against Black women, the oppression of slavery and its afterlife, while interwoven with patriarchal hierarchies, are of a uniquely evil order. Black women are situated at the intersection of both racist and patriarchal forms of oppression, with the two deeply enmeshed. Womanist theologians are not in one accord on the rejection of surrogacy necessitating a rejection of sacrifice. Monica Coleman affirms the need for sacrifice in the Christian life from a process theology perspective, for example. See Coleman, "Sacrifice, Surrogacy and Salvation."

52. Williams, *Sisters in the Wilderness*.

53. Williams, *Sisters in the Wilderness*, 62–71.

54. It should be noted that the conversation around the surrogacy of Black women is highly relevant for thinking about the agency of Black women in the military. Black women are almost doubly overrepresented as a percentage of women in the US military compared to the general population. See Melin, "Desperate Choices"; also, Fox, "Aretē." In this vein, Walker-Barnes, *Too Heavy a Yoke*, stands out as important to consider.

and his death on the cross to be "in our place" imagine Jesus as "the ultimate surrogate figure."[55] Williams worries that these images of redemption sacralize surrogacy and asks "whether the image of a surrogate-God has salvific power for Black women or whether this image supports and reinforces the exploitation that has accompanied their experience with surrogacy. If Black women accept this idea of redemption, can they not also passively accept the exploitation that surrogacy brings?"[56] Williams thinks not and rejects previous atonement theologies dependent on surrogacy and looks away from the cross and toward Jesus' life of resistance.[57]

At the center of the tainted legacies of the Christian tradition on sexism and slavery are the ways in which atonement theology has been weaponized in support of patriarchal and white supremacist social and political structures and relationships. The subjection of women and slaves (and other colonial subjects) were not only justified with Christian Scripture and theology, but were also used to form and discipline the subjectivity of women and slaves toward self-sacrifice, primarily for the purposes and betterment of powerful, white men. Along with the feminist critiques of sacrifice, womanist critiques such as Williams's shed light on the problematic ways in which Christian theology has funded and continues to fund oppression.

As I noted earlier, Karen Guth names these tainted legacies as morally injurious. She finds a resonance and formal similarity between the phenomenon of moral injury and the moral complexity of the aftermath of tainted legacies such as sexism and racism.[58] My contention is that the resonance can be heard in both directions. The phenomenon of moral injury in the arena of war is itself bound up with the tainted legacy of the Christian tradition on war. Not only have Scripture and theology been deployed to justify war, but they also have been used—significantly—to form, discipline, and direct the subjectivity of soldiers toward self-sacrifice. Not only are soldiers placed in feminine roles within the state *oikos*, but the very same weaponization of atonement theology in the *oikos* that feminists and womanists have so rightly critiqued shows up in narrating and inculcating the sacrificial virtues of soldiers in the *polis* as *oikos*. In America, Christian theology—especially as it has been taken up into civil religion—has been

---

55. Williams, *Sisters in the Wilderness*, 143.

56. Williams, *Sisters in the Wilderness*, 143.

57. Williams, *Sisters in the Wilderness*, 148.

58. Guth, "Moral Injury," 174.

used to articulate both the formal logic and grammar for going to war and for the formation of soldiers as sacrificial agents of war.[59]

AMERICAN CIVIL RELIGION AND SOLDIERLY SACRIFICE

In his 1967 essay "Civil Religion in America," Robert Bellah uses the term "civil religion" to describe the religious dimension that is discernible in the political life and history of America.[60] This religious dimension is expressed in "beliefs, symbols, and rituals."[61] In *Broken Covenant*, he defines civil religion as the "religious dimension, found I think in the life of every people, through which it interprets its historical experience in light of transcendent reality."[62] In *War and the American Difference*, Hauerwas writes, "War is a moral necessity for America because it provides the experience of the 'unum' that makes the 'pluribus' possible. War is America's central liturgical act necessary to renew our sense that we are a nation unlike other nations."[63] It is in and through war that we are healed as a nation. War is "America's altar"[64] and it is "constitutive of the substance of our civil religion."[65] The liturgy of American war is our national soteriology. Moreover, it is not just that war is the means by which Americans constitute themselves as a people, but as a people in relation to all other people. American war making is not only central to our soteriological story about ourselves, but it is also at the heart of our role in the world ("a nation unlike other nations"). If America is a city on a hill and a light to the nations, then American war and its sacrifices are made on behalf of the world.

59. This is not to say that Christian leaders and communities in America are solely responsible for the ills of soldiers (or women). Christian theology both reflects the social order (and how that order obeys Christ or not) and can influence change. I am not arguing for a causal relationship in one direction, i.e., problem = bad theology, solution = good/better theology. I am arguing that Christian communities and theology are part of and contribute to the maintenance of the political ecology I describe.

60. Bellah, "Civil Religion," 43.

61. Bellah, "Civil Religion," 42.

62. Bellah, *Broken Covenant*, 3.

63. Hauerwas, *War*, 4. This, of course, begs the question of who is included in the unum. The service of Black men in segregated units in World War I certainly did not result in their participation in the unum.

64. Hauerwas, *War*, 33.

65. Hauerwas, *War*, 5.

In *GI Messiahs*, Jonathan Ebel writes that soldiers are not just "protectors and preservers of the nation and its ideals, but incarnations of those ideals—the Word of the nation made flesh—whose willingness to suffer and die brings salvation to an often wayward but nevertheless chosen people."[66] With Hauerwas's more global sense of the soteriological function of American war, we can extend Ebel's argument to suggest that within American civil religion, American soldiers function not just as saviors of America, but of the world.[67]

Ebel goes to great lengths to establish how deep the soldiers-as-saviors trope runs in American life and in the lives of American soldiers. The motif is written not just in speeches but in the rock hewn into monuments and tombs. This trope is almost exclusively bound up with Christian images of sacrifice, analogies to Christ, and highlights the ways in which soldiers participate in the work of atonement. The veneration of fallen soldiers is then a cult of martyrs and the blood of soldiers functions as a "seedbed" for America. Central to his argument is the reality that the civil religious role that soldiers are called upon to play functions to erase their stories and embodied identities (this is particularly true for soldiers who are not white men, but for them too). He writes,

> The symbol of the soldier and the soldier as symbol facilitate a "not knowing" of the soldier . . . a hiding of the visible body, a forgetting of the remembered personality. To the extent that individuals involve themselves in the mytho-symbolic discourse of soldiering and the rituals through which that discourse reaches the nation, they become simultaneously unknown and known, symbol and person.[68]

As civil-religious symbols, soldiers often need to transgress the "orthodoxy" of civil religion to reckon with the reality of their soldierly identities and experiences in war.[69] The trope of soldiers as saviors flattens, even erases, the identities of the very soldiers it is supposedly lifting up as heroes. The bodies and sacrifices of American soldiers are subsumed into the national narrative wholly apart from the particular context of their story. Soldiers themselves are rendered invisible behind their messianic role. The public

66. Ebel, *GI Messiahs*, 2.

67. This narrative is taken up again and again since World War I and continues in the Global War on Terror.

68. Ebel, *GI Messiahs*, 65.

69. Ebel, *GI Messiahs*, 18.

accolade and recognition of soldiers (and the theology that supports it) serves to eclipse the underlying political reality that places soldiers under patriarchal domination in the *polis* as *oikos*.

In light of the near deification of soldiers within American civil religion, it might seem that the sacrifices of women are farther apart than ever from the sacrifices of soldiers.[70] Traditionally, women are called to sacrifice in the private realm of the *oikos* under patriarchal domination. Soldiers, by contrast, sacrifice for the public good with public veneration. However, as I have argued, this contrast hides a deeper connection. The civil-military distinction troubles the wife/soldier binary and brings together the oppressive sacrifices of women in the *oikos* and the sacrifices of soldiers for the *polis*. Soldiers, like women, are subject to patriarchal relationships of command and obedience. The moral formation for soldiers, like women, is similarly oriented toward sacrificial agency. Like women in the *oikos*, the subordination of soldiers is likewise inculcated in the context of the overarching political fact of their existence that *as soldiers* they stand under authority and in service to their *paterfamilias* (i.e., the president and their chain of command). The domination and subordination of soldiers, as with women in the *oikos*, is also not an end in itself. Soldiers, too, are formed for sacrifice and formed to embody sacrificial agency.

The moral formation of soldiers, like women, is similarly oriented toward sacrifice for the political community. Like women, soldiers are not political agents themselves. Rather, it is through their exclusion, subordination, and sacrifice that they serve their country. Just as women are formed for sacrifice in the context of the *oikos*, so too are soldiers formed for sacrificial agency in the *polis* as *oikos*. In contrast with women in the *oikos*, the sacrifices of soldiers in the *polis* as *oikos* do, at first blush, appear political. The civil religious narrative is precisely that the surviving and flourishing of the political community relies on the sacrifices of its soldiers *pro nobis*. What this narrative elides is how the sacrifices of soldiers, like the sacrifices of women in the *oikos*, occur in the context of domestic relationships of care.

Relationships within the military get coded in familial terms. The soldiers in a given team, squad, or platoon are brothers and sisters and the platoon sergeant is often affectionately (or otherwise) referred to as the platoon daddy. Junior (and senior) leaders also code their relations with

---

70. Of course, there are many ways in which motherhood and its sacrifices are, if not deified, highly honored. The month of May provides us with the juxtaposition of two extra-ecclesial examples that have nonetheless been taken up into the life and liturgy of many American churches, Mother's Day and Memorial Day.

subordinates as familial relations and their leadership as a matter of taking care of their children (babysitting) or as older brothers/sisters. To the extent the sacrifices of women and soldiers are legible in voluntaristic terms (and in the context of relationships of subordination and domination this is not straightforward), just as women do not abstractly sacrifice for The Family, neither do soldiers sacrifice abstractly for The Nation (the civil religious story). They "lay down their lives" for their friends and brothers in what amounts to a militarization/weaponization of care. None of this negates the bonds of affection, trust, and intimacy that form in the military, but rather sharpens Shay's initial account of moral injury.

In Shay's telling, moral injury is a wound of betrayal and a rupture of trust in the context of the exercise of hierarchical power. Betrayal in the context of war is so significant not just because of the "high stakes" of war (and, we might add, training for war), but also because the relationships of domination and subordination required for war that are gendered (as previously described) are also coded in familial terms and oriented toward sacrifice for some higher good. Wiinikka-Lydon rightly presses beyond the narrower institutional context of Shay and toward a consideration of the "political causes of such injuries."[71] My argument is that, for soldiers, the *polis* as *oikos* (and the sacrificial agency it entails) *is* the political context in which moral injury occurs. The *polis* as *oikos* defines the relationships of soldiers with the military, the state, and the rest of society. War is certainly the beating heart of this relationship and provides the lifeblood to perpetuate it. But it is the deeply problematic dynamics of the relationship itself that provide the context for moral injury. So it is that moral injury phenomena play out in the lives of soldiers from basic training to military sexual assault to the battlefield and even to the experience of homecoming. Adding trauma to trauma, the betrayal of soldiers is further bound up with the way that Christian theology and Christian leaders (including military chaplains) serve to buttress the legal, political, social, and moral ecology that undergirds their sacrificial agency.

CONCLUSION

At the outset, I framed this study with Rambo's compelling suggestion that our various crosses might be sites of crossing. Rambo argues that our histories of trauma, rather that provoking competition, might instead be sites

71. Wiinikka-Lydon, "Moral Injury," 222.

of meeting, connection, and deep knowing. Moreover, our wounds might serve to build bonds of compassion and open up the possibility for cooperative action. In this study, I have attempted to see and know the wounds of soldiers in and through the wounds of women and Black women, in particular. I have argued that the very same theologies of sacrifice that have been deployed to buttress the legal, political, social, and moral ecology that undergirds the sacrificial agency of women in the *oikos* (against which feminists and womanists have rightly protested) are mobilized against soldiers in the *oikos* of the *polis*. Moral injury, I have argued, is thus a wound of sacrificial agency, of soldiers in the *polis* as *oikos* and women in the *oikos*. The resonance, then, that feminists like Herman find between the traumas of men at war and women in the home (or Guth and others find between the moral injury of soldiers and the tainted legacies of the Christian tradition around the oppressive sacrifices of women) is more than a faint echo, it is, in fact, the same moral frequency.

As Virginia Woolf long suspected, the tyrannies, servilities, (and traumas) of women in the private world of the *oikos* are also the tyrannies, servilities, (and traumas) of soldiers. I do not pretend that this conclusion solves anything. Soldiers and veterans, mostly men, have been formed to know women as the enemy and feminists and womanists have looked askance at the military as the site of the production of a particularly vehemently toxic form of masculinity (and too often, concomitant racism) and bear the wounds of it in their bodies and souls. My hope is that I have at the very least opened a door. I do not know what awaits us on the other side, but I know who awaits us. It is with the risen Christ, and in his wounds, that we might come to know together what it means to live, as Rambo puts it, "in the afterlife of trauma."

BIBLIOGRAPHY

Agamben, Giorgio. *Homo Sacer: Sovereign Power and Bare Life*. Translated by Daniel Heller-Roazen. Stanford, CA: Stanford University Press, 1998.

Andolsen, Barbara Hilkert. "Agape in Feminist Ethics." *The Journal of Religious Ethics* 9 (1981) 69–83.

Bellah, Robert. *Broken Covenant: American Civil Religion in Time of Trial*. New York: Seabury, 1975.

———. "Civil Religion in America." *Daedalus* 134 (2005) 40–55.

Bretherton, Luke. *Christ and the Common Life: Political Theology and the Case for Democracy*. Grand Rapids: Eerdmans, 2019.

Cerwonka, Allaine, and Anna Loutfi. "Biopolitics and the Female Reproductive Body as the New Subject of Law." *feminists@law* 1 (2011). https://doi.org/10.22024/UniKent/03/fal.18.

Coleman, Monica. "Sacrifice, Surrogacy and Salvation: Womanist Reflections on Motherhood and Work." *Black Theology: An International Journal* 12:3 (2014) 200–212.

Currier, Joseph, et al. "Introduction to Moral Injury." In *Addressing Moral Injury in Clinical Practice*, edited by Joseph Currier et al., 3–18. Washington, DC: American Psychological Association, 2021.

Deutscher, Penelope. "The Inversion of Exceptionality: Foucault, Agamben, and 'Reproductive Rights.'" *South Atlantic Quarterly* 107 (2008) 55–70.

Diagnostic and Statistical Manual of Mental Disorders. 3rd ed. Washington, DC: American Psychiatric Association, 1980.

Drescher, Kent and Jacob Farnsworth. "A Social-Functional Perspective on Morality and Moral Injury." In *Addressing Moral Injury in Clinical Practice*, edited by Joseph Currier et al., 35–52. Washington, DC: American Psychological Association, 2021.

Ebel, Jonathan. *GI Messiahs: Soldiering, War, and American Civil Religion*. New Haven: Yale University Press, 2015.

Elshtain, Jean Bethke. *Public Man, Private Woman: Women in Social and Political Thought*. Princeton: Princeton University Press, 1981.

———. *Women and War*. Chicago: University of Chicago Press, 1987.

Fassin, Didier, and Richard Rechtman. *The Empire of Trauma: An Inquiry into the Condition of Victimhood*. Princeton: Princeton University Press, 2009.

Fox, Nancy. "Aretē: 'We as Black Women.'" *Journal of Veteran Studies* 4 (2019) 58–77.

Goff, Stan. *Borderline: Reflections on War, Sex, and Church*. Eugene, OR: Cascade, 2015.

Goldstein, Joshua. *War and Gender: How Gender Shapes the War System and Vice Versa*. New York: Cambridge University Press, 2001.

Guth, Karen. "Moral Injury, Feminist and Womanist Ethics, and Tainted Legacies." *Journal of the Society of Christian Ethics* 38:1 (2018) 167–86.

Hauerwas, Stanley. *War and the American Difference*. Ada, MI: Baker Academic, 2011.

Herman, Judith. *Trauma and Recovery: The Aftermath of Violence—From Domestic Abuse to Political Terror*. New York: Basic, 1992.

Kalbian, Aline H. *Sexing the Church: Gender, Power, and Ethics in Contemporary Catholicism*. Bloomington: Indiana University Press, 2005.

Kinghorn, Warren. "Challenging the Hegemony of the Symptom: Reclaiming Context in PTSD and Moral Injury." *The Journal of Medicine and Philosophy* 45:6 (Dec. 2020) 644–62.

———. "Combat Trauma and Moral Fragmentation: A Theological Account of Moral Injury." *Journal of the Society of Christian Ethics* 32 (2012) 57–74.

———. "Moral Engagement, Combat Trauma, and the Lure of Psychiatric Dualism: Why Psychiatry Is More Than a Technical Discipline." *Harvard Review of Psychiatry* 23:1 (2015) 28–37.

Lifton, Robert Jay. *Home from the War: Learning from Vietnam Veterans*. New York: Other Press, 2005.

Litz, Brett T., et al. "Moral Injury and Moral Repair in War Veterans: A Preliminary Model and Intervention." *Clinical Psychology Review* 29 (2009) 695–706.

Mahedy, William P. *Out of Night: The Spiritual Journey of Vietnam Vets*. Knoxville, TN: Radix, 2004.

Mann, Bonnie. *Sovereign Masculinity: Gender Lessons from the War on Terror*. New York: Oxford University Press, 2014.

McCracken, Peggy. *The Curse of Eve, the Wound of the Hero: Blood, Gender, and Medieval Literature*. Philadelphia: University of Pennsylvania Press, 2003.

Melin, Julia. "Desperate Choices: Why Black Women Join the US Military at Higher Rates Than Men and All Other Racial and Ethnic Groups." *New England Journal of Public Policy* 28 (2016). https://scholarworks.umb.edu/nejpp/vol28/iss2/8.

Michael, Louis. "Hypermasculinity Is a Plague on the Modern Man." *Huffington Post*, Nov. 29, 2016. https://www.huffingtonpost.co.uk/louis-michael/hyper-masculinity-man_b_13280034.html.

Niebuhr, Reinhold. *Love and Justice: Selections from the Shorter Writings of Reinhold Niebuhr*. Louisville: Westminster John Knox, 1992.

Nygren, Anders. *Agape and Eros*. Translated by Philip S. Watson. New York: Harper and Row, 1969.

Parsons, Graham. "Contract, Gender, and the Emergence of the Civil-Military Distinction." *The Review of Politics* 82:3 (2020) 416–37.

Pateman, Carole. *The Sexual Contract*. Stanford: Stanford University Press, 1988.

Pin-Fat, Véronique, and Maria Stern. "The Scripting of Private Jessica Lynch: Biopolitics, Gender, and the 'Feminization' of the US Military." *Alternatives* 30 (2005) 25–53.

Powers, Brian. *Full Darkness: Original Sin, Moral Injury, and Wartime Violence*. Grand Rapids: Eerdmans, 2019.

Rambo, Shelly. *Resurrecting Wounds: Living in the Afterlife of Trauma*. Waco, TX: Baylor University Press, 2017.

Schmitt, Carl. *The Concept of the Political*. Translated by George Schwab. Chicago: University of Chicago Press, 1996.

———. *Political Theology: Four Chapters on the Concept of Sovereignty*. Translated by George Schwab. Chicago: University of Chicago Press, 1985.

Shay, Jonathan. *Achilles in Vietnam: Combat Trauma and the Undoing of Character*. New York: Scribner, 1994.

———. "Moral Injury." *Psychoanalytic Psychology* 31.2 (2014) 183.

Tietje, Adam. "War, Masculinity, and the Ambiguity of Care." *Pastoral Psychology* 70 (2021) 1–15.

van Creveld, Martin. "Less Than We Can Be: Men, Women, and the Modern Military." *Journal of Strategic Studies* 23 (2000) 1–20.

Walker-Barnes, Chanequa. *Too Heavy a Yoke: Black Women and the Burden of Strength*. Eugene, OR: Cascade, 2014.

Wiinikka-Lydon, Joseph. *Moral Injury and the Promise of Virtue*. London: Palgrave Macmillan, 2019.

———. "Moral Injury as Inherent Political Critique: The Prophetic Possibilities of a New Term." *Political Theology* 18:3 (2017) 219–32.

Williams, Delores. *Sisters in the Wilderness: The Challenge of Womanist God-Talk*. Maryknoll, NY: Orbis, 1993.

Wollstonecraft, Mary. *A Vindication of the Rights of Woman*. New York: Penguin, 1992.

Yandell, Michael. *War and Negative Revelation: A Theoethical Reflection on Moral Injury*. Lanham, MD: Lexington, 2022.

Young, Allan. *The Harmony of Illusions: Inventing Post-Traumatic Stress Disorder*. Princeton: Princeton University Press, 1995.

"Swallowed by the Earth"

Trauma and Universalism in the Theology of Jürgen Moltmann

SAMUEL J. YOUNGS

IN THE MID-1970S, JAMES McClendon argued that *biography is theology*, claiming that lived praxis, rather than subtlety of theorem or volume of proclamation, was the true demonstration of one's doctrine: "The truth of faith is made good *in the living of it* or not at all."[1] He also made the dialectical observation that an individual's given theology not only shapes their life's expression, but that their theology is itself shaped by that same lived experience. For theology must be recognized as "a self-involving task," forged in its unique contours by our "irremediably *varied* selves."[2] Such late-modern acknowledgment of the reciprocal conditioning of theology and life has infused foundationalist and absolutist renderings of theology with instability while legitimizing more local and personal expressions.[3] Moreover, it has highlighted the fact that Christians never simply inherit confessional "theology" as a static monolith from the past. Rather we inherit a dynamic interplay of *biographies*—the *lives* of a cloud of witnesses

---

1. McClendon, *Biography as Theology*, viii.

2. McClendon, *Biography as Theology*, 171. Johann Baptist Metz made a similar point by inverting the phrase—theology is biography—and thus gave even more forceful attention to the personally contextualized nature of theology: Metz, "Theology as Biography?," 219–28.

3. Postcolonial theologies emerge from this milieu, see, e.g., Kim-Kort, *Paper Cranes*, ix; Pedraja, *Tealogia*, 11; Ngong, *Construction of Piety*, xi. The emergence of theopoetics can also be situated here; see Keefe-Perry, *Way to Water*, introduction.

which have all, in their turn, added a hue to the picture of doctrine and given rise to a vibrant array of theological perspectives.[4]

Recent developments in the study of mental health complicate this picture in an important way. It is now widely recognized that between 70 and 90 percent of adults have experienced a traumatic event at some point in their lives.[5] Traumatization rates in earlier history, while impossible to enumerate precisely, were likely similar given the confluence of two factors: more *violence* in the past balanced against more *resilience* in the past.[6] The overall implication is striking: Christians do not simply inherit the biographies of the theological past but also the *traumas* cabined within them. The history of the church is made up of people, and insofar as those people have transited a broken world, the development of Christian thought and practice bears the marks of their trauma.[7]

Literature in theology and trauma is nascent but growing.[8] In relation to the theological past, it has at least two tasks to pursue. One task—very important but not our concern in the present essay—is the doctrinal analysis of "theological trauma," that is, the manner in which theological discourse can incubate social circumstances wherein certain types of traumatization more readily occur.[9] The second task, which is the focus of this

4. An attempt to detail the prevalence of Christian theological pluralism need not detain us here; one of the most well-known presentations can be found in Smith, *Bible Made Impossible*, ch. 2.

5. See Benjet et al., "Epidemiology"; Kirkpatrick et al., "National Estimates." Indeed, widely respected psychiatrist Bessel van der Kolk has called trauma "our most urgent public health issue" (*Body Keeps the Score*, 356). He also names trauma a "hidden epidemic" and discusses the related statistics at considerable length (pp. 145–70).

6. Illustrative studies of more violent, harsher, and less humane societal conditions can readily be found; of note are Foucault, *Discipline and Punish*; Pinker, *Better Angels*, ch. 1; as well as in Dwyer et al., *History of Violence*, especially the sections and essays pertaining to social, collective, interpersonal, and intimate violence. For the likely deeper resilience of the past, see Southwick and Charney, *Resilience*, 16–19, and cited works.

7. Realism in discussing church history has grown in recent years, as embodied in works like Dickson, *Bullies and Saints*. These works remain impoverished, however, insofar as they do not pursue interdisciplinary insights from psychology and trauma studies, ultimately rendering much of their analysis overly moralistic (as seen in Dickson's title, for example).

8. See, e.g., Jones, *Trauma and Grace*; Rambo, *Spirit and Trauma* and *Resurrecting Wounds*; Baldwin, *Trauma-Sensitive Theology*; Harrower, *God of All Comfort*; Harrower et al., *Dawn of Sunday*.

9. I set out an example of this work in Youngs, "Ways to Sin." Theology of the body, bibliology, providence, and personal eschatology are all be fertile fields for immediate work on theological trauma, though all *loci* could be productively explored with this focus.

present essay, relates to what we have indicated above: the exploration of "traumatized" theology, that is, tracing the plausible connections between a given theologian's traumatic experience and their concomitant handling of doctrine.[10] The goal of this sort of exploration would be, initially, very modest, aiming simply to throw mutual light upon both theological biography and biographical theology. Its central and probing question would be: *To what degree does traumatic experience influence theological expression?*

This essay applies such an illuminative exploration to the life and thought of Jürgen Moltmann, focusing particularly on his soteriological universalism.[11] This study contends that the rhetoric of Moltmann's universalism is deeply colored by his traumatic experiences during and after World War II. Moltmann is an exemplary candidate for this kind of analysis on at least three fronts: (1) he is a highly influential theologian across several global contexts;[12] (2) he has been overt and honest about the role of his biography in shaping his theological developments;[13] and (3) he has supplied readership with myriad statements about his personal life (not least in his autobiography, *A Broad Place* [ET, 2008]) which often serve to illuminate his traumatic experiences.

While not arguing that these experiences are somehow *causative* for Moltmann's universalism, this study contends that the particular manner in which Moltmann frames his universalism bears an indelible impress from certain overwhelming elements of his life experience. Moltmann himself speaks of his general theology in this way, with characteristic poignancy and candor:

> For me the Christian faith is fundamentally bound up with the experiences of a particular existential situation. . . . Anyone who has had to cry out to God in the face of the mutilation and death of so many who were comrades, friends, and relatives no longer

10. Such an undertaking is not novel in the main; psychologically oriented analyses of key theologians have been usefully pursued, if criticized by some: e.g., Erikson, *Young Man Luther*. However, foregrounding *trauma* as the lodestone of such pursuits is relatively novel.

11. A stance acutely associated with Moltmann, especially following his publication of *Coming of God* in 1995.

12. An impact that is well-summed up in Bauckham's "Introduction" to the recent Bauckham and Kohl, *Jürgen Moltmann*; in terms of global reach, see Moltmann, *Broad Place*.

13. See, e.g., *Experiences in Theology*, xv-xix, 3–9.

has any withdrawn, individual approach to theology. . . . This sense of no longer being able to talk of God and yet of having to talk of God in the face of the specific experiences of an oppressive burden of guilt and cruel meaninglessness in my generation is presumably the root of my theological concerns, for reflection about God constantly brings me back to that *aporia*.[14]

We will proceed by first detailing some oddities in Moltmann's expression of universalism, namely, his pronounced dogmatism. Thereafter, we will take a biographical trek through his wartime experiences, analyzing them from a trauma-informed perspective. Finally, we will draw the threads of universalism and trauma together by examining an oft-neglected episode in the middle of Moltmann's life: his vision at the Maidanek concentration camp.

THE CERTAIN HOPE: MOLTMANN'S STRANGELY DOGMATIC UNIVERSALISM

From the more subtle notes in *Theology of Hope* (1964) to the sustained crescendo of *The Coming of God* (1995), Moltmann's commitment to universalism—what he often calls "God's universal future"—is unmistakable.[15] As with all of his theological reflection, the centering locus is christology and the suffering solidarity of the incarnate God that leads to hope for new life.[16] It is the resurrection of the suffering Christ that "signifies a new factor which opens our world, locked up in guilt and death, toward the future."[17] This new future is for *everything* and *everyone*, unreservedly, for God has promised to be "all in all" (1 Cor 15:28).[18] Moltmann sometimes draws on the powerful sermons of Christoph Blumhardt to drive the point home: "If I must give up a man, or give up hope for an area or an earth, then Jesus is not risen for me. You are not the light of the world if I must give up a man anywhere."[19]

14. Moltmann, "My Theological Career," 166.

15. E.g., *Theology of Hope*, 190–97, 278–79; *Coming of God*, throughout, but especially 240–55.

16. On all of Moltmann's theology as christological in basis and extension, see Youngs, *Way of the Kenotic Christ*, 3–6.

17. "Resurrection as Hope," 52, punctuation added; see also p. 61.

18. One of Moltmann's most-cited biblical passages across his corpus; see, e.g., "God and Resurrection," 50; *Sun of Righteousness*, 141; *Coming of God*, 294; *In the End*, 149–151.

19. "God and Resurrection," 49. Moltmann is here quoting Blumhardt's Easter sermon of 1899. See also Blumhardt's appearance in *Sun of Righteousness*, 140.

Like many contemporary universalists, Moltmann has endured salvos from evangelical, conservative, and traditional thinkers across the ecumenical spectrum.[20] These critiques follow predictable lines, as does Moltmann's responsive discourse that offers apologetics for universalism,[21] and these do not overly concern us here. Rather, I am interested to highlight certain features in Moltmann's rhetoric of universalism that betray a mysterious decontextualization, stridency, and inconsistency—or, in short, dogmatism.

More Certain Than Others

The luminaries of Moltmann's immediate and most influential theological contexts—Barth, Rahner, and von Balthasar—all expressed some variation on the theme of universal salvation. But they all did so with a layer of vagueness and hesitancy, resisting a dogmatic or overly confident assertion. Barth's doctrine of election certainly seems to imply universalism, but he left his discourse here "open" in important (and still-debated) regards.[22] Rahner's "anonymous Christianity" certainly begged the question of universalism, but deferred a conclusive word.[23] And von Balthasar famously circumscribed his own tentative universalism with a controlling theme that is deeply germane to Moltmann: *hope*.[24]

Given Moltmann's indebtedness to these three thinkers on a variety of scores,[25] it is notable to find him espousing his own universalism in a manner decidedly more strident and even, at times, doctrinaire.[26] As Ryan Neal

20. E.g., Williams, "Moltmann on Jesus Christ," 121–25.

21. Much of which can be found in *Coming of God*, 235–55.

22. See Barth, *Church Dogmatics*, 2/2:306–8. Oliver Crisp has written one of the most lucid analyses of Barth's "universalism" and its attendant issues; see Crisp, "I Do Teach It."

23. E.g., Rahner, *Theological Explorations*.

24. Von Balthasar, *Dare We Hope*.

25. Barth deeply influenced Moltmann's view of revelation and the nature of theological speech; von Balthsar's impact is felt in Moltmann's manifold treatments of both Trinitarian kenosis and perichoresis; and Rahner's dictum on the immanent-economic Trinity was hugely directive for Moltmann's thought. Note that Moltmann sometimes conscripts Barth as a partner in his universalism, see *Sun of Righteousness*, 145; *Coming of God*, 239.

26. Universalism can be found readily across Moltmann's early work (e.g., *Theology of Hope*, 190–97; *Crucified God*, 101–2, 176–80, 194–95), but his later statements are even more forceful; see in particular *Coming of God*, 235–55; "Logic of Hell"; and *Sun of Righteousness*, 127–48.

rightly says, Moltmann "does not invoke an agnostic claim of uncertainty regarding future salvation."[27] His surety applies no matter the condition of those under salvific consideration; all difference of life and belief is "caught up" in God's universal and eschatological saving action:

> The all-embracing hope for God's future is based on the boundlessness of his love. Why should we take different belief, disbelief, or superstition of other people more seriously than God's mercy on them? . . . The differences between believers, people of other beliefs, and unbelievers exist, but they are caught up and absorbed in the frame of reference which is God's mercy on all.[28]

Statements like this certify the accuracy of Neal's assessment regarding Moltmann's view: "[Universal salvation] is not a *possibility*, but an eschatological *certainty*."[29]

Missing Humility

This certainty in Moltmann, besides placing him in contrast to many of his peers, has the additional effect of countermanding his own stated ethos of humility. This ethos is deeply apparent in most of his theological discussions and is, in fact, symptomatic of his general methodology. Moltmann has always framed his theological questing as "contributions" to ongoing dialogue, explicitly eschewing "the seductions of the theological system and the coercion of the dogmatic thesis."[30] Rather than fortressing his own opinions or promulgating a tired defense of old ideas, Moltmann typically embraces a rhetoric of "suggestion" and "exploration" in staging his theology.[31]

Ironically it is Moltmann's eschatological commitments that normally empower his theological humility. He maintains that since God's future is not yet fully revealed, all theological pronouncements must be tentative,

27. Neal, *Theology as Hope*, 203.

28. *Sun of Righteousness*, 145.

29. Neal, *Theology as Hope*, 205 (emphasis added).

30. *Trinity and the Kingdom*, xii. See also Youngs, *Way of the Kenotic Christ*, 22–26.

31. It is worth quoting him at-length on this score: "I have never done theology in the form of a defense of ancient doctrines or ecclesiastical dogmas. It has always been a journey of exploration. Consequently my way of thinking is experimental—an adventure of ideas—and my style of communication is to suggest. I do not defend any impersonal dogmas, but nor do I merely express my own personal opinion. I make suggestions within a community" (*Coming of God*, xiv).

open, and unfinished. He writes, "No concept in history is ever final and complete. Indeed in the history of Christian theology the openness of all knowledge and all explanations is actually constitutive, for it is their abiding openness that shows the power of their eschatological hope for the future."[32] This noted provisionality enables Moltmann's self-labeling of his theology as *theologia viatorum*, a pilgrim theology, a theology on-the-road, with final judgments suspended.

Against this humble methodological backdrop, then, it is all the more surprising that Moltmann could voice his universalism so stridently. Granted, in the *Coming of God*, Moltmann strikes a more balanced tone.[33] But in subsequent work his tenor shifts drastically, producing statements like those found in his "Dialogue Between Faith and Grace." In that essay, (divine) Grace is personified as a loving and capacious universalist and (human) Faith as a judgmental particularist, as below:

> Faith: God can only help those who let themselves be helped. . . . The person who rejects [God's] offer is lost. The person who seizes it will be saved. Faith is the presupposition for salvation; unbelief leads straight to hell.

> Grace: My dear Faith, do you think that God's will is so feeble that even though he wants to help all human beings, he is unable to do so without their cooperation? Do you think that human beings are so strong that they can do what they like with God's gracious will? Who are you, human Faith, that you can set yourself up like this over God's will, and make God your servant?[34]

Suspicion of Freedom

The "dialogue" above highlights one final oddity in Moltmann's presentation of his universalism: his surprising suspicion of human freedom. He associates dual-outcome soteriology with a misplaced emphasis on human subjectivity and agency.[35] But across his larger theological oeuvre, he

---

32. *Trinity and the Kingdom*, xiv. Again, see Youngs, *Way of the Kenotic Christ*, 13–27.

33. *Coming of God*, 135–55, although this section still contains several more-strident moments. For instance, double-outcome judgment is at one point compared to a customer (human) who has to choose what the vendor (God) is selling (grace).

34. "Dialogue Between Faith and Grace," 235.

35. "Dialogue Between Faith and Grace," throughout; "Logic of Hell"; *Coming of God*, 244–46.

vibrantly espouses a broadly construed understanding of human freedom that bears out real impacts on the world, to the ends of either great blessing or great devastation. The creaturely situation, scientifically and otherwise for Moltmann, is marked by agency, complexity, and indeterminacy.[36] God, in fact, wills it to be so, and the divine commitment to human agency is such that God *withdraws* his very omnipotence in order to "make room" for creaturely freedom.[37] As Moltmann writes, "[Divine love] cannot compel a response by violence. For the sake of freedom, and the love responded to in freedom, God limits and empties himself. He *withdraws his omnipotence* because he has confidence in the free response of men and women."[38]

But, in contexts where his universalism is broached, all of these commitments are subsumed in a kind of eschatological determinism, in which all things will become "what God has destined for them."[39] Ryan Neal is incisive in his overall analysis of Moltmann's universalism, seeing its finality to run athwart Moltmann's core commitment to *hope* itself. Neal writes, "Dogmatic universalism cannot be hopeful, because it does not *hope* for salvation, it *presumes* it."[40] Though Moltmann speaks often of an "open future" in his discussions of *freedom* and *possibility*, his soteriology seemingly collapses both categories: "the still-to-be-determined open future is actually closed. . . . Moltmann's conception [of the future] . . . contains no surprises."[41]

Thus, whether in terms of his theological peers, his ostensible commitment to theological humility, or his own emphasis on the significance of creational agency, Moltmann's "monophonic" rhetoric of universalism raises perplexing issues.[42] What is most remarkable is not the inconsistency

36. "Creation and Redemption," 131.

37. On this and a few additional scores, Moltmann's language and thinking resonate deeply with that of C. S. Lewis; on the point of creaturely agency involving "divine abdication" in Lewis, see "Efficacy of Prayer," in *World's Last Night*, 1–10.

38. *Trinity and the Kingdom*, 119. Also, in *God in Creation*, 86–87: "In order to create a world 'outside' himself . . . God withdraws his presence and restricts his power." Moltmann is here drawing on the Kabbalistic notion of *zimsum*, a "contraction" or "concentration" of Godself. The fullest mature statement is found in "God's Kenosis." This is his famous perspective on creational kenosis, which entwines his providential, christological, and anthropological commitments on numerous fronts; see, e.g., Youngs, *Way of the Kenotic Christ*, 72–74, 88–95.

39. Moltmann, "God's Kenosis," 151.

40. Neal, *Theology as Hope*, 209.

41. Neal, *Theology as Hope*, 208–9.

42. See Richardson, "Moltmann's Communitarian Trinity," 38–39.

per se; Moltmann's methodology entails a certain ambiguity (and, again, provisionality) in his theological pronouncements.[43] But what *is* mysterious is the dogmatism, the supreme confidence, which can verge close to condescension in its treatment of other views on the final judgment.[44] As Neal says, "[Moltmann's] lack of resistance toward dogmatic universalism is a self-assured confidence that disallows mystery; there are no dark corners of theology, everything is clearly in view."[45]

Frankly, this is not like Moltmann. His tenor in the contexts of universalism sits in noteworthy tension with other facets of his work.[46] In noting this, we have not yet said much new. As mentioned above, various quarters have critiqued Moltmann's universalism, often via some iteration of points we have outlined above.[47] But what such critiques lack, even among nuanced commentators like Neal, is an earnest attempt to *account* for the oddly overstated nature of Moltmann's universalism. In what follows, I suggest that Moltmann's traumatic experiences may hold the key. I propose that Moltmann's universalism is not an example of simple theological overconfidence, but rather it is an example of *adaptive* theology,[48] emerging from concrete experiences in his history and religious development, funded by the dual-wound of both psychological trauma and spiritual grief.

THE DICTATORSHIP OF THE NIHIL: MOLTMANN'S TRAUMATIC EXPERIENCES

Moltmann was born in Germany in 1926, a geographical and temporal fact that would predetermine his history in painful ways. He was a child when

43. Not to mention that he sees overly systematic thinking to shut down and ossify theology that ought to always stand ready for revision in light of God's coming future; see *Experiences in Theology*, 102–6.

44. The most clear examples are: "Logic of Hell," 44–45; "Dialogue Between Faith and Grace," throughout; and *Sun of Righteousness*, 142–44.

45. Neal, *Theology as Hope*, 208.

46. In Neal's treatment, many of the tensions I've highlighted here are raised, but Neal is persuaded that Moltmann's universalism is a natural consequence of both Moltmann's theology of hope and his trinitarian thinking; see Neal, *Theology as Hope*, ch. 8. Given the evident tensions with other dimensions of Moltmann's his work, I'm less convinced of the necessity of this sort of universalistic expression.

47. That is, if they elect to actually engage Moltmann's thought, rather than simply attempting to "debunk" universalism via prooftexting or other superficial operation.

48. Or, we could say, "therapeutic" theology.

the Third Reich rose to power, and his early worldview, unmoored from any notable attachment to Christianity,[49] was conditioned by nationalism and propaganda.[50] As Berhard Giesen writes, "The generation [of Germans] born between 1920 and 1933 were raised in a world that provided few alternatives to National Socialism. . . . They had few choices to oppose Nazi power."[51] His involvement in the war, and indeed his very identity as a German, constitutes for Moltmann the great weight of what he later calls the "burdens and traumas" of his generation.[52]

The Inferno—War Trauma

Moltmann was conscripted into Hitler's army at the age of seventeen. Stationed in a variety of capacities, but first on antiaircraft artillery, he bore witness to and experienced not just generalized suffering but what he later called "annihilation."[53] In 1943 he lived through Operation Gomorrah—the fire-bombing of Hamburg, in which over forty thousand people, mostly civilians, were burned to death in one horrific night. The conflagration scarred itself deep into Moltmann's young psyche, and he would refer to it often in later writing as "the inferno."[54]

Standing next to Moltmann on an artillery platform, his friend Gerhard Schopper was ravaged by an explosion of wood shrapnel, his head torn from his body. Alongside the seizing terror of this grisly moment, surrounded by the screams and roar of the burning city, Moltmann was also struck by piercing guilt: "Why am I alive and not dead, too, like the friend at my side?"[55] While Operation Gomorrah would not be the final traumatic wartime experience for Moltmann, it seems to have been the most

---

49. Moltmann details the general Enlightenment humanism of his family in *Broad Place*, 6–12.

50. See the description of his experience as a member of the Hitler Youth in *In the End*, 24–25.

51. "Trauma of Perpetrators," 122; see also von Kellenbach, *Mark of Cain*, 200.

52. "Crucified God in Context," 2.

53. Moltmann, *Broad Place*, 189.

54. See *Broad Place*, 16–17, 189–90; *Experiences in Theology*, 3–4; "Crucified God in Context," 3; "My Theological Career," 166.

55. Moltmann, *Broad Place*, 17.

disturbing to him overall, and it is the only event in light of which he labels himself a "survivor."[56]

Following the mass death of Hamburg, Moltmann found himself in an infantry company, pinned down near the village of Asten: "All night long, grenades howled over our heads . . . only half the company was still alive [in the morning]."[57] A short time later he endured the death of another friend, Günther Schwiebert:

> Suddenly out of the clear sky, grenades began to rain down on us, and we made a rush for the bunkers. I reached them but . . . all at once the roof of the bunker was open, and a splinter hit the back of Günther's head. I tried to bandage him . . . but he only screamed and stammered. I finally got him onto a cart and brought him to a dressing station, but he died in my arms.[58]

On a march to Cleves, gunfire suddenly bombarded Moltmann and his troop from all sides. Pinned down again, terrified, Moltmann saw more of his companions shot dead before finally surrendering. He never shot an enemy combatant—a fact for which he was grateful in later life—but in the moment, nineteen years old and captured as a POW, he felt only fear, helplessness, and guilt, as well as something emergent and dreadful: "*Cold despair* laid an iron ring round the heart and took away the air we needed to breathe. Each of us [who had been captured] tried to conceal his bleeding heart. . . . That was the inward imprisonment of the soul which was added to the outward captivity."[59]

The Train—Perpetrator/Bystander Trauma

Many German soldiers only became aware of the horrific extent of the concentration camps as the Allied Forces discovered them. This was the case with Moltmann. While he was a POW in Scotland, the atrocities dawned on him as they dawned on the wider world. He returned one day to his prisoner's quarters to find hideous pictures affixed to the walls:

> [Pictures of Belsen and Buchenwald] were pinned up in the huts.
> . . . Slowly and inexorably the truth seeped into our consciousness,

56. Moltmann, *Broad Place*, 17.

57. Moltmann, *Broad Place*, 22.

58. Moltmann, *Broad Place*, 23.

59. Moltmann, *Broad Place*, 26 (emphasis added).

and we saw ourselves through the eyes of the Nazi victims. . . . Depression over the wartime destruction and captivity with no end in sight was compounded by a feeling of profound shame at having to share in shouldering the disgrace of one's people. That really choked me, and the weight of it has never left me to the present day.[60]

While much trauma discourse has rightly focused on the experience of victims, it is becoming evermore apparent that an additional category is needed: perpetrator trauma. Such a focus does not at all serve to diminish or silence victims, nor does it make "victims" out of perpetrators, but rather it focuses even more thoroughly on trauma's pervasive distortionary effects, which radiate outward and affect all parties involved in the traumatizing event.[61]

Though a newer domain of study, trenchant analysis of perpetrator trauma has been published, focusing on individual, group, and national manifestations.[62] Of the latter category, post-Holocaust Germans are one of the foremost examples, and serve as the main subject for the investigations of Berhard Giesen's work on the subject.[63] Analogous in many ways to individual traumas, Giesen notes that "[national] traumas remember a moment of violent intrusion or collapse of meaning that the collective consciousness was not able to perceive or grasp in its full importance when it happened."[64] Germans, especially young soldiers captured on the front, were confronted by "the unspeakable or incomprehensible horror, the dark abyss into which the German nation had been precipitating. . . . The trauma is insurmountable. As a moral subject the person is dead."[65] Moltmann, while not a direct perpetrator of specific acts of anti-Semitic genocide, belongs to the German nation, and thus he falls within a plausible scope of post-Holocaust perpetrator trauma, hinted at in many of his reflections: "Fate had—against

---

60. Moltmann, *Broad Place*, 29.

61. From the standpoint of Christian trauma theology, a trauma-informed hamartiology will need to take account of sin's decreational effects on perpetrators as well as victims; see further, Youngs, "Sin in the Therapeutic Circle."

62. On individual perpetrator trauma, see Mohamed, "Monsters and Men;" on group (military, in this case) perpetrator trauma, see Eyerman, "Collective Guilt;" on national perpetrator trauma, see Giesen, "Trauma of Perpetrators."

63. Giesen, "Trauma of Perpetrators."

64. Giesen, "Trauma of Perpetrators," 111.

65. Giesen, "Trauma of Perpetrators," 121.

my will—made me a member of the generation of perpetrators. I had to bear the shame of the mass murder of the Jews."[66]

But the application of perpetrator trauma to Moltmann, while plausible, is not exact. There is yet another related and important category, that of "bystander trauma,"[67] which may more accurately encompass his experience. Bystander trauma can befall those who "know about the crime or watched it being done without intervening or preventing it."[68] While Moltmann did not participate in the death camps or know the details of the Final Solution, he did hear of Jewish massacres from his father, who had actually seen mass graves.[69] After this revelation, Moltmann attests to have no longer been "willing" to serve in the war, but he did continue in military service until his capture, mired by "a sense of my own helplessness."[70]

That felt helplessness was darkly augmented on a fateful day before his capture, when he and some other German soldiers saw a train passing on nearby tracks. As it rolled by, they were shocked to see human faces staring darkly out of the cars.[71] Reflecting on this moment with all the guilt of retrospect, Moltmann writes, "We could see that these people were not wearing uniforms like us but were wearing the striped clothing of the concentration camps. . . . This dictatorship of the Nihil [Nothingness] was for me so incomprehensible because the abyss of the mass annihilation is such a bottomless pit."[72] As a bystander to unfathomable suffering, Moltmann bore a wound, a trauma; as Giesen writes, "Bystanders' ambivalent position between guilt by non-action, voluntary inattention, and lack of courage is especially prone to collective trauma."[73]

---

66. "Crucified God in Context," 4.

67. Featured sometimes in the "trauma triangle" of victim-victimizer-bystander, as seen in Ringel et al., *Trauma*, e.g., 284–85, 305, 335, 347.

68. Giesen, "Trauma of Perpetrators," 110.

69. Moltmann, *Broad Place*, 20.

70. Indeed, as Giesen writes of this generation of Germans, "Few knew all the horrible facts, but almost everybody knew something. Most German deliberately or inadvertently avoided focusing their attention on the disappearance of the Jews from public life. They did not want to get involved in piercing moral questions, for fear, negligence, or resentment" ("Trauma of Perpetrators," 122).

71. This was in 1944; see *Broad Place*, 190.

72. Moltmann, *Broad Place*, 190.

73. "Trauma of Perpetrators," 110.

THE UNCLOSED WOUNDS: MOLTMANN'S TRAUMATIC SYMPTOMOLOGY

It is now well recognized that trauma reshapes us psychologically and physiologically. It changes our experience of ourselves and our world. Moltmann is no exception. His mental, emotional, and embodied existence was thrown into turmoil, resulting in various manifestations of traumatized symptomology.[74]

Freezing/Numbing

In a Belgian POW camp shortly after his capture, the young Moltmann found himself imprisoned not only with his own trauma, but also with a new threat: captured Nazi zealots who terrorized the less "dedicated" Germans by night in the prisoners' bunker.[75] Overwhelmed by the shame and terror of his recent and ongoing experiences, Moltmann would scarcely move from his bunk. As he continued in this state, he readily developed a case of boils and took no action to remedy them, even as the sores deepened all over his body. His case eventually became so severe that a fellow prisoner carried him to medical attention. The boils had progressed so drastically that, though he recovered, Moltmann's flesh would bear scars for the rest of his life.[76] This lack of attention to his hygiene, health, and physical pain reflects the "numbing" response that can be characteristic of the deeply traumatized.[77] In this state, as Bessel van der Kolk notes, "[We become] unresponsive to the environment. . . . Awareness is shut down, and we may no longer even register physical pain."[78]

Suicidality

It was later, as a POW in Scotland, that Moltmann fully learned of the death camp horrors, and it was there that his psychological condition approached a nadir of such depth that he seemingly contemplated ending his own life. He refers to these days as his "valley of the shadow of death" and his

74. See Perry and Winfrey, *What Happened to You?*, 87–92, 168–69.

75. Moltmann, *Broad Place*, 27.

76. Moltmann, *Broad Place*, 27.

77. See van der Kolk, *Body Keeps the Score*, 78–79, 89–104.

78. *Body Keeps the Score*, 85; see further 89–104, 268.

"experiences of death."[79] In the midst of this, a chaplain gave him a Bible, and in Mark's Gospel Moltmann discovered a world-altering solidarity in the forsaken cry of Jesus on the cross.[80] Solidarity that leads to hope, God with us in our dark present summoning us toward his good future—this is the fountainhead of Moltmann's most sustained theological concerns.[81]

> Jesus is the one who delivers us from the guilt that weighs us down and robs us of every kind of future. And I became possessed by a hope when in human terms there was little to hope for. I summoned up the courage to live, at a point when one would perhaps willingly have put an end to it all. This early companionship with Jesus, the brother in suffering and liberator from guilt, has never left me since.[82]

Nightmares, Flashbacks, Guilt, and Shame

"Traumatic events recondition the human nervous system,"[83] writes Judith Herman, and van der Kolk's work has emphasized that in our bodies, our very flesh, the "score is kept." Moltmann's faith in the co-suffering Christ rescued him from the brink of death, yes and gratefully, but the wounds of his wartime and bystander traumas remained with him, perhaps less acute, but still unclosed. Throughout his career, his writing has attested to intrusive sensations, flashbacks, and nightmares, reflecting the temporal fracture so distinct of traumatic memory.[84]

When Moltmann describes his nightmares—"Sleepless nights when the tormenting memories rose up, and I woke soaked in sweat, when the faces of the dead appeared and looked at me with their quenched eyes"—it aligns with the PTSD symptoms war veterans commonly recount in clinical

79. Moltmann, *Broad Place*, 30 and 31, respectively.

80. Moltmann, *Broad Place*, 30.

81. As is well known and broadly evidenced across his corpus; see, e.g., his first two major publications, *Theology of Hope* and *Crucified God*. See also Youngs, *Way of the Kenotic Christ*, 28–44.

82. Moltmann, *Jesus Christ*, 2–3. Elsewhere he writes, "[I] found a new hope in the Christian faith, which brought me not only spiritual but also (I think) physical survival, because it rescued me from despair and from giving up" (*History and the Triune God*, 166).

83. Herman, *Trauma and Recovery*, 36.

84. On which see Herman, *Trauma and Recovery*, 37–42; van der Kolk, *Body Keeps the Score*, 173–201.

settings.[85] He describes what seem to be flashbacks, or at least recurrent, detemporalized fragments of traumatic experience:

> Even today I can still feel shaken by the terror of early experiences of death, even if I am no longer consciously aware of them, and even though "the activity of my reason" tells me that these experiences are forty-seven years old, and go back to the fire-storm that raged through Hamburg in 1943. But for all that, these experiences are present with me still. I can feel myself back into them, and they still plunge me into the same terror as they did then. Ever since, my life has been hung over by the tormenting, insistent questions: "Where is God?" and "Why am I not dead too?" In the depths of experiences like this, there is apparently no such thing as "time the great healer," and no merciful forgetting. So we can never say about an experience of this kind "I had it" as if it were finished and done with, something past and gone.[86]

For much of Moltmann's professional and theological life, he has not had the toolkit of "trauma language" available to him. Given this, he does not refer to his wounding experiences as *traumatization*. But this technical precision is hardly needed, as what is recounted above accords deeply with the well-known presentation of unintegrated traumatic moments, which emerge in consciousness "as though [they] were continually recurring in the present . . . with all the vividness and emotional force of the original event."[87]

A significant further component of complex trauma, especially in the aftermath of war, can be survivor's guilt. Such guilt is "especially severe when the survivor has been a witness to the suffering or death of other people . . . [it] creates a tremendous burden of conscience," and this even more so in the case of young soldiers.[88] This sort of guilt, as we've seen, has plagued Moltmann across his lifetime.[89] But when the survivor also sees themselves as a perpetrator of, or at least a bystander to, horrific atrocity, the psychological load accumulates to a potent degree. Moltmann goes so

---

85. Van der Kolk recounts "the nightmares war veterans had reported to me: seeing the precise, unadulterated images of faces and body parts they had encountered in battle. These dreams were so terrifying that they tried not to fall asleep at night" (*Body Keeps the Score*, 137).

86. Moltmann, *Spirit of Life*, 21.

87. Herman, *Trauma and Recovery*, 37.

88. Herman, *Trauma and Recovery*, 54, 60–61.

89. E.g., Moltmann, *Spirit of Life*, 21; *Broad Place*, 17, 381.

far as to associate himself with the original murderer, Cain, and he asks poignantly, "[What] about the life of the people burdened by guilt, and about the future of Cain, and those whose collective biography bears the mark of Cain. . . . Is there any reconciliation for those who bear the burden of guilt?"[90] Indeed, Moltmann seeks the perpetrator's and bystander's liberation from self-hate; for him, such liberation has to be possible, has to be found, for to live without it was "unendurable."[91]

I have arrayed Moltmann's experiences with careful deliberation. On the heels of discussing his oddly dogmatic universalism, the reader can likely detect an implicit case: the depth of Moltmann's pain and guilt points yearningly toward an understandable hope for universal redemption. Moltmann has seen his view of the world, his country, his friends, his very identity, his moral agency, his own body, unseated and thrown into chaos. Surely, if God could seek and find the young Jürgen—the *Hitlerjunge* sitting in a POW camp and nearly lost—then God can and will bring all to himself. Such would not be an inaccurate etiology of Moltmann's soteriology. But to stop there would not tell the whole story. For Moltmann's trauma also engendered a startling and liminal experience when he visited a concentration camp in 1961. This experience, so little accounted for in scholarship on Moltmann, sheds a final ray of light on his vigorous universalism.

THE SWALLOWING EARTH: MOLTMANN'S VISION IN MAIDANEK

In 1961, three years before submitting the manuscript of his first major work, *Theology of Hope*, Moltmann visited a concentration camp in Maidanek, Poland. He recounts the difficult experience in an essay several years later:

> With each step it became physically more difficult to go further and look at the thousands of children's shoes, clothing remnants, collected hair, and gold teeth. At that moment from shame I would have preferred to be swallowed up by the earth, if I had not believed: "God is with them. They will rise again."[92]

---

90. Moltmann, *God for a Secular Society*, 173; see also pp. 186–90.

91. Moltmann, *Spirit of Life*, 133. See also von Kellenbach, *Mark of Cain*, 200.

92. Moltmann, "Apathetic Man," 72–73.

Though it is concise, there are many notable elements in the account from a trauma-informed perspective. His indication of physical difficulty in movement implies a disconnection from his body, and the vivid image of being swallowed by the earth—of being taken away from present circumstances and eclipsed in a dark space—speaks of overwhelm and dissociation. Given what we know of Moltmann's traumatic history, none of these elements are surprising. They are not rhetorical but deep and real features of his experience, for Moltmann repeats them when he recounts the story at later times.[93]

But in those repetitions, Moltmann's account does shift, especially in its treatment of the theme of the resurrection. His earliest account, 1971, is cited above. In his autobiography, over thirty years later, he writes the following:

> At the time [as I walked through Maidanek] I wanted to sink into the ground for shame, and would have suffocated in the presence of mass murder, if on one of the roads through the camp I had not suddenly had a vision. I looked into the world of the resurrection and saw all these dead men, women, and children coming towards me. Since then I have known that God's history with Auschwitz and Maidanek has not been broken off, but that it goes further with the victims and with the perpetrators. Without hope of the "new earth in which righteousness dwells" (2 Peter 3.13), this earth, which has suffered Treblinka and Maidanek, would be unendurable.[94]

Three features of this account must be highlighted. The first we have already alluded to, Moltmann's repetititon of the dissociative image of disappearing into the earth, as well as his mention of physical difficulty (here seemingly related to his breathing—"suffocated"). The second feature, quite obviously, is the vision, a wholly new element in the account, which Moltmann clearly understands as a look into the future, the "world of the resurrection." Third is Moltmann's extrapolation of universalism in this moment, emerging from the overwhelming feelings of the experience and freighted with all the burden of his traumas. To live, to "endure" in that place, which encapsulates all that he most dreads in his own history, Moltmann must believe, and is blessed to see, that all the dead will rise again to life in God. No one is lost.

93. Moltmann writes of Maidanek at least three more times: *Broad Place*, 84, 191; "In Context," 4.

94. Moltmann, *Broad Place*, 84.

Judith Herman's reflections on remembrance and mourning in the process of trauma recovery shed fascinating light on Moltmann's Maidanek experience. In formal, therapist-led sessions, the traumatized individual "reconstructs" a narrative of their experience, making a choice "to confront the horrors of the past."[95] This reconstructed narrative did not issue from Moltmann himself, and his walk through the death camp was not a therapy session. And yet, what he saw, in visible, dramatic, and disturbing ways, generated a living narrative of horrors:

> The plank beds in the barracks were the last resting place of starv-ing and tormented men, women, and children. Behind glass lay the little shoes of the murdered Jewish children, and hair that had been cut off from the gassed women. We saw the pits in which more than 10,000 people had been shot on a single day.[96]

Hyperarousal, dissociation, failure of language, physical discomfort, or agi-tation can all mark the reconstruction process as the "patient" is flooded with sensations related to the past trauma.[97] These physiological markers may explain Moltmann's allusions to physical difficulty in movement and breathing during his visit to Maidanek. Traumatic reconstruction also helps to make sense of his later recall of his visionary experience; as Herman writes, "In the course of reconstruction, the story may change as missing pieces are recovered."[98]

The eventual goal of such reconstruction in a therapeutic setting is to "integrate these experiences into a fully-developed life narrative."[99] Such in-tegration may be detected in Moltmann's latest recounting of his Maidanek experience, in which he writes: "I saw the children's shoes, the cut off hair, and I was overwhelmed by shame. And as I walked alone through one of the camp's streets I had a vision: I saw the murdered children walking toward me in the fog. *Since then I have been convinced that there is a resurrection of the dead.*"[100] The difference in this third recounting is striking: Moltmann now fully claims the rootedness of his soteriology in the Maidanek expe-rience. Of course, he had learned from Barth, Blumhardt, and others; of

95. Herman, *Trauma and Recovery*, 174.

96. Moltmann, *Broad Place*, 84.

97. Herman, *Trauma and Recovery*, 176–79. Of course, in the later writing of his expe-rience, Moltmann is able to engage in further reconstruction, and in a safer environment.

98. Herman, *Trauma and Recovery*, 179.

99. Herman, *Trauma and Recovery*, 184.

100. Moltmann, "In Context," 4 (emphasis added).

course he *knew* of universalism before Maidanek. But *his* universalism, his convicted assurance of the resurrection of all, takes its unique impress from his trauma, that trauma's reconstruction, and the images he perceived in the death camp, issuing forth in a declaration of eschatological restoration for all that had been lost.[101] This movement, the "reconnection" which can follow the long process of facing the traumatic past, does not necessarily cure or fix trauma but transforms it. Again Herman: "The old beliefs that gave meaning to [the patient's] life have been challenged; now [they] must find anew a sustaining faith. . . . In accomplishing this work, the survivor regains [their] world."[102]

CONCLUSION

What follows from the foregoing analysis? It bears within it at least a two-fold contribution, each of distinct value for different conversations in theological scholarship.

First, from the perspective of trauma-informed theology more generally, this study has contributed an example of a specifically new type of theological analysis. Such analysis takes the biographically formed nature of theology seriously, and therefore takes the biography seriously, being especially attentive to experiences and symptomology that can be reasonably associated with trauma. Not all theologians have experienced trauma, and many theologians do not leave us enough details of their lives from which we might responsibly draw conclusions. But in cases in which both things—biographical detail and plausible trauma—are present, trauma-informed theology can perceive connections between trauma and doctrinal expression that illuminates both past lives and past theologies.

Second, from the perspective of the ever-burgeoning scholarship on Moltmann's life and thought, this study contributes a proposal for the origin of his seemingly "dogmatic" universalism. His rhetoric of universalism is not a product of abstract soteriological rumination or theological hubris, but an expression of life; life seized in the maw of suffocation and shame, life affirmed by grace against the unfathomable horrors of trauma. Moltmann speaks the restoration of all things without equivocation, for to equivocate

101. His visionary experience in Maidanek could be examined even more fully than we have done here. It could represent an involuntary self-enablement of guided imagery, a known tool in the treatment of PTSD; see LeDoux et al., *Post-Traumatic*, 264–67.

102. Herman, *Trauma and Recovery*, 197.

would be to deny the life and the new story he has discovered within it. The mending of all creation—this was the theological idea that comforted the boy who survived the inferno and bore the guilt of the passing train; it was the affirmation of hope that closed the yawning earth which threatened to swallow him; it moved him from terror to consolation:

> "The Last Judgment" is not a terror. In the truth of Christ it is the most wonderful thing that can be proclaimed to men and women. It is a source of endlessly consoling joy to know, not just that the murderers will finally fail to triumph over their victims, but that they cannot in eternity even remain the murderers of their victims.[103]

BIBLIOGRAPHY

Baldwin, Jennifer. *Trauma-Sensitive Theology: Thinking Theologically in the Era of Trauma.* Eugene, OR: Cascade, 2018.

Barth, Karl. *Church Dogmatics.* Vol. 2/2: *The Doctrine of God.* Edinburgh: T&T Clark, 1957.

Bauckham, Richard, and Margaret Kohl. *Jürgen Moltmann: Collected Readings.* Philadelphia: Fortress, 2014.

Benjet, C., et al. "The Epidemiology of Traumatic Event Exposure Worldwide: Results from the World Mental Health Survey Consortium." *Psychological Medicine* 46:2 (2016) 327–43.

Crisp, Oliver. "I Do Teach It, but I Also Do Not Teach It: The Universalism of Karl Barth (1886–1968)." In *"All Shall Be Well": Explorations in Universal Salvation and Christian Theology,* edited by Gregory McDonald, 305–24. Cambridge: James Clarke & Co., 2011.

Dickson, John. *Bullies and Saints: An Honest Look at the Good and Evil of Christian History.* Grand Rapids: Zondervan, 2021.

Dwyer, Philip, et al. *The Cambridge World History of Violence.* 4 vols. Cambridge: Cambridge University Press, 2020.

Erikson, Erik H. *Young Man Luther: A Study in Psychoanalysis and History.* New York: Norton, 1958.

Eyerman, Ron. "Perpetrator Trauma and Collective Guilt: The My Lai Massacre." In *Memory, Trauma, and Identity,* 167–94. London: Palgrave Macmillan, 2019.

Foucault, Michel. *Discipline and Punish: The Birth of the Prison.* Translated by Alan Sheridan. New York: Vintage, 1995.

Giesen, Bernhard. "The Trauma of Perpetrators: The Holocaust as the Traumatic Reference of German Identity." In *Triumph and Trauma,* 109–54. London: Routledge, 2004.

Harrower, Scott. *God of All Comfort: A Trinitarian Response to the Horrors of This World.* Bellingham, WA: Lexham, 2019.

Harrower, Scott, et al. *Dawn of Sunday: The Trinity and Trauma-Safe Churches.* Eugene, OR: Cascade, 2022.

103. Moltmann, *Coming of God,* 255. See also *In the End,* 149–50.

Herman, Judith. *Trauma and Recovery: The Aftermath of Violence—From Domestic Abuse to Political Terror.* New York: Basic, 1997.

Jones, Serene. *Trauma and Grace: Theology in a Raptured World.* Louisville: Westminster John Knox, 2009.

Keefe-Perry, L. Callid. *Way to Water: A Theopoetics Primer.* Eugene, OR: Cascade, 2014.

Kilpatrick, Dean G., et al. "National Estimates of Exposure to Traumatic Events and PTSD Prevalence Using DSM-IV and DSM-5 Criteria." *Journal of Traumatic Stress* 26:5 (2013) 537–47.

Kim-Kort, Mihee. *Paper Cranes: Toward an Asian American Feminist Theology.* St. Louis: Chalice, 2012.

LeDoux Joseph, et al. *Post-Traumatic Stress Disorder: Basic Science and Clinical Practice.* Totowa, NJ: Humana, 2009.

Lewis, C. S. *The World's Last Night and Other Essays.* San Francisco: HarperOne, 2017.

McClendon, James. *Biography as Theology: How Life Stories Can Remake Today's Theology.* Eugene, OR: Wipf & Stock, 2002.

Metz, Johann Baptist. "Theology as Biography?" In *Faith in History and Society: Toward a Practical Fundamental Theology,* 219–29. Translated by J. Matthew Ashley. New York: Crossroad, 2007.

Mohamed, Saira. "Of Monsters and Men: Perpetrator Trauma and Mass Atrocity." *Columbia Law Review* 115:5 (2015) 1157–1216.

Moltmann, Jürgen. *A Broad Place: An Autobiography.* London: SCM Press, 2007.

———. *The Coming of God: Christian Eschatology.* Minneapolis: Augsburg, 2004.

———. "Creation and Redemption." In *Creation, Christ, and Culture,* edited by R. W. A. McKinney, 125–35. Edinburgh: T&T Clark, 1976.

———. *The Crucified God.* Minneapolis: Fortress, 1993.

———. "The Crucified God and the Apathetic Man." In *The Experiment Hope,* 69–84. Eugene, OR: Wipf & Stock, 2003.

———. "The Crucified God in Context." In *Theology—Descent into the Vicious Circles of Death,* edited by Zoran Grozdanov, 1–18. Eugene, OR: Cascade, 2016.

———. *Experiences in Theology: Ways and Forms of Christian Theology.* Philadelphia: Fortress, 2000.

———. "God and Resurrection." In *Hope and Planning,* 187–96. New York: Harper & Row.

———. *God for a Secular Society: The Public Relevance of Theology.* Philadelphia: Fortress, 1999.

———. "God's Kenosis in the Creation and Consummation of the World." In *The Work of Love,* 137–55. Grand Rapids: Eerdmans, 2001.

———. *History and the Triune God.* London: SCM Press, 2012.

———. *In the End, the Beginning.* Minneapolis: Augsburg Fortress, 2004.

———. *Jesus Christ for Today's World.* Philadelphia: Fortress, 1995.

———. "The Logic of Hell." In *God Will Be All in All: The Eschatology of Jürgen Moltmann,* edited by Richard Bauckham, 43–48. Philadelphia: Fortress, 2001.

———. "My Theological Career." In *History and the Triune God,* translated by John Bowden, 165–82. London: SCM Press, 1991.

———. "Resurrection as Hope." *Harvard Theological Review* 61:2 (1968) 129–47.

———. *The Spirit of Life: A Universal Affirmation.* Philadelphia: Fortress, 2001.

———. *Sun of Righteousness, Arise! God's Future for Humanity and the Earth.* Philadelphia: Fortress, 2010.

———. *Theology of Hope: On the Ground and the Implications of a Christian Eschatology.* Philadelphia: Fortress, 1993.

———. *The Trinity and the Kingdom.* Philadelphia: Fortress, 1993.

———. "Will All Be Saved, or Only a Few? A Dialogue Between Faith and Grace." In *Theology as Conversation*, edited by Bruce L. McCormack and Kimlyn J. Bender, 235–40. Grand Rapids: Eerdmans, 2009.

Neal, Ryan A. *Theology as Hope: On the Ground and Implications of Jürgen Moltmann's Doctrine of Hope.* Eugene, OR: Wipf & Stock, 2009.

Ngong, David T. *Theology as Construction of Piety: An African Perspective.* Searcy, AR: Resource, 2013.

Pedraja, Luis G. *Teologia: An Introduction to Hispanic Theology.* Nashville: Abingdon, 2004.

Perry, Bruce D., and Oprah Winfrey. *What Happened to You? Conversations on Trauma, Resilience, and Healing.* New York: Flatiron, 2021.

Pinker, Steven. *The Better Angels of Our Nature: Why Violence Has Declined.* New York: Penguin, 2012.

Rahner, Karl. *Theological Investigations.* Vol. 6. Baltimore: Helicon, 1969.

Rambo, Shelly. *Resurrecting Wounds: Living in the Afterlife of Trauma.* Waco, TX: Baylor University Press, 2017.

———. *Spirit and Trauma: A Theology of Remaining.* Louisville: Westminster John Knox, 2010.

Richardson, Kurt Anders. "Moltmann's Communitarian Trinity." In *Jürgen Moltmann and Evangelical Theology: A Critical Engagement*, edited by Sung Wook Chung, 17–39. Eugene, OR: Pickwick, 2012.

Ringel, Shoshana, et al. *Trauma: Contemporary Directions in Theory, Practice, and Research.* Thousand Oaks, CA: Sage Publications, 2012.

Smith, Christian. *The Bible Made Impossible: Why Biblicism Is Not a Truly Evangelical Reading of Scripture.* Ada, MI: Brazos, 2012.

Southwick, Steven, and Dennis Charney. *Resilience: The Science of Mastering Life's Greatest Challenges.* Cambridge: Cambridge University Press 2012.

van der Kolk, Bessel. *The Body Keeps the Score: Brain, Mind, and Body in the Healing of Trauma.* New York: Penguin, 2015.

von Balthasar, Hans Urs. *Dare We Hope That All Men Be Saved? With a Short Discourse on Hell.* San Francisco: Ignatius, 1988.

von Kellenbach, Katharina. *The Mark of Cain: Guilt and Denial in the Post-War Lives of Nazi Perpetrators.* Oxford: Oxford University Press, 2013.

Williams, Stephen. *Jürgen Moltmann: A Critical Introduction.* Westmont, IL: Theological Students Fellowship, 1987.

———. "Moltmann on Jesus Christ." In *Jürgen Moltmann and Evangelical Theology: A Critical Engagement*, edited by Sung Wook Chung, 104–25. Eugene, OR: Wipf & Stock, 2012.

Youngs, Samuel J. *Way of the Kenotic Christ: The Christology of Jürgen Moltmann.* Eugene, OR: Cascade, 2019.

———. "Ways to Sin: Thinking About Hamartiology and Trauma with Moltmann." *The Other Journal* 33 (2022). https://theotherjournal.com/2022/01/sin-trauma-moltmann/.

Traumatic Love

Religious Trauma and the Atoning Christ

MICHELLE PANCHUK

I. INTRODUCTION

A small child sits in Sunday School.[1] The teacher chooses them as the central example for the lesson. This is a great honor—the height of social status in their small second-grade world. Ms. Anna announces that she is going to tell a story to illustrate just how much Jesus loves us all. "Imagine," she says, "that I'm still a little girl and that I have been very naughty. My mom tells me that I have earned a spanking for being bad. But, I have a very good friend, Alex," she continues, gesturing at the child. "Alex loves me so very much that they don't want me to have to get a spanking, so Alex says, 'Ms. Anna's Mommy? please forgive Ms. Anna for being bad. I don't want her to get a spanking.' But my mom says, 'No.' She cannot just excuse my behavior because that wouldn't be fair. Actions always have consequences. Someone *has* to get a spanking. But my friend loves me so much that they get another idea. They ask, 'Ms. Anna's Mommy, can you spank *me* instead of Ms. Anna?'"

At this point Alex is blushing deeply and has broken into a cold sweat. They try not to squirm too noticeably in their seat, not wanting their friends

---

1. I would like to thank Michael Rea and the fellows at the Center for Theological Inquiry, particularly Jessica Coblentz, Andrew Shepherd, Sheryl Overmyer, and Michael Bräutigam, for their helpful comments on early drafts of this paper, as well as Blake Hereth for being such an insightful conversation partner on this topic.

to see how terrified they are in real life of being hit with a belt or dowel rod. It's just a story, but it's also not *just* a story. The thought of the teacher describing this scene to the whole class fills Alex with shame. There is an unspoken code among the children. They never speak of being punished. It's a matter of basic respect. Still, Alex feels a little proud of the version of themself that Ms. Anna describes. They sound incredibly brave—braver than Alex feels—and deeply kind and caring.

Ms. Anna continues, "My mom thinks about it for a minute and decides that she can spank my friend instead of me. So my friend accepts my spanking, even though it hurts and even though I deserve it and they don't. That is how much Jesus loves us—only, he didn't just take our spanking for us. The Bible says that the wages of sin is death. We really deserve punishment that is much, much worse than a spanking. We deserve to die for our sins and burn forever in hell, separated from God. Jesus died in our place, just like Alex took my spanking in the story." Alex is moved by Jesus's self-sacrifice, but they decide that they don't like Ms. Anna's mom at all. She sounds like the sort of grown-up who enjoys hurting kids—and any child will do.

In "big church," Alex hears a similar story, only this time it involves an only son and an uncle sentenced to the electric chair for murder. Again, Alex finds the hero's courage and love inspiring. If this boy is an example of Jesus, then Jesus seems like someone they could trust. The judge and the father, on the other hand, sound neither kind nor smart. Where in the world does the judge get the cruel idea to ask the father to kill his son? Why does the father agree to the horror? Alex decides that if God is like the judge, like the father, and like Ms. Anna's mommy, then God must just be really into hurting humans. After all, he doesn't care so much *who* he gets to hurt as long as he gets to hurt *someone*. But then again, he is God, so they *have* to love him and his ways.

These purported illustrations of the dynamics of the atonement, the atoning Christ, and the character of God were central to Alex's understanding of themself in relation to God. The unspeakable torture of ancient Roman crucifixion, the stoning of rebellious children (Deut 21:18–21), not to mention eternal conscious torment in hell, were all presented to them not only as what they *deserved*, but as what God was obliged, indeed *wanted*, to do to them. He was just as happy, though, to torture Jesus instead. As a result, when human abusers claimed to act in the divine name, Alex had little reason to doubt that their abuser's actions were god-like. They had the same conflicting feelings toward those humans that they did toward God: love, fear, trust, disgust, confusion. But instead of questioning others' actions or those others' account of God, Alex wondered what their inability to wholeheartedly embrace the *goodness* of either revealed about their own character. Their relationship to God, to Jesus's saving love, and to their own worth became deeply entangled with their relationship to abuse, to fear, and to shame. It was not until years later that this entanglement became clear as a central component of their experience of trauma and as a barrier in their relationship with God—that is, as a form of *spiritual and religious trauma*.[2]

To identify a connection between theories of atonement—particularly the family of views often labeled "satisfaction theories"—and justification for abuse is not original. Feminist and womanist theologians, among others, have long criticized the way that atonement theories valorize self-sacrificial suffering and sanctify violence and abuse.[3] This chapter extends such work in two ways. First, for those already rejecting satisfaction theories on moral or practical grounds, I identify *religious and spiritual trauma* as additional, previously neglected, harms that satisfaction theories often inflict. I show that they not only render people more vulnerable to abuse and more likely to passively accept oppression, but that they often harm abuse survivors specifically in their relationship with God and in their capacities as spiritual beings. Second, my argument anticipates a common response to feminist critiques of atonement theories—namely, that the fact that a theory can be misapplied or used as a tool for oppression does not, by itself, prove that the account is false.[4] I argue that the connection between satisfaction theories of the atonement and religious and spiritual trauma is not accidental, as a popular misunderstanding or misapplication, but that it arises from the central features of the standard forms of these theories.[5] They portray God

2. Although a true story used with permission, names have been changed both to respect privacy and because the experience is neither unique nor anomalous. Countless similar stories could be told. I count among my closest friends people whose parents explicitly encouraged this sort of "self-sacrifice" from their children, purportedly to help them develop in Christlikeness. Unlike Alex, they *actually* took their siblings' place for countless beatings. While they don't regret doing so, they also now recognize it as a deep source of trauma.

3. Cf. Brown and Parker, "For God So Loved the World?"; Williams, *Sisters in the Wilderness*; Brock and Parker, *Proverbs of Ashes*; Pineda-Madrid, *Suffering and Salvation in Ciudad Juárez*; Weaver, *Nonviolent Atonement*.

4. I thank Michael Rea for encouraging me to make this point more explicit.

5. Although given the diversity of views that fall broadly under the label "satisfaction

as acting in ways familiar to humans primarily in the behavior of human abusers and oppressors. Such portrayals are beneath God and lead many further away, rather than closer to, an accurate understanding of God's salvific work in Christ.

I begin by providing a brief account of satisfaction theories of the atonement and some exemplary feminist critiques of them. I then describe the central features of spiritual and religious trauma in order to show that there are (at least) two ways in which the standard satisfaction theories contribute to them by portraying God in the image of a human abuser. I end by suggesting that thinking of theology and philosophy of religion as engaged, at least in part, in the project of conceptual engineering gives us reasons to think that it is unfitting for human theologians and philosophers of religion to develop theories that attempt to communicate the truth of Jesus's atoning love in a way that portrays God as acting *in the same way* as human abusers. This is true, as I shall show, even if one thinks that such theories do not portray God as acting immorally.

II. SATISFACTION THEORIES OF THE ATONEMENT

While there are a number of important differences among models of the atonement that I am here broadly calling "satisfaction theories,"—among which I include Anselmian satisfaction theory and penal substitutionary theories—a key feature that unites them is that, unlike other accounts, such ransom theories, *Christus Victor*, and moral influence models, satisfaction theories see the primary work of atonement as directed Godward—that is, as making satisfaction for human sin *to God* in some way.[6] They are generally regarded as owing their rise to prominence to the work of Anselm of Canterbury in the eleventh century, although the motif has roots that date much earlier. In *Cur Deus Homo?* or *Why the God Man*, Anselm mounts an impressive argument against the claim that it would unfitting

---

theory" it is possible that some versions may escape my critique. I do not regard this as a failing of my argument.

6. Weaver, *Nonviolent Atonement*, 258; one might say that on penal substitionary accounts, it isn't so much God as the demands of justice that are being satisfied. However, insofar as the justice in question is usually understood as divine justice, grounded in the divine nature, and the penalty for sin as one that God metes out in God's capacity as judge, there is still a fundamental sense in which atonement is directed Godward, as opposed to toward the devil (ransom theory), toward defeating death (*Christus Victor*), or toward changing humans (moral influence).

for God to lower himself to become human, suffer, and die as the Christian story maintains. According to Anselm, God's honor has been besmirched by human sin. Humans, in virtue of their creation by God, owe God their absolute obedience and allegiance, and have failed to render it. While it is not logically or morally impossible for God simply to forgive humans, Anselm argues that to do so would be *unfitting*.[7] It is unfitting for God to suffer dishonor either because his purposes for creation are frustrated by human sin or because he remains uncompensated for humanity's failure to give him his due. God's honor can be restored either by punishing sinners or by humans repaying him with some other sufficiently meritorious act.[8] Humans are incapable of doing the latter because anything they can render to God, including their own obedience, is no more than what they already owe, but if humans bear the penalty for their sin, God's purposes in creation would be frustrated. However, because Jesus, as the God-Man, is the only human who does not owe his life to God on account of his own sin, his obedience to God unto death is both supererogatory and meritorious. Although scholars diverge on the contours of exactly how Anselm thinks that Jesus's death restores God's honor, what is clear is that the voluntary death of the innocent—obedience unto death—is *meritorious* and pleasing to God, in some way. The merit Jesus obtains through his suffering and death plays an essential role in restoring God's honor and creation's relationship with God.[9]

7. Fittingness, for Anselm, has to do not only with what God has reason to do, and what is appropriate for God to do, but also with broader aesthetic properties like beauty and symmetry. Further, it is determined in the current context in relation to three categories: the character of God, God's aims with respect to humanity, and the human condition (Johnson, "Fuller Account," 304). For Anselm, that something would be fitting for God to do x (God has reason to do x and it would be beautiful if God did x) does not by itself prove that God does x. But that something is unfitting for God to do x is sufficient reason to deny that God has done x (I.4).

8. Katherine Sonderegger offers a very sympathetic read of Anselm, pointing out that one need not read the necessity of satisfaction here as one would a mob boss's demand for respect, but more in line with the oppressed person's insistence that what is wrong with the world must be made right ("Anselmian Atonement," 186). For my purposes in this chapter, what is at issue is less the insistence that things be put right and more that things can be put right through suffering and death, either of the wrongdoer or of the one who freely gives his life.

9. Given the constraints of this paper, this overview elides important debates in Anselmian interpretation. For an introduction to those conversations, see Hopkins, *Companion to the Study of St. Anselm*; Sonderegger, "Anselmian Atonement"; Cross, "Atonement Without Satisfaction"; Rea, "Introduction."

Nancy Pineda-Madrid's engagement with Anselm in her landmark work *Suffering and Salvation in Ciudad Juárez* is paradigmatic of feminist critique of atonement theory. She argues that it is impossible to fully understand or interpret a theory of the atonement apart from its practical impact throughout history.[10] Without laying the responsibility for that impact fully at Anselm's feet, she points out that the legacy of his work is decidedly mixed, having been used and abused in support of everything from the crusades in Anselm's own time and "to prolong, if not tacitly condone, situations of domestic violence and many other forms of violence—all under the banner of 'carrying one's cross' in our own."[11] She agrees with J. Denny Weaver that "it is not that the satisfaction motif promotes violence per se," but that "the motif lends itself to easy accommodation of violence and projects little that specifically opposes violence."[12] The problem, as Pineda-Madrid sees it, is that regardless of what Anselm may have intended, by placing almost exclusive emphasis on Jesus's suffering and death as the "source and summit of salvation,"[13] his theory suggests that passive submission to violence is not only sometimes pleasing to God, but intrinsically good.[14] The call to be imitators of Christ can serve to undermine victims' of domestic violence or social oppression (like the victims of feminicide in Ciudad Juàrez who concern Pineda-Madrid) ability to exercise agency in opposition to their own suffering.

Later satisfaction theories such as penal substitutionary theory[15] tend to use a legal/judicial, rather than a shame/honor, lens through which to conceptualize the atonement.[16] William Lane Craig defines penal substitutionary theory as "the doctrine that God inflicted upon Christ the suffering that we deserved as the punishment for our sins, as a result of which we

---

10. Pineda-Madrid, *Suffering and Salvation in Ciudad Juárez*, 83.

11. Pineda-Madrid, *Suffering and Salvation in Ciudad Juárez*, 86.

12. Weaver, *Nonviolent Atonement*, 97, cited in Pineda-Madrid, *Suffering and Salvation in Ciudad Juárez*, 87.

13. Pineda-Madrid, *Suffering and Salvation in Ciudad Juárez*, 89.

14. Pineda-Madrid, *Suffering and Salvation in Ciudad Juárez*, 90.

15. And according to Stephen R. Holmes, first fully worked out by Calvin. See Holmes, "Penal Substitution," 304.

16. Whether to consider penal substitution a kind of "satisfaction theory" is itself controversial, but it is common enough that I set aside this debate for present purposes. If one has strong views to the contrary, one can view my thesis as that both satisfaction and penal substitution theories tend to cause religious trauma.

no longer deserve punishment."[17] Historically, the penalty for sin has been understood as eternal separation from God, often involving the experience of divine wrath against sin. God incarnate, who is infinite but also innocent and, thus, not liable for punishment, can bear the penalty for which human beings are liable. On this model, Jesus voluntarily takes on the suffering of condemned humans—or something commensurate to the suffering their punishment would have involved—for human sin on the cross so that justice is satisfied and humans are reconciled to God, because their debt has already been paid.[18] Although penal substitution is far from the dominant view among academic theologians or across the history of the church, it has a significant degree of purchase in evangelical circles where it is often regarded as a fundamental or even necessary doctrine of the faith. Indeed, Craig claims that any "biblically adequate atonement theory must include penal substitution at its center"[19] and harshly criticizes Eleonore Stump for thinking about "at onement" with God primarily through the lens of the reconciliation of interpersonal alienation and wrongs rather than seeing God as a ruler and judge who must exact retributive justice in response to human sin.[20]

In addition to concerns about encouraging submission to violence like those raised by Pineda-Madrid, Rebecca Parker objects to the image of God portrayed in penal substitutionary theories as a God "appeased by cruelty." Such an image, she claims, cannot but help to shape the values and behaviors of those who follow and worship such a God. For example, she writes, "If God is imagined as a fatherly torturer, earthly parents are also justified, perhaps even required, to teach through violence."[21] In an earlier work she writes with Joanne Brown:

> The image of God the father demanding and carrying out the suffering and death of his own son has sustained a culture of abuse and led to the abandonment of victims of abuse and oppression.

17. Craig, *Atonement and the Death of Christ*, 147. Theorists differ on the question of whether or not forgiveness for sin is, in principle, *possible* without punishment and also on whether Jesus is rightly understood as being punished for human sin or merely bearing the penalty (or harsh treatment) that would have constituted punishment if undergone by the humans who deserve it. But those debates take us beyond the scope of this paper.

18. Holmes, "Penal Substitution."

19. Craig, *Atonement and the Death of Christ*, 147.

20. Craig, *Atonement and the Death of Christ*, 167.

21. Brock and Parker, *Proverbs of Ashes*, 31.

Until this image is shattered it will be almost impossible to create a just society.[22]

Analytic theologians and philosophers of religion may be inclined to agree with William Lane Craig that when assessing a theory of the atonement one should attend to "(1) their accord with biblical teaching and (2) their philosophical coherence,"[23] perhaps adding a third about compatibility with the tradition handed down through the church. As we saw from Pineda-Madrid, feminist scholars tend to add an additional criteria that encourages attention to the *practical consequences* of believing and acting as if the theory were true. And it is on this point that conflicts in methodology tend to arise. While feminist scholars often assume that demonstration of harmful results constitutes conclusive evidence of the falsity of a theory (the tacit assumption seems to be that believing the truth about God shouldn't produce bad consequences), analytics tend to regard such demonstrations as weak evidence at best and, at worst, as utterly irrelevant to the conversation. The question, they assume, is whether the claims are true, not whether they would make the world a better place if believed.[24] Analytics often point out that almost any idea can be abused or misapplied, and it is exceedingly difficult to demonstrate that any particular theory or proposition strictly entails the permissibility of any particular form of abuse or a moral obligation to submit to it. In what follows, I argue that it is not merely one-off features of specific versions or misunderstanding and misapplication of satisfaction theories at the popular level that result in religious and spiritual trauma, but rather that central features of the most prominent extent theories cause the harm. In order to do so, I first provide an account of spiritual and religious trauma and then return to the features of satisfaction theory that perpetuate them.

III. RELIGIOUS AND SPIRITUAL TRAUMA

One way of reading the feminist critique of satisfaction theories is that they encourage or at least fail to guard against both violence itself and passive

22. Brown and Parker, "For God So Loved the World?," 6–7.

23. Craig, *Atonement and the Death of Christ*, 7.

24. I sympathize with this inclination although I don't entirely endorse it. I often find it off-putting when my therapist says that I should believe P because believing P would have some positive psychological effect. Of course it makes me feel bad to believe that I am selfish, but it might be true for all that! Sometimes the truth is ugly and unpleasant.

submission to it. On this read, satisfaction theories promote concrete physical and psychological suffering. However, the account with which I began this chapter suggests that regardless of whether the feminists are right about the causal claims, the harms they point to actually run much deeper. Yes, Alex continues to experience some of the classic symptoms of post-traumatic distress related to childhood physical abuse, such as recurring nightmares, heightened startle response, and difficulty regulating emotions in the face of scenarios and topics connected to the abuse. But the abuse also harms them in a specifically spiritual way not fully captured by mainstream discourse surrounding trauma, PTSD, or moral injury. Their relationship with God, with themself in relation to God, and with their religious community is also damaged because their understanding of the abuse is so deeply entangled with their understanding of how God relates to humans. This psycho-spiritual wound is the hallmark of religious and spiritual trauma. I have proposed elsewhere that religious and spiritual trauma paradigmatically involves:

> religiously or spiritually significant traumatic experience(s) that 1) causes religiously or spiritually significant post-traumatic effects and 2) harms the individual in their capacity as a religious or spiritual being.[25]

A traumatic experience may be religiously or spiritually significant because the trauma is caused by something that the individual closely associates with the religion (e.g., clergy member, religious parents, or religious teachers), is experienced for religious reasons (e.g., as part of a religious ritual or motivated by religious reasons), or because the religious or spiritual frame of reference through which the subject experiences or interprets the event explains why the experience constitutes a violation (as in the case of a forced violation of a religious rule or obligation). Post-traumatic effects, in turn, can be religiously or spiritual salient because they are triggered by, or bound up in some other way with, one's religion or spirituality. Unwanted memories might intrude on one's consciousness during Mass. Overwhelming emotions might erupt unbidden during meditation. The body might rebel with vomiting, aching head, or racing heart upon entering a mosque. Fear and dread might overwhelm during prayer. The sight of clerical garb might spark panic. One might avoid the mikva (ritual bath) or skip passages from the Tanakh or Talmud used to justify abuse. Finally, these

---

25. Panchuk, *Defiant Spirituality: Suffering and Flourishing in the Aftermath of Religious and Spiritual Trauma*, unpublished manuscript.

post-traumatic effects harm the person in their capacity as a religious or spiritual being, by undermining spiritual agency, destroying or diminishing certain religious or spiritual capacities, making aspects of one's spiritual life emotionally fraught, calling into question the truth of religious claims, or casting doubt on the goodness of one's religious tradition, just to name a few possibilities.

Although little empirical research on the topic has been done, what little exists increasingly bears out that religiously and spiritually significant traumatic events tend to impact people in ways that are significantly different from the impact of trauma in other contexts. For example, one study found that individuals who had experienced religion-related physical abuse as children had significantly worse mental health along a number of dimensions (depression, anxiety, phobic anxiety, hostility, psychoticism, and paranoid ideation) as adults than both those who had never been physically abused and those physically abused in a non-religious context,[26] and another that women abused by Catholic clergy reported less trust in God as adults than both those who had never experienced sexual abuse and those who had been sexually abused by non-clergy.[27] Similarly, a national randomized sample of active Catholic nuns found that those who reported sexual abuse or exploitation by a clergyman or nun were more likely to report difficulty praying, disruption in their relationship with God, and difficulty imagining God as Father as a result of the abuse than those abused by lay people.[28] And a recent study found that religious and spiritual abuse accounted for a full 18 percent of the sample's spiritual struggles beyond what was accounted for by other traumatic experiences.[29]

Few people would deny that religious and spiritual trauma exist, given the weight of anecdotal and the empirical evidence that has emerged in recent decades, as well as the glut of documentaries about abuse and cover-up in high profile contexts such as the Duggars' community led by the now-disgraced Bill Gothard and news reporting about accusations against well-known Christian figures such as Jean Vanier (founder of L'Arche), Jonny Hunt (former president of the Southern Baptist Convention) and Marko Rupnik (Slovenian, Jesuit priest and internationally renowned sacred artist). What is harder to discern is what, if any, role particular theological

26. Bottoms et al., "Religion-Related Child Physical Abuse."
27. Rossetti, "Impact of Child Sexual Abuse."
28. Chibnall et al., "National Survey of the Sexual Trauma Experiences."
29. Ellis et al., "Religious/Spiritual Abuse."

commitments, such as atonement theory, play in experiences of religious traumatization. Our question is whether religious or spiritual trauma often results from something central to satisfaction theories or whether the connection is merely incidental—the result of unfortunate, but misguided (mis)applications of otherwise innocent theories.

IV. SATISFACTION THEORY AND RELIGIOUS TRAUMA

If it is true that satisfaction theories of atonement encourage, or at least fail to guard against, the use of violence and passive submission to it, why might this be? While there are many features of these theories to which we could attend, the two I consider here are the value and scope satisfaction theories place on punishment (or harsh treatment) in response to wrongdoing. First, satisfaction theories of the atonement canonically assume a retributive model of justice—not just as a model for merely human, concrete justice systems, but as part of the divine order and even of the divine nature.[30] That is, they assume that punishing wrongdoers is *intrinsically good* because in committing a moral wrong, wrongdoers come to deserve punishment.[31] While other considerations might weigh against this intrinsic good constituting an ultima facie reason in favor of punishment in individual cases (which is why some satisfaction theorists are not necessitarians—they do not think that Jesus's substitutionary death is strictly necessary in order for God to forgive sin), it is a prima facie reason in favor of always punishing wrongdoers. Second, satisfaction theories take severe, one might even say *ultimate* consequences—physical death and spiritual separation from God

30. William Lane Craig, for example, argues that retributive justice is part of the divine nature, and so not something that God can set aside, while a prohibition on punishing the innocent could arise only out of divine command, and so God has no duty of justice not to punish the innocent (cf. Craig, *Atonement and the Death of Christ*, 177). A notable possible exception to this tendency is Jonathan Rutledge's non-retributive penal substitution theory (Rutledge, *Forgiveness and Atonement*). I say "possible exception" because it is not entirely clear whether, when penal substitution serves restorative rather than retributive justice, it is properly classified as a *satisfaction* theory, although it clearly remains an instance of penal substitution.

31. This should not be confused with the claim that punishment for sin is *necessary* for the reconciliation of sinful humans to God (although this is likely the view most familiar to evangelical readers), as some proponents of divine retributivism hold that the intrinsic good of punishing the wrongdoer is merely one reason among many. God could have chosen to forgive sin in some other way, but chooses to do so by the vicarious death of Jesus.

at the very least, but usually also infinite suffering in hell—to be the harsh treatment wrongdoers deserve for their *finite* wrongs.[32] Both features of satisfaction theory are evident in Calvin's words: "God's wrath and curse always lie upon sinners until they are absolved of guilt. Since he is a righteous Judge, he does not allow his law to be broken apart from punishment, but is equipped to avenge it."[33] Indeed, Paul Dafydd Jones describes Calvin's understanding of the cross as "an 'unleashing' of wrath," an "expression of holy indignation," and "a vehement assault, long deferred."[34] For Anselm too, torture is also a morally appropriate response to wrongdoing: "For either man renders due submission to God of his own will, by avoiding sin or making payment, or else God subjects him to himself by *torments*, even against man's will."[35] Nor is such violence conceived of as contrary to the communication of perfect divine love. "He loved us, even while he hated us," says Calvin.[36] Although neither the value nor the scope of punishment is *unique* to satisfaction theories, both are *central* to them, and it is these features that, for victims and survivors of abuse, cast God in the image of human abusers in a way that contributes to religious and spiritual trauma.

In our human interactions we not only overlook or excuse minor wrongs on a regular basis, we generally regard it as *virtue* to do so. No one wants a partner, a colleague, or a boss who feels a compulsion (or judges it intrinsically good) to point out, or worse—make us pay—for every failing or mistake. Indeed, some of us believe that the goal in responding to wrongdoing is to promote moral change, re-connection between parties, and positive growth. This doesn't require the complete absence of boundaries or permissiveness toward those for whose moral development we are partially responsible, but it does require that we are not focused on making sure others always "get what they deserve." Within such a framework, insofar as consequences are sometimes necessary, it is as a deterrent to protect the innocent or because the consequences help the wrongdoer to see the error of their ways, to change, or to make amends. Many in what is known

32. Even if it is true that one of the parties wronged by human sin is infinite and that there is, thus, as sense in which the weight of the wrong is infinite, given that the morally responsible wrongdoer is always finite, I will assume without argument that the wrong is finite in some morally relevant sense.

33. Jones, "Fury of Love," 217, citing Calvin, *Institutes* II.xvi.1.

34. Jones, "Fury of Love," 222.

35. Anselm, *Cur Deus Homo?*, I.xiv.

36. Calvin, *Institutes* II.xvi.4.

as the "restorative justice movement" maintain this understanding of the demands of justice even in the context of formal justice systems.

While proponents of penal substitution often claim that it would be a miscarriage of justice for a judge to let a guilty criminal go without punishment, those within the restorative justice movement give a more nuanced account. Leading restorative justice theorist John Braithwaite is keen to point out that restorative justice is not morally neutral about injustice. He insists that moral wrongs not be called mere "conflicts" or by any other word that portrays an attitude of neutrality toward harm done to others.[37] So, for those within the movement, what would be a miscarriage of justice, and indeed an affront to harmed parties, is for a judge to declare that no wrong has been committed, contrary to the evidence. But the intrinsic goods to be pursued in response to wrongdoing are (1) the restoration of the harmed party, as much as possible, to a state of flourishing and (2) acknowledgment, accountability, and change, when possible, for the offender.[38]

Indeed, Judith Herman goes to great length in her book *Truth and Repair: How Trauma Survivors Envision Justice* to show that survivors of sexual and domestic violence tend to be surprisingly uninterested in the *punishment* of their perpetrators.[39] Instead, they more often want acknowledgment from both the wrongdoer and their community that what they experienced was intolerable, they want accountability for wrongdoers, and they desire, when possible, restitution, apology, and the rehabilitation of the offender. On the view of many victims, punishment is not the only, and indeed often not the best, means of pursuing these ends.

This view stands in sharp contrast to the retributive justice in satisfaction theories. When we think about the human persons we know who cannot let any wrong, any mistake, any perceived slight to their ego go without making someone pay, it is usually *not* those we love, trust, or respect who come to mind. It is the abusive parent, the unreasonable teacher, the mob boss, the controlling partner. Given this, we should not be surprised when we encounter stories of people who accepted this vision of justice as divinely approved who inflict or accept harsh punishment, up to and including what most of us would call abuse, on theological grounds.

Consider, for example, the testimony of Vitaline Elsie Jenner, who was physically and sexually abused at the Fort Chipewyan school for indigenous

---

37. Braithwaite, "Fundamentals of Restorative Justice," 38.

38. Braithwaite, "Fundamentals of Restorative Justice," 38.

39. Herman, *Truth and Repair*, 110.

children in Alberta, Canada. A priest repeatedly stabbed her outstretched hand with a headpin so that she would "feel what Jesus felt on the cross . . . feel the same pain."[40] This punishment was for the egregious crime of talking with a friend during class. Jesus's suffering on the cross is held up to her as an explicit example of what she deserves for her childish infraction. The crucifixion, rather than a symbol of the love and grace of God, or of God's solidarity with her in suffering, is for Jenner a horrifying symbol of why it is good for her to be abused. Furthermore, Jenner recounts how worthiness of divine punishment becomes emotionally associated for her not just with her concrete "sins," but also with her identity as an indigenous person. She identifies this as a source of deep and ongoing shame, disclosing to interviewers through tears that she used to do everything from dying her hair to drinking excessively to hide and forget her identity. What and who she is are tied up with the feeling that she deserves suffering.

In response to the examples I and other feminist scholars have offered, where satisfaction theories of atonement are implicitly and explicitly used to justify religious abuse, theologians are likely to point out that, however the doctrine gets distorted and misapplied at the popular level, nothing about satisfaction theories entail that *humans* may torture, torment, or otherwise abuse fellow humans. There are all sorts of things that are appropriate for God to do that no Christian would say that humans should imitate. God may accept worship, but it is sacrilege for humans to do the same. Therefore, claiming that it is morally appropriate for God to find humans repugnant and loathsome in their sin or for God to punish them with eternal conscious torment doesn't entail that humans may act similarly.

Such a response fails in at least two ways. First, even if satisfaction theories do not entail that human abusers do no wrong, they do entail, at least in cases where the abuse is precipitated by some wrongdoing on the part of the victim, that the treatment is *not undeserved*. Humans should not visit horrific suffering on other humans for their sins not because human wrongdoing does not merit it, but because humans lack the proper standing to mete out the deserved punishment. Furthermore, the distinction becomes harder to maintain when the abuser is taken to have appropriate standing, and even responsibility, to censure the victim for their wrongs: parents, teachers, the state, etc. Satisfaction theorists might be willing to bite this bullet, however, and insist that the lack of standing is sufficient to

---

40. Truth and Reconciliation Commission of Canada, *Survivors Speak*, 87–88.

allay any *in principle* objections and that sufficient attention to application can resolve any remaining concerns.

However, the response also fails in a second and, to my mind, more significant regard. It fails to appreciate that even if, according to satisfaction theories, human abusers lack standing to impose the suffering they do, their mistake is one of usurping a divine role—that is, in acting *too much like* the God they worship. We may be able to tell Jenner that her teacher never should have stabbed her with a pin for talking to her friend in class, but when she is taught about God's wrath against sin—including her sin of disobeying her teacher—she may well experience a pang of familiarity. The description of God may be familiar to her because God acts so much like the human who abused her, or, put differently, because her human abuser acts so much like the God he teaches her about. Even if wrath in response to wrongdoing is not, in principle, objectionable in the divine case in the same way it is in the human case, what can we expect such descriptions to do to the faith of children like Jenner and Alex? Alex recognizes their human abusers in examples meant to illustrate God's love. As feminist theologians have argued, this makes it exceedingly difficult for them to understand that they are not morally obligated to passively accept abuse. But it also makes it difficult for children like Alex to engage with God in a manner characterized by love, trust, and vulnerability. Their only frame of reference for God's relationship to them is found in abusive human relations. For children like Jenner, like Alex, and like countless other survivors of abuse, it will be difficult, if not impossible, to relate to God without seeing in God the image of those who have hurt them most deeply, and it is not difficult to see how this might undermine their religious and spiritual wellbeing. As such, it may often contribute in direct and essential ways to religious trauma.

One might also object to my line of argument by pointing out that the fact that certain ways of talking about God "misfire" for some people does not, by itself, show that this way of speaking about God is false or that we have any broad practical reasons to avoid doing so. To see why this objection fails, it will be helpful to consider two different things we might mean when we say that a portrayal of God "misfires." First, a way of speaking about God can "misfire" because the hearer has a distorted or mistaken concept associated with the relevant words, or because the concept has, for them, taken on connotations not intended by the one using it. For example, when Jesus describes God as Father, this is often read as communicating God's loving care: "If you who are evil know how to give good gifts to your children, how much more will your heavenly Father give good things to those who ask him."[41] For the survivor of incestuous sexual abuse at the hands of a father, thinking of God *as Father* may seem to them to entail, or merely trigger, connotations of violence, abuse, manipulation, and exploitation. Such associations might be epistemic (e.g., the person believes that fathers act violently and therefore that God acts violently) or they might be affective (e.g., the person just feels distant or afraid when trying to think of God as Father). However, none of these associations are supported by the textual evidence for what Jesus intended to communicate in his use of the word "Father." Whatever account we give of what is going on in the world-concept-mind nexus in such cases, clearly the survivor is getting the wrong epistemic or affective message. An otherwise helpful metaphor leads them further away from what Jesus arguably affirms about the nature of God. It seems to me that how we should respond to misfirings of this kind is context-dependent. In the case of speaking of God as Father, I'm inclined to say that while it is understandable for the person for whom a concept has become so corrupted to avoid using it in association with the divine, there is also nothing inherently problematic with others continuing to use it, because the affective and cognitive associations that make the concept problematic for some are not inherent in the concept itself. However, I do not think that this is the sense in which satisfaction theories of the atonement harm abuse survivors.

A second case that we might call a "misfire" is when the content *actually communicated* by the speech is what elicits the negative response. In this case the metaphor has successfully led the person to what the speaker wishes to communicate about God, but the hearer finds that vision of God morally or emotionally intolerable. Indeed, it isn't clear to me that such cases are rightly regarded as "misfirings," except insofar as one regards the individual's assessment and response as somehow mistaken (even if psychologically understandable). I suggest that this is what is happening in the current case: the vision of God presented in the account of the atonement being offered, even when understood correctly, mirrors the behaviors and attitudes of human abusers. Importantly, the mirroring of behavior here is not idiosyncratic or accidental, but the result of central features of the theories themselves.[42] Unlike the metaphor of God as Father that will help some

41. Matt 7:11, Common English Bible translation.

42. At least those versions in which retributive justice and severe punishment are central components.

better understand God's love and misfire for others, there is something *inherent* in this way of portraying God that I and other feminist object to. It is the *salience* of the mirroring of human abusers that may be idiosyncratic or accidental to survivors or their allies. That the person has been devastatingly harmed by humans acting *in the very same way* as the doctrine describes God as acting may explain why this person is more likely to notice the similarity between God and abusers and, perhaps, why they are more averse to such descriptions than those for whom such relations are mere abstractions. But the similarity is inherent in the theory, and it is there for anyone to observe.

V. ATONEMENT THEORY AND CONCEPTUAL ENGINEERING

The question, then, is whether this mirroring of God in the face of human abusers and the harm it causes some constitute good reasons to reject the theory. Are survivors repulsed by the image of God presented in these theories like a survivor who doesn't want to picture Jesus as having dark hair because they were assaulted by a dark haired person (understandable, not probably not a good epistemic reason for forming beliefs about the historical Jesus), or are they recognizing something more akin to Anselm's notion of fittingness—that there is something in the idea of God acting in a particular way that is unfitting, beneath, or unworthy of God? I claim that the latter is true. More specifically, I claim that it is inappropriate for human theologians to construct theories of the divine nature and action that portray God as acting in ways familiar to many of us primarily in some of the worst human behavior we have encountered.

To see why, it may be helpful to take a step back and think about what theologians do when they construct theories of atonement. That Jesus was God incarnate, who suffered, died, and rose again to save humans are articles of the Christian faith. But how atonement is accomplished and its relationship to the incarnation, birth, life, and death of Jesus has always been a matter of significant theological debate. No particular account has ever enjoyed credal status.[43] In thinking about the atonement, theologians take a series of diverse metaphors from the Christian scriptures, the interpretations of these metaphors in the tradition, and their own moral commitments, informed by both scripture and the tradition, to try to make

43. Crisp, "Methodological Issues in Approaching the Atonement," 314–33.

sense of how God saves, and what the meaning of Jesus's life and death is. In mapping the different ways that one might think about models of the atonement, Oliver Crisp cites Ian Barbour's account of models and theories in science:

> Models and theories are abstract symbol systems, which inadequately and selectively represent particular aspects of the world for specific purposes. This view preserves the scientist's realistic intent while recognizing that models and theories are imaginative human constructs. Models, on this reading, are to be taken seriously but not literally; they are neither literal pictures nor useful fictions but limited and inadequate ways of imagine what is not observable. They make tentative ontological claims that there are entities in the world something like those postulated in the models.[44]

If something like this is a helpful way of thinking about theological models, then while the truth about God and the nature of the atonement is not up to us, it is up to us to some degree which stories and models of atonement we offer to partially and imperfectly, but still accurately and faithfully, capture a reality not fully within our ken. It is probably no accident that a medieval theologian like Anselm uses metaphors reminiscent of the feudal system to explain the atonement while an early modern one uses something more akin to legal theory. This is not to say that Anselm's or Calvin's account was nothing more than a product of its time, but that it was *also* a product of its time, drawing on the intellectual resources and conceptual apparatuses available within their context to do theology. The biblical authors before them also drew on their own context and conceptual resources to communicate the ways of God to humans.

This way of describing the project of theology aligns with recent scholarship that sees a major aspect of the project of theology and philosophy as conceptual engineering or conceptual mapping.[45] In conceptual engineering, as in other forms of engineering, certain values shape design choice. Truth and accuracy are among them. If one's formulas are wrong, the bridge might not stand and the program might not function. But design choices are also guided by other values. Functionality and aesthetic value

---

44. Barbour, *Religion and Science*, 115, cited in Crisp, "Methodological Issues in Approaching the Atonement," 326.

45 Reichel, *After Method*; Kidd and Rinderknecht, *Putting God on the Map*; Chalmers, "What Is Conceptual Engineering?"

are virtues as well. Does the building or the program do what it is designed to do optimally? Does the bridge not only stand but allow a sufficient flow of traffic? Is the living room cozy and inviting? Does the word processor facilitate the writer's flow? Can people who are hard of hearing use it?

In theology and philosophy of religion the truth about God and God's work in the world matters. But functionality and aesthetics do too. If the stories we tell about God are always partial, finite attempts to describe how the infinite God interacts with humans, we must do our best to construct models that are accurate *and* communicate the truth about God in a way that allows people to see the truth as the good news that it is. As a result, we should probably avoid constructing models and metaphors that portray God in a negative light, even if the actions they attribute to God would not be, strictly speaking, immoral if performed by God. To use a silly and admittedly superficial example: even if I could say something true about God and God's work in the world by saying God's work is like the animal body's elimination of feces, "fecal elimination theory of divine action" would probably not be an example of a good theological model. This would be the case even if the things that I attribute to God would not be "gross" when God did them, even if they are "gross" when humans do something similar.

A central question I raise in this paper is whether it is functional and fitting to put forward theories that portray God as acting in ways familiar to many of us primarily through the behavior of human abusers. Is it fitting to account for God's love for us in a way that makes it tremendously difficult for survivors and victims of abuse to see God's atoning act as an act of love and care, one characterized by extravagant grace and welcome, especially when other metaphors and other stories that have just as much claim to being true and accurate—grounded in the Christian scriptures and the tradition—are available? Some readers will answer this question with an easy "no," because they reject retributive justice as inherently immoral or because they believe that God never acts violently or because they are convinced along with many feminist theologians that the truth about God wouldn't cause the harm that satisfaction theories seem to have. For these readers I hope to have shown that, in addition to the aforementioned harms, satisfaction theories also contribute to religious and spiritual trauma. For those who do not think that retributive justice and severe punishment are inherently morally problematic, particularly in the divine case, I want to suggest that perhaps satisfaction theories of the atonement are the equivalent of building a church that can only be entered through a staircase. There is nothing *inherently* bad about stairs or anything wrong with building them. But in a world with people with mobility disabilities—especially when people with disabilities have been systematically excluded from society—there is something inherently wrong with building such a church. It unnecessarily and unjustly harms people in their relationship with God by denying them opportunities to worship.

But even this may not go far enough because it treats the problem of satisfaction theory as problematic in the sense of the first sort of misfiring I mentioned above. It suggests that they are harmful for some—the minority of people who find themselves in situations of violence—but not the majority. I argue that the retributive God imagery of satisfaction theory is akin to a church surrounded by a wide mote, filled with ravenous crocodiles. Neither moat nor crocodiles are inherently bad. No doubt they serve a function. And those who happen to be skilled swimmers might successfully traverse the waters, skirting violent attack to experience God in worship unscathed. But the fact that some escape the moat unwounded doesn't negate the inherent hostility of the church's design. Even if one takes oneself to have no direct moral argument for the conclusion that it would be immoral for God to enforce retributive justice, and even if one thinks that God would not act abusively if God were to endlessly punish humans for their finite wrongs, or if God were pleased by Jesus's obedience unto suffering and death, it would seem that reverence for God and care for those who seek to worship God would preclude the theologian from concluding that the best account of the atonement is one where God acts as human abusers. Whatever other virtues the theories have, they tell the story of God's saving work in a way that wounds and cuts off some of us from relating to a God who has revealed Godself to us not as an abuser, but in the image of a mother chicken, a gentle shepherd, and a loving human father.

BIBLIOGRAPHY

Anselm of Canterbury. *Cur Deus Homo?* Translated by Sidney Norton Deane. Chicago: Open Court, 1903.

Barbour, Ian G. *Religion and Science: Historical and Contemporary Issues.* San Francisco: HarperCollins, 1997.

Bottoms, Bette L., et al. "Religion-Related Child Physical Abuse: Characteristics and Psychological Outcomes." *Journal of Aggression, Maltreatment and Trauma* 8.1–2 (2004) 87–114.

Braithwaite, John. "The Fundamentals of Restorative Justice." In *A Kind of Mending: Restorative Justice in the Pacific Islands*, edited by Sinclair Dinnen et al., 38–60. Canberra: ANU Press, 2010.

Brock, Rita Nakashima, and Rebecca Ann Parker. *Proverbs of Ashes: Violence, Redemptive Suffering, and the Search for What Saves Us.* Boston: Beacon, 2015.

Brown, Joanne Carlson, and Rebecca Parker. "For God So Loved the World?" In *Christianity, Patriarchy, and Abuse: A Feminist Critique*, edited by Joanne Carlson Brown and Carole R. Bohn, 1–30. New York: Pilgrim, 1989.

Calvin, John. *Institutes of the Christian Religion.* Translated by Henry Beveridge. Peabody, MA: Hendrickson, 2008.

Chalmers, David J. "What Is Conceptual Engineering and What Should It Be?" *Inquiry* (Sept. 2020) 1–18.

Chibnall, John T., et al. "A National Survey of the Sexual Trauma Experiences of Catholic Nuns." *Review of Religious Research* 40.2 (1998) 142–67.

Craig, William Lane. *Atonement and the Death of Christ: An Exegetical, Historical, and Philosophical Exploration.* Waco, TX: Baylor University Press, 2020.

Crisp, Oliver D. *Atonement.* Cambridge: Cambridge University Press, 2020.

———. "Methodological Issues in Approaching the Atonement." In *T&T Clark Companion to Atonement*, edited by Adam J. Johnson, 314–33. London: Bloomsbury, 2017.

Cross, Richard. "Atonement Without Satisfaction." In *Trinity, Incarnation, and Atonement*, edited by Michael C. Rea, 328–47. Vol. 1 of *Oxford Readings in Philosophical Theology.* Oxford: Oxford University Press, 2009.

Ellis, Heidi M., et al. "Religious/Spiritual Abuse and Psychological and Spiritual Functioning." *Spirituality in Clinical Practice* 12.1 (2025) 136–45.

Herman, Judith L. *Truth and Repair: How Trauma Survivors Envision Justice.* New York: Basic Books, 2023.

Holmes, Stephen R. "Penal Substitution." In *T&T Clark Companion to Atonement*, edited by Adam J. Johnson, 304–20. London: Bloomsbury T&T Clark, 2017.

Hopkins, Jasper. *A Companion to the Study of St. Anselm.* Minneapolis: University of Minnesota Press, 1972.

Johnson, Adam J. "A Fuller Account: The Role of 'Fittingness' in Thomas Aquinas' Development of the Doctrine of the Atonement." *International Journal of Systematic Theology* 12.3 (July 2010) 302–18.

Jones, Paul Dafydd. "The Fury of Love: Calvin on the Atonement." In *T&T Clark Companion to the Atonement*, edited by Adam J. Johnson, 213–35. London: Bloomsbury T&T Clark, 2017.

Kidd, Erin, and Jakob Karl Rinderknecht, eds. *Putting God on the Map: Theology and Conceptual Mapping.* Lanham, MD: Fortress Academic, 2018.

Panchuk, Michelle. *Defiant Spirituality: Suffering and Flourishing in the Aftermath of Religious and Spiritual Trauma.* Unpublished manuscript.

———. "Religious Trauma, Spiritual Violence, and the Moral Authority of the Church." In *Harm, Healing, and Human Dignity: A Reader on the Church and Social Transformation*, edited by Christine Firer Hinze and J. Patrick Hornbeck II, 128–42. New York: Fordham University Press, 2022.

Pineda-Madrid, Nancy. *Suffering and Salvation in Ciudad Juárez.* Minneapolis: Fortress, 2011.

Rea, Michael C. "Introduction." In *Trinity, Incarnation, and Atonement*, edited by Michael C. Rea, 1–18. Vol. 1 of *Oxford Readings in Philosophical Theology*. Oxford: Oxford University Press, 2009.

Reichel, Hanna. *After Method: Queer Grace, Conceptual Design, and the Possibility of Theology*. Louisville, KY: Westminster John Knox, 2023.

Rossetti, Stephen J. "The Impact of Child Sexual Abuse on Attitudes Toward God and the Catholic Church." *Child Abuse and Neglect* 19.12 (1995) 1469–81.

Rutledge, Jonathan. *Forgiveness and Atonement: Christ's Restorative Sacrifice*. New York: Routledge, 2022.

Sonderegger, Katherine. "Anselmian Atonement." In *T&T Clark Companion to Atonement*, edited by Adam J. Johnson, 175–93. London: Bloomsbury, 2017.

Stump, Eleonore. *Atonement*. Oxford: Oxford University Press, 2018.

Truth and Reconciliation Commission of Canada. *The Survivors Speak: A Report of the Truth and Reconciliation Commission of Canada*. Winnipeg: Truth and Reconciliation Commission of Canada, 2015.

Weaver, J. Denny. *The Nonviolent Atonement*. 2nd ed. Grand Rapids: Eerdmans, 2011.

Williams, Delores S. *Sisters in the Wilderness: The Challenge of Womanist God-Talk*. Maryknoll, NY: Orbis, 2013.

If God Can Forgive, Why Can't I?

A Christology of Forgiveness

ROGER P. ABBOTT

WHEN JOHN MOSEY, A Pentecostal Church pastor, took Helga, his nineteen-year-old daughter, to London Heathrow Airport on December 21, 1988, to catch her flight, Pan Am 103, to New York, he looked forward to seeing his only daughter again soon. Days later, sat alongside his wife Lisa in their home in the English Midlands, a visiting TV reporter asked them, "How can you forgive animals like that?" The "animals" the reporter was referring to were the people rumored to have been responsible for placing a bomb on the flight carrying Helga and 258 others, which had exploded 31,000 feet above the Scottish Borders town of Lockerbie, killing all on board and eleven more in the town.

John recalls that it was Lisa who responded first to the reporter's question. Almost instantly she said, "Sir, Jesus said in the Sermon on the Mount, 'If you do not forgive men their trespasses, neither will your heavenly Father forgive you your trespasses.' We haven't murdered anyone, but we are big sinners who are having to trust in the death and resurrection of Jesus Christ as our only hope of forgiveness and heaven. We dare not fool about with not forgiving." Echoing Lisa's words in his own heart, John recalled that for both of them their commitment to forgive whoever was responsible for their daughter's murder was *immediate*. In John's view, that instantaneous commitment was "miraculous."[1] This "miraculous" choice to forgive

---

1. Mosey, "Disasters, Blame and Forgiveness," 98–99.

those who had committed terrible crimes, though rare, is not unique to John and Lisa Mosey.[2]

Lest readers think this is a chapter about highlighting "miracles" of forgiveness that occur *instantaneously*, as if this immediacy should be the only truly Christian way, it isn't. It isn't necessarily the Moseys' usual way.[3] I do not question that such miracles of this kind do happen; however, this chapter is for the majority of trauma survivors who find forgiveness to be a sticky ingredient to the trauma that remains with them long after the original event. Forgiveness for many trauma victims is just an additional weight to the already great burden of trauma. Sometimes this weight is carried around for years, gnawing not just at their physical health, but more so at their psychological and spiritual health. For some, forgiveness is the last remaining ingredient to their trauma. These are survivors living an apparently normal life again; and it is normal for most of the time, until something inside them reignites the painful challenge of forgiveness. It is this aspect of the *trauma that remains* which the Mosey family still feel spared from, but many others don't.

As a Christian who has worked as a trauma responder and now as a practical theologian in the field of natural hazard related disasters,[4] I have found it encouraging to read the works of other theologians who have found reading the Bible through the lens of trauma to be both encouraging and challenging.[5] In fact, the Bible abounds with traumatic events and traumatized people; events where suffering "overwhelms a person's normal capacity to cope" and where a very real threat to life is perceived, and which creates "a sense of spiritual disorientation or loss of faith."[6] In their classic work on traumatic stress, Bessel van der Kolk and Alexander McFarlane remind us that "experiencing trauma is an essential part of being human;

2. For other instances of instantaneous forgiveness, see Kasdorf, "To Pasture," 328–47; McKittrick, "Obituary"; Malone, "If I Had Carried On."

3. Personal interview, March 2021.

4. Since 2012 I have researched some of the most catastrophic disasters in modern times, in New Orleans, Haiti, the Philippines, and the COVID-19 pandemic.

5. See Warner et al., *Tragedies and Christian Congregations*; Barker, *Tackling Trauma*; Jones, *Trauma and Grace*; Boase, and Frechette, *Bible Through the Lens*; Carr, *Holy Resilience*; McFadyen and Sarot, *Forgiveness and Truth*.

6. Boase and Frechette, *Bible Through the Lens*, 9; Koenig, *In the Wake of Disaster*, 142.

history is written in blood."[7] The gospel of forgiveness was literally written in blood (Eph 1:7; Col 1:20; 1 John 1:7).

Shelly Rambo is another contemporary theologian who has helpfully argued that reading the Bible's record of the Easter weekend through the lens of trauma can be a useful, hermeneutical method for shedding light on the Scripture texts that narrate the traumatic experience of Jesus, particularly through "Holy Saturday."[8] In her perspective, Rambo sees in the original event of the crucifixion a kind of living death, since the wounds of the crucifixion remain. I suggest that forgiveness, for some, can be a significant ingredient to this remaining, the ingredient that remains for the longest. For such people the trauma narrative formation of a pathway to freedom and flourishing cannot be complete until forgiveness is addressed. To be clear, I am not arguing that forgiveness is required for all forms of post-traumatic flourishing. But it is true that many survivors value the path to forgiveness as an important task in their own journey of recovery. In this chapter I seek to provide some directions towards completing that important task.

INTRODUCTION

For the Christian particularly, forgiveness can feel an extra weight to their burden of trauma—especially when they read of the instantaneous experience of the Mosey family. It may be helpful, therefore, to be assured by Deborah Hunsinger's words that "forgiveness, though freely given by God, does not seem to be a human possibility for us in turn. Try as we might, it does not seem subject to our human will." And yet, as she insists, "Forgiveness rarely happens apart from an active decision to forgive." Therefore, when it does happen, it feels as if it were "as a miracle of God."[9] But the added weight Christians can feel comes from something much more challenging than the Moseys' example, or from anyone else's experience of an *instant* commitment to forgive someone who has committed some unbearable evil against them. The added weight can also come from the very nature of the gospel message itself. It can come from the gospel's claim to convict us of *our* own evil and of *our* need of forgiveness from God. This is why Jesus is

---

7. Van der Kolk et al., *Traumatic Stress*, 3.

8. Rambo, *Spirit and Trauma*.

9. Hunsinger, *Bearing the Unbearable*, 21, and in McFadyen and Sarot, *Forgiveness and Truth*, 71–98.

called *Savior*, a title that in itself identifies us as needing saving from the plight of our sin (Matt 1:21).

That can feel confusing and difficult for trauma survivors, to say the least. To put this confusion in perspective, in this case, a survivor is the one who may desire to find freedom in forgiving a traumatic offender, and yet the broader theological narrative in which they are situated is one that places them primarily as the offender in need of forgiveness. How is a trauma survivor to make sense of the vocation to forgive in a complex arrangement like this? These aspects will be the focus of attention in what follows, as I suggest a complementarity between forgiveness and lament, modeled by Jesus on the cross.

FORGIVENESS AS ETHIC, HEALTH, AND THEOLOGY

Forgiveness as Christian ethic

That forgiveness is at the very heart of the gospel is inescapable when viewed in the canonical text. It is a golden thread running through Jesus' name, teaching, and practice of communion with God and the godly life (Matt 6:5–15, 18:21–35; Mark 2:5). Crucially, forgiveness was crystallized in Jesus' own attitudes and words as he suffered the agonizing death of his crucifixion: "Father, forgive them, for they know not what they do" (Luke 23:34).[10] Jesus' example could well have been in the forefront of the first Christian martyr, Stephen, when he was being stoned to death by the Jews and as he cried out, "Lord, do not hold this sin against them" (Acts. 7:60). This centrality of forgiveness became a key aspect of Pauline Christology and soteriology as well, as represented in statements such as, "in whom we have redemption, the forgiveness of sins" (Col 1:14; also Eph 1:7). For Prof. Greg Jones, in his seminal work, *Embodying Forgiveness*, it is *the* topic guaranteed a central place in Christian theology.[11] The late New Testament theologian Donald Guthrie saw "a close correlation between God's forgiveness and man's forgiveness" regarding what we may also call the ethics of Jesus.[12]

---

10. These words are disputed by textual scholars. See the additional note in Plummer, *Critical and Exegetical Commentary*, 545.

11. Jones, *Embodying Forgiveness*, 36.

12. Guthrie, *New Testament Theology*, 904. See also Brock, *Singing the Ethos of God*, 291–93.

Turning from scriptural texts to lived experience, forgiveness also plays a prominent role in the lives of Christians today. For instance, the Indian Christian scholar and pastor, Kethoser Kevichusa, sees forgiveness as "the most appropriate response" to the reality of a world that is created good but fallen, redeemed but not yet fully redeemed, according to the drama of Scripture. For navigating such a broken world then forgiveness as an ethic is essential: "In order for humans to live in consonance with reality, and in order for human actions to respond appropriately to broken reality, they must be forgiving. Thus, forgiving is the most appropriate existential posture, mind-set and roadmap for negotiating life in this world." Given the world is a fallen domain then the reality is that life abounds with disruption and evil, and so "forgiveness is an ethic of realism that takes into account the reality of living in a fallen and broken world."[13] Given such an essential need of an ethic of forgiveness, there is a concomitant need for forbearance and empathy.

Forgiveness and health

Theologically, health can be simply defined as being in a right relationship with God. An exposition of this idea can be seen in Ps 130. Here is a person crying out to Yahweh, "out of the depths" (v. 1). Walter Brueggemann's commentary on these opening words is powerful. He speaks of the customary manner by which a significant dignitary is addressed: "from a posture of obedience, or at least from a situation of prosperity and success" and "suitably dressed." But in fact, he adds, these opening words are "the miserable cry of a nobody from nowhere" who is addressing *God.*[14] What is of importance, therefore, is that even the most devastated person has hope of crying out to God and being heard if they are positioned in a state of moral and spiritual poverty (v. 3a) and in recognition of the need for divine forbearance. Of note, mere relief from torment is not the chief end for which forgiveness is required or intended in this passage. The end really is that "[God] may be feared" (v. 4).

Forgiveness is now a significant therapeutic concept in trauma theory.[15] Forgiveness can be defined as having certain therapeutic components: the cessation of negative feelings; the cancellation of perpetrator debt; a

13. Kevichusa, "Forgiveness in a Broken World," 121–22.

14. Brueggemann, *Message of the Psalms*, 104.

15. Noll, "Forgiveness," 372–75; McCullough et al., *Forgiveness*.

reduced increase in motivation for retaliation and estrangement from the perpetrator; and a pro-social change toward a blameworthy transgressor.[16] With this conception, however, there is an almost exclusive focus upon addressing the negative psychological impacts of unforgiveness on unresolved trauma from a strictly psychotherapeutic perspective.[17] For Harold Koenig, trauma also includes the spiritual dimension because trauma can give rise to theological questions and spiritual needs that faith can help meet.[18]

This growing attention to the psychotherapeutic benefit to addressing trauma that religion and spirituality can provide was highlighted more recently by Andrew Serazin, of the Templeton World Charity Foundation, when he announced a funding stream for research under the Templeton's Forgiveness Project.[19] Conscious that "there is a dramatic worldwide effort to create new tools to fight COVID-19," Serazin introduces a "tool" he feels is vitally important for the healing of the many mental and spiritual wounds he believes will result from the COVID-19 pandemic.[20] The project invites proposals for research that produce scientific empirical evidence for neurological mechanisms facilitating forgiveness for healing trauma and other psychomedical ailments.

It is worth noting briefly that the focus on using religion as a therapeutic utility has been contested on both scientific, medical, and theological grounds.[21] In his *Embodying Forgiveness: A Theological Analysis,*

16. Noll, "Forgiveness," 364.

17. Worthington, "Power and Meaning of Forgiveness."; Noll, "Forgiveness," 372–74; Koenig et al., *Handbook of Religion and Health.*

18. Koenig, *In the Wake of Disaster,* 115.

19. Serazin, "After a Year." Claims are made of there being over four thousand scientific articles on forgiveness. See Tavia Gilbert's compelling interview with Prof. Everett Worthington, clinical psychologist and pioneer of the REACH Forgiveness method, a product of the scientific research Worthington has conducted. A professing Christian, Worthington claims his method can have success among religious and non-religious people because the method employs strategies that all humans can deploy by: recalling the hurt; empathizing with the offender; committing to forgiveness; holding on whenever you doubt. Worthington, "Power and Meaning of Forgiveness."

20. For example, see Sample, "Covid Poses 'Greatest Threat'"; O'Shea, "Covid-19."

21. Four authors are worth mentioning for readers' attention. These are Gregory Jones, Dean of Duke Divinity School, Durham, North Carolina; Richard Sloan, Professor of behavioral medicine at the Columbia University Medical Center; Joel Schuman, Assistant Professor of Theology at King's College in Wilkes-Barre, Pennsylvania; and Keith Meador, Clinical Professor of Psychiatry and Behavioral Science at the School of Medicine, and Clinical Professor of Psychiatry and Behavioral Science at the School of Medicine, and Professor of the Psychiatry and Health Policy at Vanderbilt University, Nashville, Tennessee.

Gregory Jones critiques the conflation in the American Christian church of secular psychology and Christian theology around the matter of forgiveness, and the way in which the Christian communities have secularized the language of forgiveness by permitting secular psychology logical priority in constructing theologies of forgiveness that highlight individualism. Jones strongly renounces the conflation of theological with psychological paradigms as a kind of theological and pastoral sell-out.[22] In *Blind Faith*, Richard Sloane likewise argues that a narrow focus on religion as a therapeutic utility is irrational, has a questionable scientific research methodology, and amounts to bad science, bad medicine, and bad theology.[23] Schuman and Meador, in their *Heal Thyself: Spirituality, Medicine and the Distortion of Christianity*, though they push back on Sloan, still argue that religion as a therapeutic utility idea necessarily degenerates into requiring a generic concept of religion that is theological problematic.[24] They maintain that issues of health raise theological questions as well as empirical medical ones, namely: What are the criteria "of an ultimately Good human life"? They argue that questions on what constitutes health need to be answered with perspectives from "boundaries set by theological tradition."[25]

Schuman and Meador remind us that "religions make truth claims. . . . Such claims are not only substantive but frequently totalizing." They are claims that do not have human physical health as their primary focus, but rather the "proper conduct, nature, and destiny" of human lives. Such emphases have more to say about how to live and to die faithfully to God than about maintaining good and prolonged physical health. A healthy forgiveness in a theological sense is concerned with the divine-human relationship (Ps 130:3–4), not merely with medical criteria specific to each individual.

To be clear, I would not wish to suggest that a psychotherapeutic focus on the treatment of trauma is outside a Christian's ethical interest, nor am I suggesting that a generic sense of forgiveness cannot be a significant psychotherapeutic tool for healthcare purposes. My concern at this point is with the use of religion and spirituality as generic concepts being theologically legitimate for *Christological* forgiveness. Against what I would call the "religion as a healthcare utility" thesis, there are theological criteria that

---

22. Jones, *Embodying Forgiveness*, 35–70. I am grateful to Prof. John Swinton for recommending this book to me.

23. Sloan, *Blind Faith*.

24. Schuman and Meador, *Heal Thyself*, 107–9.

25. Schuman and Meador, *Heal Thyself*, 45.

far outstrip the psychotherapeutic benefits of forgiveness. These teleological criteria need to be considered in themselves without total reduction to psychological categories.

Of course, emotions and cognitions are integral to our relationship with God both for good and ill, and can be profoundly disturbed and disorientated by trauma. Fear, anger, despair, anxiety, and depression can pose significant threats to that relationship (e.g. Elijah's post-Mount Carmel trauma, 1 Kgs 19:4–14). Therefore, addressing these relational aspects through pastoral care involving psychotherapeutic tools can undoubtedly be helpful, as Jesus' teaching on anxiety for example, shows (Matt 6:25–34). Yet in such cases therapy comes from applying principles that fit within particular theological boundaries.[26] Similarly, the psalms record people interrogating themselves and reminding themselves of theological truths (Ps 42:5) and of taking themselves in hand with spiritual exercises in the care of their relationship with God: prayer and meditation. The huge compilation of lament psalms is another example of resources Christians have used in the care of a healthy relationship with God, a point I will focus on more concertedly below.

Hunsinger's reflection, in the light of childhood abuse, is salient in regard to the "religion as a healthcare utility" thesis. She maintains that, theologically, for the practice of the gospel of grace and mercy, forgiveness suggests much more than just a personal therapeutic end is in mind. Rather, from the perspective of Christian theology, forgiveness could never be such an instrumental value, because it is an end in itself. Forgiveness is God's unfathomable gift of grace to humanity, a gift that enables us to be set free from the power of guilt and sin to destroy us. Emotional healing, from this perspective, would be understood within the context of forgiveness, rather than the other way around. Healing in this view would be considered a sign of God's mercy and grace that points beyond itself to the salvation accomplished apart from us in Jesus Christ. That is to say, emotional healing would be understood as a kind of inbreaking of the kingdom, a little light that would encourage hope for the greater light of salvation promised to break forth at the end of all things.[27]

---

26. See Abbott, *Sit on Our Hands*.

27. Hunsinger, "Forgiving Abusive Parents," 94.

A theologically bounded forgiveness

Thus, we can say that Christians have an ethical responsibility to forgive others arising from their theological boundary for receiving forgiveness from God: forgiveness for a debt that is so incredibly out of proportion to anything the Christian can be asked to forgive (Matt 18:21–35). Awareness of this huge disproportionality is what should lead to fearing and glorifying God in a healthy way.

In the rest of this chapter I propose an approach to the work of forgiveness that conforms to the theological boundaries that contain the purpose for a flourishing relationship with God, namely one that has the glory of God as its final telos (John 9:3), a purpose that involves mercy, grace, and hope as essential ingredients. The compassionate mind of the Trinity becomes the manner of the incarnate Son's disposition and action (Gal 4:4–7).

My proposal combines a focus upon the two cries that Jesus uttered from the cross of crucifixion: the first is the plea for the Father to forgive the Son's assailants, "Father forgive them, for they know not what they do." (Luke 23:34); the second is Jesus' lament to God about his experience of desertion, "My God, my God, why have you forsaken me?" (Matt 26:27), a lament so poignant that the Gospel author also chose to record it in the original Aramaic. These cries were not random utterances, much less were they the incoherent ramblings of someone disoriented with pain. They were focused, theological utterances. There is even a chronological pattern to their sequence that suggests a connection between the two sayings. In the first plea there is the incarnate Son's commitment to obedience to the Father in the act of forgiveness, since forgiveness was at the heart of the work Jesus had come to achieve and the purpose for him being on the cross to atone for sins and to provide forgiveness (Matt 1:21; Eph 1:7). So Jesus' plea for his assailants to be forgiven by God was his enactment of that forgiveness in his own case. Furthermore, this obedience was much more than a commitment of duty, it was a commitment of love for the glory of God (John 17:1). But then the second cry, coming sometime after the first, from Jesus' suffering abandonment by God, was a lament of anguished horror and bewilderment.

To what benefit is this connection between the two sayings for Christian pastoral care of trauma? I suggest it models a pastoral trajectory which, on the one hand, affirms that it is an wholly appropriate act from loving obedience to God, to forgive those complicit in causing our trauma. To have such a commitment to forgive, for God's sake first and foremost, is to glorify God irrespective of whether it gives medico- or psychotherapeutic benefits to the forgiver and / or to the offender. To forgive is to glorify God. However, the link between the sayings is salient because it also recognizes that just as the suffering that the work for forgiveness cost Jesus, so the commitment to forgiveness will cost his disciples, even when they have been traumatized (Col 3:13).[28] The spontaneity of Jesus to forgive his assailants was not an easy commitment; there was theological and emotional struggle. Lament was the resource Jesus brought to that struggle.

I propose there is, therefore, a theological and pastoral strategy here for Christians to address trauma with: forgiveness through lament. My proposal will argue that forgiveness is an issue no Christian should ignore or bypass in addressing their trauma; however, it acknowledges that the work of forgiveness is often far from being straightforward or an instantaneous miracle; it can involve a huge struggle, involving confusion, resistance, and a sense of unfairness, anger, and the anguish of wrestling with the question, "Why?"

I consider forgiveness first because it is the primary aim of my proposal. However, I am aware that in some Christian circles there can be covert, if not overt pressure to ensure that forgiveness is achieved expeditiously. Carla Grosch-Miller, considering trauma in the context of congregations and sexual scandal, warns that "pressure to forgive is often an unconscious ploy to cover up denial or to put a plaster on the deep wound of betrayal."[29] Therefore, I fully recognize that for many experiencing trauma forgiveness may *not* be *their* primary concern or their first action. In fact, the act of forgiveness may come at the end of a process that is prolonged and one may have to accept that it will not be fully accomplished in this life; the *desire* to forgive will have been there, but not the full act.[30] If forgiveness is the end then lament is a powerful means to that end.

FORGIVENESS

The Moseys' instantaneous act of forgiveness must not be taken to suggest that the exercise was easy for them. Forgiveness is complex because it throws up so many painful issues: a true understanding of what happened,

28. See also Jones's focus on the cost and the hard work necessarily inherent from a Christian theology of forgiveness in Jones, *Embodying Forgiveness*, 5–25.

29. Grosch-Miller, "Sexual Scandals in Religious Settings," 249.

30. Volf, *Exclusion and Embrace*.

who to forgive, when to forgive, the right to withhold forgiveness, addressing one's anger and the impulse for retribution.[31] Space will not permit responding to all these questions, but I want to acknowledge the complexity as an assumption in what follows.

Forgiveness as a praxis of godliness

The Christian doctrine of divine forgiveness is a formative doctrine. That is, forgiveness is not just a gift of God's grace we receive, the donation of that gift is also to be formative of our identities, formative of who Christians are and what they do, what Scripture calls "godliness." (2 Pet 1:3, 6). On Ps 130:4 and Dan 9:9, Brian Brock comments, "In these passages we hear God's chosen crying for God to return his care to a people lost in the byways of unfaithfulness. In such a state, the fear of God is, to use Luther's image, the chisel knocking away the old man's reliance on other powers. As fear removes reliance on powerless forces, the new man being built up by the Spirit can emerge, a sculpture of hope in Yahweh alone made from the rough stone of fear and idolatry." On Ps 130, Brock comments, "In these verses the psalmist indicates that it is God's action of forgiveness that opens human perception and creates human identity."[32] Jesus' obedience of love to the Father is also a formative strategy for our identity in showing an obedience of love to be forgiving, even from within our trauma (Matt 6:14–15).

Forgiveness and memory.

One definition of forgiveness is "surveying the damage one incurred through the harmful actions of another and eventually remembering it differently rather than trying to erase it from memory."[33] While just wanting to forget all the pain of trauma can provide an analgesic, it is a deceptive one where temporary pain relief gives way to the unpredictable and terrifying recollections and flashbacks that inhabit trauma. However, theology can provide a refiguration of the trauma narratives memory feeds on. Volf's appeal to the experience of Joseph, in the book of Genesis, is an example of

---

31. Ouei, "Bad," 142.

32. Brock, *Singing the Ethos of God*, 291, 292.

33. Schults and Sandage, *Faces of Forgiveness*, 3, cited in Barker, *Tackling Trauma*, 144.

a form of remembering differently.[34] In the struggle from meeting his abusive brothers, Joseph's theological reading of the providence of God enabled him to memorialise his traumatic experience tangibly by naming his son, Manasseh ("making to forget"). This way of "forgetting" was a refigured narrative concerning all his hardship that he had endured from his "father's house" (Gen 41:51).

In Isa 43:25, Yahweh assured his covenant people that though they had burdened and wearied him with their sins, he would blot out theirs sins and "not remember" them. If forgiveness is to be formative of godliness, then the remembering of the traumatic incident(s) is hugely challenging if forgiveness is to be so absolute. Traumatic memories are often unstable, lingering affairs. They can seem uncontrollable when they come out of the blue in the form of flashbacks or when they resurrect in their raw forms at anniversaries, when randomly meeting people, or while watching news clips. Volf's theological counsel on the "affliction of memory" is instructive and helpful. He suggests that repenting and forgiving needs to lead "to a certain kind of forgetting." He thinks that only those who are *willing* to forget can be safe to remember aright.

Paradoxically, in this life a certain form of remembering is necessary because if we forget too soon we shall not learn the lessons of the past, but also refiguring memories now helps forget later (in heaven). There is a form of forgetting that can be redemptive, but in a way that is a form of an "anti-theodicy," that is "an abandonment of all speculative solutions to the problem of suffering."[35] Volf's fear is that insisting on the search for a theodicy that satisfies the human mind is doomed to failure and is more likely to keep traumatic memories alive in the wrong form. It also risks creating an academic distraction from the more painful process that forming a new trauma narrative for forgiving often involves.

Complementing these recognitions of the struggle in forgiveness is the point Douglas Hall made when he reflected on reconciliation as a process and a hope that might take us beyond this life for a complete resolution. Hall warns us against the Western culture's lust for immediate resolution and "closure" and "expectations that are humanly absurd, standards that God himself does not apply *to us.*" Hall encourages a greater approach of realism, where the "refusal to demand finality is born of the compassion [to] feel for imperfect and flawed creatures who, [like ourselves], could

34. Volf, *Exclusion and Embrace*, 139.

35. Volf, *Exclusion and Embrace*, 131–40.

only fall into despair were [we] confronted by the full demands of a finally reconciled creaturehood. Such Christians content themselves with 'proximate goals' on the way to the ultimate reconciliation that *God* will bring to pass."[36] Though reconciliation is an advance on forgiveness, Hall's alert applies equally to the process of forgiveness, in that it validates Volf's view that the only truly pastoral way to refigure traumatic memories is through the cross as a paradoxical, eternal memorial in heaven to the divine forgetting, namely the Lamb of God who takes away the sin of the world.[37]

Forgiveness as justice

Questioning justice and meaning is one of so many facets of trauma,[38] since trauma seems to "precipitate a crisis of telos and shatters cherished beliefs that life is fair and orderly."[39] Trauma often arises out of our experiences of extreme vulnerability, where we assumed either we were strong enough to cope, or someone we trusted would be there to protect us (God and / or a parent, spouse, friend, professional). We can see elements of this in Jesus' experience on the cross as revealed in his lament: his sense of desertion by the Father, and in his desperate desire for meaning in the midst of acute loneliness and disorientation in his suffering: "why have you forsaken me?" (Matt 27:46). Since the precipitating event(s) for his trauma were so horrendous and unjust, the call to address forgiveness seemed a mockery of justice and only deepened the wounds of trauma already sustained.

However, in Jesus' case, his suffering unto death was in itself part of the divine plan to address the issue of justice for such an "horrendous evil,"[40] to provide forgiveness of sins (Col 3:13). I maintain that the order of the two cries of Jesus on the cross under consideration in this chapter implies that Jesus' plea for the Father to forgive his assailants held primacy over him gaining relief for himself.

Volf is right to aver that "every act of forgiveness enthrones justice."[41] This is the meaning of the words of the apostle Paul, when he wrote of the redemption in Christ on the cross as being "to show God's righteousness

36. Hall, "Preaching Reconciliation," 14 (emphasis mine).

37. Volf, *Exclusion and Embrace*, 140. Also John 1:29; Rev 22:1–4.

38. Roberts and Ashley, *Disaster Spiritual Care*, xx.

39. Abbott, *Sit on Our Hands*, 125.

40. Adams, *Horrendous Evils*, 26.

41. Volf, *Exclusion and Embrace*, 123.

[justice] at the present time, so that he might be just, and the justifier of the one who has faith in Jesus" (Rom 3:26). Jesus' death was not bypassing justice, nor denying justice, nor was it merely pardoning the evils of the guilty ones, it was also most certainly not a mere forgetting of their evils. Instead, it was God offering up the incarnate Son to be the recipient of justice in *our place.* In the words of the suffering servant song of Isa 53:5, "He was pierced for our transgressions; he was crushed for our iniquities; upon him was the chastisement that brought us peace."

In Christian theology, forgiveness can never be an escape from justice; the whole basis for forgiveness is underwritten by the justice of the crucified Christ: "In Christ God was reconciling the world to himself, not counting their trespasses against them. . . . For our sake he [God] made him [Christ] to be sin who knew no sin, so that, in him [Christ] we might become the righteousness of God" (2 Cor 5:19, 21).[42] Jesus embraced the justice upon himself and in so doing could plead for forgiveness for his perpetrators.

Another complicating factor that we can bring into the arena of forgiveness as justice is the assumption or protest of innocence; what Volf terms "the politics of the pure heart."[43] This protest can work in at least two directions: either in the interests of the traumatized pleading innocence as a reason for them seeking revenge, or in the interests of the traumatizer who is in denial, pleading their innocence at needing to ask forgiveness. However, in both cases these are misguided pleas. Escaping the hard process of forgiveness for fear it evades or softens justice is theologically errant, as Volf explains: "Every act of forgiveness enthrones justice; it draws attention to its violation precisely by offering to forego its claims."[44] Richard Hays concludes that the Matt 18 parable of the unforgiving servant "is nothing other than a logical extension of God's mercy. And yet the threat of future judgement hangs over those who despise God's grace."[45] The Lamb of God lives alongside the one sitting on the white horse (Rev 19).

Yet, the Scriptures do seem to endorse a certain claim to innocence (Pss 10:8, 15:5, 94:21, 106:38). The book of Job records the traumatized Job narrating his innocence before God. Yet Job was also acutely aware that if it came to trial before God he was never innocent: "I am afraid of

---

42. While reconciliation, as such, is not the subject of this chapter, theologically, reconciliation must involve forgiveness; forgiveness is part of the process of reconciliation.

43. Volf, *Exclusion and Embrace*, 111–19.

44. Volf, *Exclusion and Embrace*, 123.

45. Hays, *Moral Vision*, 104.

all my suffering, for I know you will not hold me innocent" (Job 9:28). In Luke 13:1–5, where Jesus addresses the temptation to "interpret" tragedy as divine punishment for the victims (an all too common phenomenon in religious circles), he turns attention away from the victims to the religious spectators on the tragedies, implying *their* non-innocence before God.

How should Christians reconcile such an apparent theological and experiential inconsistency? The reconciliation rests with the concept of innocent non-innocence. That is, in respect of a specific event (e.g., a rape, violent burglary, terrorist attack, disaster) victims may be innocent. However, when one's whole life is reviewed in the light of God's light, we have to confess, "all have sinned and fall short of the glory of God" (Rom. 3:23).

Helpful to recognizing this innocent non-innocence is the way Alistair McFadyen explores the Augustinian doctrine of original sin in his *Bound in Sin*.[46] He contends that the modern preoccupation with theologies of freedom involve an implicit rejection "of the view that we are subject to a profound, pre-personal distortion at the very heart of our beings, which destroys our freedom to avoid sinning; that sin encompasses us, determining our situation before God already as one of guilt, prior to and independently of anything we will or do." Greg Jones describes this fundamental "always-already brokenness" as human nature's rejection of communion with the Triune God, "which collapses into a series of isolated and divided individuals obsessively concerned with preserving or sustaining a sense of 'self.'" Together, as humanity, we have scorned "God's self-giving communion" in preference for this obsession with the "poor *victim*" of self.[47]

Intriguingly, original sin doctrine rarely appears in theological works on trauma theory despite being so central to the Pauline theology in Rom 1–7. Yet in trauma narratives regarding forgiveness, something very akin to a recognition of this theological underpinning in human experience of trauma and forgiveness is revealed. David Self's interview with Marian Partington, whose sister Lucy was kidnapped and brutally murdered by Fred and Rosemary West in December 1973, is very telling. Marian only came to know the truth about her sister's disappearance and death in March 1994. In the interview she describes how, after a time on a Buddhist retreat, she made a vow to try and forgive her sister's murderers. Yet immediately after making the vow she experienced an involuntary feeling of rage that frightened her because, in her words, "it was just a huge eruption beyond logic

46. McFadyen, *Bound in Sin*, 28.
47. Jones, *Embodying Forgiveness*, 61–62.

or words, which was terrifying because I knew at that moment that I was capable of killing." This realization led to her recognizing how much like Rosemary West she was also capable of becoming. So pertinent to the subject of this chapter, she explained, "At that moment I knew that part of the process of forgiveness was facing within myself my own potential for perpetuating abuse or being a victim."[48] It is this conviction of non-innocence, through a very similar experience, that led Everett Worthington to come to forgive his mother's murderer.[49]

The Christian doctrine of original sin does provide a Christological explanatory framework for the trauma narrative of innocent non-innocence, which can helpfully service the work of forgiveness. In Volf's words, "But no-one can be in the presence of the God of the crucified Messiah for long without . . . transposing the enemy from the sphere of monstrous humanity into the sphere of shared humanity and herself from the sphere of proud innocence into the sphere of common sinfulness."[50] A conviction of this kind, forged out of Rom 1–3, can create an empathy, which while it calls for evil to be exposed and justice served it also calls for a willingness to try and understand the bondage of the will of we whose lives are "so mangled that they do not know they are doing wrong, let alone have the capacity to repent and confess."[51]

Forgiveness and the ekklesia

The Christian community, as a theo-social organism, can play an important role in the formation of trauma narratives.[52] Just as trauma can be considered a social construct in psychological diagnoses, Joanna McGrath believes it can offer a hopeful prognosis for post-traumatic growth.[53] McGrath traces the growth of the early church out of the trauma of witnessing Christ's death and resurrection, and analyses the New Testament narratives from a psychological and phenomenological perspective. She argues that the early Christians as a collective were able to construct a narrative around

48. Self, "Enfolding the Dark," 159. See also Partington, *If You Sit Very Still*.

49. Worthington, "Power and Meaning of Forgiveness."

50. Volf, *Exclusion and Embrace*, 124.

51. Kevichusa, "Forgiveness in a Broken World," 122.

52. Abbott, "Trauma, Compassion, and Community."

53. Alexander, *Trauma*, 1–6; McGrath, "Post-Traumatic Growth," 291–306. Also Boase and Frechette, *Bible Through the Lens*, 10–23.

the events of Jesus' death, based on eyewitness accounts, which provided an alternative interpretative framework for seeing things. This framework included such points as the necessity of Jesus' death and the emergence of hope from something that seemed, initially, to shatter all hope. Such hope is bolstered by the events vindicating Jesus as Messiah, namely his resurrection and ascension. Armed with this hermeneutic there developed a collective wisdom that viewed suffering and trauma in positively refigured ways, which was instrumental in attracting new converts. McGrath concludes that the strength of this collective interpretation "seems to have been a developing spirituality that saw suffering and adversity as means of thriving."[54] However, resisting the pressure to rush through this process is important pastorally for a church body involved in forgiveness.

Inhabiting this theologically bounded location in our cognitive and emotional states, we can move towards forgiveness in a manner that is appropriate to a healthy relationship with God where we can both receive and offer forgiveness for the glory of God.

LAMENT

Prioritizing the praxis of forgiveness in addressing trauma is rarely easy and is often counterintuitive. If the praxis of forgiveness within the theological boundaries outlined above is pursued, inclusive of suffering, then what can help us continue that process through to fulfilment? It is the lamenting cry of Jesus (Matt 27:46) that promises a model for some pastoral direction. I consider the subject under three categories: authenticity; safe space; and assurance.

Lament as authenticity

Understandably, in view of our intuitive impulse to avoid struggle and pain, a mental or simple verbal commitment to forgive and to forget can provide the best tonic for putting the whole business behind us and for banishing the offence in the oblivion of the past and sustaining aloofness for the future. But this conception of forgiveness is so cheap it has to be a rejected. The real business of forgiveness involves cost, and this lament of Jesus reveals that to us. As Volf reminds us, "More than just a passive suffering of

54. McGrath, "Post-Traumatic Growth," 304.

an innocent person, the passion of Christ is the agony of a tortured soul and wrecked body offered *as a prayer for the forgiveness of the torturers*."[55] But the cost was huge: desertion! Desertion by friends (Matt 26:56) and desertion by God (Matt 27:46). Jesus' lament was the way in which he found help through the struggle of forgiveness. In so doing the same resource is authenticated for his disciples still. It does not simply authenticate the *use* of lament, it also provides a means of our *being authentic* before God in expressing our lament.

Writing in the context of extreme childhood suffering and death, Stanley Hauerwas homes in on the authenticity of lament in addressing bereavement trauma. He says lament "is an act of bold faith on the one hand, because it insists that the world must be experienced as it really is and not in some pretended way."[56] Certainly, there was no pretense in Jesus' experience of the struggle.

Jesus' example also assures that lament does not betray an unauthentic faith. Jesus laments the anguish of divine desertion and the traumatic loss of "knowing": the disorientation of being human without the compassionate presence of God. Though we shall never know the precise emotional devastation Jesus had on the cross, our traumas can bring an experience of isolation, a feeling of absence and of not knowing why what has happened has happened. The traumatic impact of what has happened to us, coupled with the apparent absence of compassion from God can be devastating. It can silence us, driving our shock, anger and self-pity deep inside until it becomes deeply toxic. Furthermore, if we really express in language how we feel, we fear it offending God and so prolonging his absence. Lament, however, is the God-ordained language permitted us to bring our deepest pain to be expressed in groans and visceral language, in the assurance that the God we lament to is not a God who has sensitivities beyond which he cannot cope.

Lament as safe space

In the light of trauma theory, there is a feature of Christ's lament from the cross that is intriguing and challenging. I refer to this feature as a *safe place*. Trauma theory and practice endorse the importance of a safe place.[57] But

55. Volf, *Exclusion and Embrace*, 125 (emphasis mine).

56. Hauerwas, *Naming the Silences*, 81.

57. Boase and Frechette, *Bible Through the Lens*, 6; Newman et al., "Assessment of Posttraumatic Stress Disorder," 246–47, 265–66.

what about situations where there is no physical or geographical safe place accessible at the time? Does the work of forgiveness have to be delayed until such a space is provided? Not necessarily so, as Jesus demonstrated on the cross.

It would seem that the cross of crucifixion, under the eyes of the mocking Roman guards and the religious leaders, must have seemed the most unsafe place any person could inhabit. Physically, this was true of Jesus, he was trapped (literally nailed) to a cross, there was no escape until a lingering death arrived. Yet, because of his relationship with God I suggest Jesus' lament indicates a sense of him creating a safe place—even safe enough to ask forgiveness on his perpetrators.

Many of the laments recorded in Scripture come from people in physically unsafe locations (e.g., Pss 3, 22, 57, 59, 60, 63), yet it was the act of faith-filled lamenting that brought them into a safe place in their relationship with God and which gave fresh perspective on the traumatizing incidents, a transformative addition to their trauma narratives. In fact, one can read many lament psalms as transformative, faith-filled trauma narratives for the glory of God.

But what is it about lamenting before God that creates a secure and safe space? The distinguishing feature of biblical lament is the fact that, as stated above, from their place in the biblical canon, we are authorized to let our authentic rage, despair, confusion, fear, doubt, and desire to be uttered, even explosively, but hope-fully, before God. I think Volf makes an important point when he argues that the main message of the imprecatory psalms is that "rage belongs before God," but "not in the reflectively managed and manicured form of a confession, but as a pre-reflective outburst from the depths of the soul."[58] This being true, Hauerwas is right when he asserts that rather than being the tool of the unfaithful, lament demonstrates that "one of the profoundest forms of faithlessness is the unwillingness to acknowledge our inexplicable suffering and pain."[59]

CONCLUSION

This chapter has focused on the value of Jesus' example for reasons much greater than personal healthcare needs, by addressing forgiveness in the face of trauma primarily for the *glory of God*, though, secondarily, this may

58. Volf, *Exclusion and Embrace*, 124.

59. Hauerwas, *Naming the Silences*, 83.

well service healthcare benefits. I have attempted this focus while embracing Volf's persuasion that Jesus on the cross needs to be foundational for us for his example to be valuable.[60] Only then will we appreciate, not just God's self-giving solidarity with the suffering of the victims, but also with the perpetrators. Psalmic lament is the resource Jesus used to achieve his struggle with forgiveness. We can use it too, to pursue the commitment to experiencing the miracle of forgiveness.

BIBLIOGRAPHY

Abbott, Roger Philip. *Sit on Our Hands, or Stand on Our Feet?* Eugene, OR: Wipf & Stock, 2013.

———. "Trauma, Compassion, and Community: Reconciling Opposites in the Interests of Post-Traumatic Growth." *Practical Theology* 5:1 (2012) 31–46. https://doi.org/10.1558/prth.v5i1.31.

Abbott, Roger, and Robert White. *What Good Is God: Crises, Faith, and Resilience.* Oxford: Monarch, 2020.

Adams, Marilyn McCord. *Horrendous Evils and the Goodness of God.* New York: Cornell University Press, 1999.

Alexander, Jeffrey C. *Trauma: A Social Theory.* Cambridge: Polity, 2012.

Barker, Paul A., ed. *Tackling Trauma: Global, Biblical, and Pastoral Perspectives.* Carlisle, UK: Langham, 2019.

Boase, Elizabeth, and Christopher G. Frechette, eds. *Bible Through the Lens of Trauma.* Atlanta: SBL, 2016.

Brock, Brian. *Singing the Ethos of God: On the Place of Christian Ethics in Scripture.* Cambridge: Eerdmans, 2007.

Brueggemann, Walter. *The Message of the Psalms: A Theological Commentary.* Minneapolis: Augsburg, 1984.

Carr, David M. *Holy Resilience: The Bible's Traumatic Origins.* London: Yale University Press, 2014.

Grosch-Miller, Carla. "Sexual Scandals in Religious Settings." In *Tragedies and Christian Congregations: The Practical Theology of Trauma,* edited by Megan Warner et al., 239–56. Abingdon: Routledge, 2020.

Guthrie, Donald. *New Testament Theology.* London: InterVarsity, 1981.

Hall, Douglas. "Preaching Reconciliation in the World of Long Memories." *Journal for Preachers* 26:7 (2007) 9–14.

Hauerwas, Stanley. *Naming the Silences: God, Medicine, and the Problem of Suffering.* Edinburgh: T&T Clark, 2004.

Hays, Richard B. *The Moral Vision of the New Testament: A Contemporary Introduction to New Testament Ethics.* New York: Harper Collins, 1996.

Hunsinger, Deborah van Deusen. *Bearing the Unbearable: Trauma, Gospel, and Pastoral Care.* Cambridge: Eerdmans, 2015.

---

60. Volf, *Exclusion and Embrace,* 22–28.

———. "Forgiving Abusive Parents: Psychological and Theological." In *Forgiveness and Truth: Explorations in Contemporary Theology*, edited by Alistair McFadyen and Marcel Sarot, 71–98. Edinburgh: T&T Clark, 2001.

Jones, L. Gregory. *Embodying Forgiveness: A Theological Analysis*. Grand Rapids: Eerdmans, 1995.

Jones, Serene. *Trauma and Grace: Theology in a Ruptured World*. Louisville: Westminster John Knox, 2019.

Kasdorf, Julia Spicher. "To Pasture: 'Amish Forgiveness,' Silence, and the West Nickel Mines School Shooting." *Crosscurrents* 59:3 (Fall 2007) 328–47.

Kevichusa, Kethoser (Aniu). "Forgiveness in a Broken World: An Exploration Through the Drama of Scripture." In *Tackling Trauma: Global, Biblical, and Pastoral Perspectives*, edited by Paul A. Barker, 121–24. Carlisle: Langham Global Library, 2019.

Koenig, Harold G. *In the Wake of Disaster: Religious Responses to Terrorism and Catastrophe*. Philadelphia: Templeton Foundation, 2006.

Koenig, Harold G., et al. *Handbook of Religion and Health*. Oxford: Oxford University Press, 2001.

Malone, Carole. "If I Had Carried on Hating . . . ." *Sunday Mirror*, July 26, 1998. https://www.thefreelibrary.com/If+I+had+carried+on+hating+it+would+have+destroyed+me...and+I+didn%27t...-a060647690.

McCullough, Michael E., et al., eds. *Forgiveness: Theory, Research, and Practice*. New York: Guilford, 2000.

McFadyen, Alistair. *Bound in Sin: Abuse, Holocaust, and the Christian Doctrine of Sin*. Cambridge: Cambridge University Press, 2000.

McFadyen, Alistair, and Marcel Sarot, eds. *Forgiveness and Truth: Explorations in Contemporary Theology*. Edinburgh: T&T Clark, 2001.

McGrath, Joanna Collicutt. "Post-Traumatic Growth and the Origins of Early Christianity." *Mental Health, Religion and Culture* 9:3 (2006) 291–306.

McKittrick, David. "Obituary: Gordon Wilson." *Independent*, June 27, 1995. https://www.the-independent.com/news/people/obituary-gordon-wilson-1588729.html.

Mosey, John. "Disasters, Blame and Forgiveness." In *What Good Is God: Crisis, Faith and Resilience*, edited by Roger Abbott and Robert White, 98–99. Oxford: Monarch, 2020.

Newman, Elana et al. "Assessment of Posttraumatic Stress Disorder in Clinical and Research Settings." In *Traumatic Stress: The Effects of Overwhelming Experience on Mind, Body, and Society*, edited by Bessel van der Kolk et al., 242–78. New York: Guilford, 1996.

Noll, Jennie G. "Forgiveness in People Experiencing Trauma." In *Handbook of Forgiveness*, edited by Everett L. Worthington Jr., 363–75. New York: Routledge, 2005.

O'Shea, Nick. "Covid-19 and the Nation's Mental Health: Forecasting Needs and Risks in the UK, October 2020." Centre for Mental Health, 2020. https://www.centreformentalhealth.org.uk/wp-content/uploads/2020/09/CentreforMentalHealth_COVID_MH_Forecasting3_Oct20_0.pdf.

Ouei, Amos Winarto. "The Bad, the Ugly, the Worst: A Reflection on Christian Forgiveness Towards Perpetrators of Traumatic Experiences." In *Tackling Trauma: Global, Biblical, and Pastoral Perspectives*, edited by Paul A. Barber, 141–50. Carlisle, UK: Langham, 2019.

Partington, Marian. *If You Sit Very Still: A Sister's Fierce Engagement with Traumatic Loss*. London: Jessica Kingsley, 2016.

Piper, John. *Providence*. Wheaton, IL: Crossway, 2020.

Plummer, Alfred. *A Critical and Exegetical Commentary on the Gospel of Luke*. Edinburgh: T&T Clark, 1910.

Rambo, Shelly. *Spirit and Trauma: A Theology of Remaining*. Louisville: Westminster John Knox, 2010.

Roberts, Stephen B., and Willard W. C. Ashley. *Disaster Spiritual Care: Practical Clergy Responses to Community, Regional and National Tragedy*. Woodstock, VT: Skylight Paths, 2008.

Sample, Ian. "Covid Poses 'Greatest Threat To Mental Health Since Second World War.'" *Guardian*, Dec. 27, 2020. https://www.theguardian.com/society/2020/dec/27/covid-poses-greatest-threat-to-mental-health-since-second-world-war.

Shults, F. LeRon, and Steven J. Sandage. *The Faces of Forgiveness: Searching for Wholeness and Salvation*. Grand Rapids: Baker Academic, 2003.

Schuman, Joel James, and Keith G. Meador. *Heal Thyself: Spirituality, Medicine, and the Distortion of Christianity*. Oxford: Oxford University Press, 2003.

Self, David. "Enfolding the Dark." In *Forgiveness and Truth: Explorations in Contemporary Theology*, edited by Alistair McFadyen and Marcel Sarot, 157–64. Edinburgh: T&T Clark, 2001.

Serazin, Andrew. "After a Year That Pushed Us to the Brink, It's Time for Forgiveness to Go Viral." *Time*, Dec. 16, 2020. https://time.com/5921505/forgiveness-viral/.

Sloan, Richard P. *Blind Faith: The Unholy Alliance of Religion and Medicine*. New York: St. Martins Griffin, 2006.

van der Kolk, Bessel, et al., eds. *Traumatic Stress: The Effects of Overwhelming Experience on Mind, Body, and Society*. London: Guilford, 1996.

Volf, Miroslav. *Exclusion and Embrace: A Theological Exploration of Identity, Otherness, and Reconciliation*. Nashville: Abingdon, 1996.

Warner, Megan, et al. *Tragedies and Christian Congregations: The Practical Theology of Trauma*. New York: Routledge, 2020.

Worthington, Everett. "S4E: Transcript: The Power and Meaning of Forgiveness." *Stories of Impact* podcast, season 4. Aired Nov. 18, 2024. https://www.youtube.com/watch?v=bqkxpwjYDA8.

The Trauma-Informed Mysteries of Mary, the Mother of Jesus

EMILIE GROSVENOR

INTRODUCTION

KAREN O'DONNELL NOTES THAT transcendent relationships with Mary the mother of Jesus,[1] characteristic of popular religiosity in Catholic and Orthodox Christian traditions, are marked by a feeling of safety.[2] Prayers of petition, often taking the form of requests for protection, have been the source of critique and reason for dismissal by theologians who view the prayers of the rosary and novenas, the wearing of scapulars and miraculous medals, as well as flower offerings to the Blessed Virgin Mary, not simply as idolatry, but as bargaining. Elizabeth Johnson describes such practices as projecting human kyriarchal structures into heaven, turning the supplicant into a child with a juvenile need for safety.[3] Despite its emphasis on popular religion, liberation theologians in Latin America in the latter part of the twentieth century differentiated between the faith of the masses and

1. Heretofore, when referring to Mary, the author is referring solely to Mary of Nazareth, the mother of Jesus. The author acknowledges the diverse contributions of unique women, by the name of Mary/Miriam, presented in Scripture. However, as no other disciples by the name of Mary/Miriam are discussed in this paper, the reader is informed that the name *Mary* in this particular chapter refers only to Mary the mother of Jesus.

2. O'Donnell, *Broken Bodies*, 180.

3. Johnson, *Truly Our Sister*, 40. Agbasiere, "Rosary," 242–54.

the devotional practices which they believed served as an avoidance of the cross, rather than an embrace of it.[4] However, these arguments speak little of the basic human need for safety in the aftermath of a traumatic event. Serene Jones defines such an event as one in which the person/s experience the threat of annihilation.[5] In her exploration of sexual ethics, x`Margaret Farley defines personhood as being characterized by autonomy and relationships.[6] In this context, therefore, the threat of annihilation may not apply specifically to an individual person, but to another whom they love. As humans find meaning and identity in relationship to others, the loss of safety in community, or the threat to the life of a child, for example, is felt as an extension of the self's sense of physical danger.

This rupture in relationships, crisis of identity when divorced from community, and direct threat of physical harm is a pattern in the story of Jesus' mother Mary. O'Donnell argues that Mary's motherhood provides a "mode of recovery," through which the individual members and larger community comprising the traumatized Body of Christ may find the sense of safety necessary in integrating traumatic experience. I add that Mary is a mode of recovery through her discipleship. The following is an exploration of Marian discipleship as a mode of recovery through the prayers and meditations of an ecumenical rosary accessible to Christians more broadly.

TOWARD AN ECUMENICAL ROSARY

The practice of praying a rosary has interreligious and ecumenical roots. Christians likely began this practice due to interactions with Muslims and Buddhists.[7] While known for its use of rote prayer, traditionally ten Hail Mary's (a decade) with an Our Father in between, what is unfortunately given less attention are the *mysteries* of the rosary. These are meditations in which the person at prayer is called to reflect upon what are often biblical scenes between each decade. Those most commonly used throughout Christian history have been the joyful and sorrowful mysteries listed below.

4. Ribas, "Liberating Mary," 125.

5. Jones, *Trauma and Grace*, 13.

6. Farley, *Just Love*, 111.

7. Kelly, "Rosary as a Tool."

Seven Sorrowful Mysteries

1. The prophecy of Simeon (Luke 2:34, 35)

2. The flight into Egypt (Matt 2:13, 14)

3. The loss of the child Jesus in the temple (Luke 2:43–45)

4. The Galilean crisis

5. The crucifixion

6. The taking down of the body of Jesus from the Cross[8]

7. The burial of Jesus

The Seven Joyful Mysteries

1. The annunciation (Luke 1:26–38)

2. The visitation (Luke 1:39–1:56)

3. The nativity (Matt 1:18–25; Luke 2:1–19)

4. Visit of the magi (Matt 2:9–12)

5. The presentation in the temple (Luke 2:25–39)

6. The finding in the temple (Luke 2:41–51)

7. The resurrection

These meditations are in the realm of mystery because the theological imagination employed by the faithful in prayer is filling in the gaps and details not attended to in Scripture.[9] Imagining the scene from the Marian perspective, one may, in compassion, imagine the smell of the stable at the birth of Christ, Mary's fear for the life of her child, the dread brought on by Simeon's prophecy, etc. The mysteries within Scripture are attended to as an exercise in prayer, empathy, and witness through remembrance. Thus, the aim is not a factual historical account, or even scriptural literalism, but using Scripture as the grounding element for a meditation on discipleship. As such, while rosaries are a devotional practice and often a form of supplicant

8. These mysteries are not part of a five-decade rosary, but added when praying a seven-decade, *Seraphic* rosary. See Szyszkiewicz, "Pray the Rosary," 30–34.

9. For more information on the use of theological imagination in interpreting Scripture see Viljoen, "Theological Imagination."

prayer for protection, they are furthermore a scriptural meditation which requires the use of one's theological imagination.

In addition, these mysteries provide a space for those praying to envision Jesus, not only as an autonomous individual, but one whose identity, like all human beings, is nourished by a web of relationships. In the mysteries of the rosary, the most cited of these relationships is that of mother and son.[10] Reflecting upon the joyful and sorrowful mysteries of Jesus' life one cannot help but also reflect upon his mother. However, I argue that the line drawn between joy and sorrow does not do justice to Mary's perspective. We may imagine that a dichotomy between joy and sorrow does not attest to the full range of emotion Mary felt. Furthermore, these mysteries were originally written down by men or celibate educated women. Thus, we are conditioned to believe that the news of Mary's pregnancy was only ever experienced as joy. Why not joy *and* fear? Why not good tidings *and* sorrow? Ivone Gebara asserts that women's experience is often a liminal one. Women must often sell their bodies to feed their children. We are often expected to stand at the borders of life, delivering children, caring for the dying.[11] Even in less extreme circumstances, women are often placed in roles in which joy/sorrow, good/evil, fear/witness are experienced and enacted simultaneously in a manner that cannot be attended to through a dualistic lens.

The holding of life's complexity, the capacity for life in the midst of death, is a recurring theme in Mary's story. She articulates this in her Magnificat, the longest speech of a woman in the New Testament. I offer an ecumenical rosary, which accounts for the complexity of human experience using the words of the Magnificat for each decade. Being a scriptural prayer demonstrative of the great reversal of the gospel, and paradoxical experience of the reign of God, the Magnificat offers words in which to rest in the aftermath of trauma, as well as words to discomfort when the call is to stand with the traumatized. In this meditative discussion on the mysteries of trauma, Mary will serve as a testament of where trauma recovery and discipleship collide. These mysteries point to Mary of Nazareth's actions as an empowering choice to witness, the opposite of disassociation, thus confronting trauma.

---

10. Goizueta, *Caminemos con Jesus*, 66.

11. Gebara, *Out of the Depths*, 18–19. See also Oakes, *Defiant Middle*.

PRESUPPOSITIONS: TRAUMA AND GOD

Prior to praying the rosary through the lens of trauma, it is necessary to set out a definition of trauma that is grounded in theological anthropology. That is, a definition which accounts for the human person as an embodied spirit whose identity is constructed through relationships within community. This autonomous identity, paradoxically constructed through mutuality, is a reflection of the divine. Trauma then, according to O'Donnell, is a rupture in self and relationships which occurs when one is made helpless by fellow creatures, political structures, or apathetic forces of nature.[12] Shelly Rambo further defines trauma as *remaining*, or "suffering that does not go away."[13] It is not easily classified. Thus, comparing traumas in terms of whether the victim's post-traumatic stress is justified or not disempowers all victims as well as human experience more generally. Trauma is therefore experienced as the breaking of one's autonomy interlaced with a rupture of self in relation to one's own body, spirit, sense of time, narratives of faith, and larger community. Recovery—herein spoken of as salvation—is therefore found in life-giving personal empowerment and a chosen affirming community.[14]

However, just as salvation is both already and not yet, recovery is never fully realized in this life. Rather, Herman notes that symptoms of post-traumatic stress will resurface due to life changes or triggers throughout one's lifetime. However, relationships which affirm the survivor's autonomy and identity allow recovery to continue alongside one's experience and understanding of trauma. Herman states that "the best indices of resolution are the survivor's restored capacity to take pleasure in her life and to engage fully in relationship with others."[15] Full recovery for the Christian is therefore bound with eschatological hope.

Furthermore, while trauma theologies have at times viewed the experience of God's inbreaking as traumatic, I argue that the God of Love and Life does not traumatize. Rather it is the *human* structures which collide with the will of God who traumatize. Gustavo Gutiérrez asserts, "As understood in the Bible, 'to live' always means 'to live with,' 'to live for,' 'to

---

12. O'Donnell, *Broken Bodies*, 6.

13. Rambo, *Spirit and Trauma*, 15.

14. Herman, *Trauma and Recovery*, 134.

15. Herman, *Trauma and Recovery*, 212.

be present to others,'; in other words life implies communion."[16] When we call our God the *living* God, when Jesus calls himself "the Life," there is an affirmation that the experience of trauma and its remaining is indeed an experience of death interfering in life, and that this is contrary to the will of God.[17] The presupposition for this ecumenical Marian meditation on trauma is that God does not will traumatic severing, rupture, and therefore death, whether it be the annihilation of a human being's physical body, the apathy and hatred that kills community, or the desecration of mind and spirit through abuse of the body.

In God, rather than a loss of self, we gain a greater sense of self in God. This threatens potential horror-makers in the world. Their reaction to the inbreaking of God, when not rooted in mutuality and discipleship, always leads to actions that demand idolatry, death, and trauma. However, that God is the God of Life, and that God is good, does not mean that the victim of trauma cannot be angry at God. Rather, this anger and doubt in the face of evil and subsequent trauma is affirmed in Scripture as an authentic and honest response to God in the midst of trauma. In sum, the malevolent rupture of sin into *Shalom* is traumatic, not the rupture of grace/*Shalom* into sin. This is not to say that fear is not a typical human response to the ineffable, but that the fear is a reminder of our own entrenchment in a fallen world when standing before the goodness of God. Because the *Shalom* of God exists we know that horrors are incongruent with mutual flourishing. This is crucial because through this presupposition we affirm our belief in our God as the God of Life and not death. In sum, God is not the one who traumatizes. God takes sides. Joel B. Green notes that Mary's Song affirms this in identifying God as "God the warrior, who engages in battle on behalf of God's people and brings them to deliverance and (2) God the merciful, who remembers the lowly and cares for the needy."[18] God is not only with the traumatized but establishes their tent among them. Thus, if the rosary is seen as a mode of recovery in prayer, connection to the divine must be affirmed as a place of safety.

It is nonetheless true that trauma often places the existence of a loving God into question. Due in part to an overemphasis of God as judge in the Middle Ages, and humanity's struggle with questions of theodicy, Christians have often found Mary's motherhood to be a place of prayerful

16. Gutiérrez, *God of Life*, 12.

17. Rambo, *Spirit and Trauma*, 16, 20.

18. Green, *Gospel of Luke*, 1854.

safety. Her womb is the place where the Body of Christ is first knit. As *Theotokos* she is not only mother of Jesus the human being, but Mother of God. As such, she is able to hold and nourish the relationship between humanity and God. Furthermore, her experiences of trauma occurred along a spectrum, culminating in the crucifixion. Thus, in meditating on her life of discipleship in motherhood, we find a soul who witnesses and relates in an embodied way to the diverse nature of human trauma. An ecumenical rosary, therefore, does not turn to Mary as divine, but as the womb/breast/ tabernacle in which mutual encounter with the Christ who bears our traumas may be nourished.

In the following section I provide guiding questions and reflections on the Seven Traumatic Mysteries.

THE SEVEN MARIAN TRAUMAS

1. Reaction against maternity

This mystery calls on the praying community to reflect upon how Mary's free consent at the annunciation places her at risk for bodily harm, shaming, and ostracization. This is not a situation confined to the past. Women's bearing of life continues to be met with the threat of being cast out of our communities and even becoming the victims of murder. In the United States homicide remains a leading cause of pregnancy-associated death, with domestic violence and workplace discrimination also presenting an increased risk to the health of both mother and child. These statistics only worsen when the pregnancy is unexpected.[19] Mary's choice to be bonded to God's will in this way also means she is choosing to bond herself to the potential wrath of the human structures which actively work against the *Shalom* of the reign of God. After the annunciation, Mary's place of safety, her kin and faith, become a place of potential danger. Reaction against her pregnancy translates to the potential severing of the relationships in which she finds her sense of identity, putting her at risk of shame, homelessness, and violence.[20]

19. Campbell et al., "Pregnancy-Associated Deaths." See also "Domestic Violence"; and Clark et al., "Pregnant and Homeless."

20. The annunciation is not included in these traumatic mysteries. Unlike the unequal power dynamics of between creatures, and the trauma which ensues when one creature or group overpowers another, discounting the autonomy of the victim, in Christianity creatures are most fully actualized as persons when their will is aligned with God's. Thus,

While promises are made regarding Jesus' life, Mary's own well-being is not guaranteed in Luke 1:26–38. At the time of the annunciation, Mary is in the first stage of Jewish marriage at this time, meaning she is betrothed but still living with her parents. She is, however, still in a legally binding contract with Joseph. In this manner, she is doubly vulnerable to ostracization. Not only can she be accused of sexual relations outside the bonds of marriage, bringing shame upon her family, but she may also be accused of adultery.

Matthew tells us that, as a righteous man, Joseph did not seek to shame her, but originally decided to divorce Mary quietly (Matt 1:19). While the reader/listener of the gospel is immediately reassured of Joseph's compassion, Mary would not have had this guarantee as she wrestled with how to tell him this news. The implication in this passage is that Joseph had the option *not* to divorce her quietly, that the option to publicly shame her was there. Mary would have been keenly aware of this. It is not surprising therefore that in Luke's gospel, Mary goes "in haste" to visit her cousin Elizabeth (Luke 1:39).

We can imagine how this announcement brought out an urgent need for Mary to plan her immediate next steps. Soon, her belly would begin to swell, but even before then, she would begin to feel the exhaustion that comes with early pregnancy. She might find herself becoming physically ill, unable to participate in the communal daily chores with the other women in her family. They would likely recognize the nature of her symptoms. Through this lens, leaving in haste becomes necessary.

---

we are truly free when we are acting as *imago Dei* and our choices reflect the will of the divine in which we live, move and have our being. Mary's consent and overshadowing by the Holy Spirit is not herein defined as traumatic for through it she becomes more herself. Marianne Katoppo states,

> We fail to realize that Mary's submission to the will of God is in no way the abject submission of the slave who has no choice. Rather, it is the receptive submission of the truly liberated human being, who put the will of God first. It is the creative submission of the fully liberated human being who, not being subjected to any other human being is free to serve. (Katoppo, "Asian Theology," 149)

Rather, the trauma and rupture of self is the reaction of those whose will is not aligned with God's over and against Mary, and therefore the child Jesus. While Katoppo emphasizes Mary's free choice, Mary nonetheless describes herself as a bondswoman, a slave to the reign of God. Katoppo's point is that being bound in will to the reign of God, marked by liberation, cannot be equated with, and is in fact the opposite of, the abject, forced submission of one human by another.

Mary is also taking part in a common practice among kinswomen, providing support in the final months of pregnancy and early weeks of postpartum recovery. In addition to providing care for her cousin, she has also found an excuse to leave the home of her immediate family, hoping perhaps that her cousin, being with child herself, will take pity on her situation. However, one can also imagine that Mary is fearful of her cousin's reaction. Will she indeed react with compassion? Will she defend Mary from detractors? Will she believe her outlandish story? Or will Elizabeth send her home to her parents in shame?

The traumatic rupture is Mary's knowledge that her "yes" to God puts her place in society, as a daughter, wife, and faithful Jewish woman, at risk. Amy-Jill Levine and M. C. Boys have both noted that an anti-Semitic strain in liberationist exegesis has often equated first-century Jewish practice with life for women under the Taliban.[21] In actuality, there is little evidence that Levitical laws were literally and uniformly enforced across each community. Interpretation of the laws and relevant situations were more common and would have varied given the diversity within Judaism in the area. However, even if Mary was not at risk of being stoned, she would have been at risk of being shamed, or even shunned, finding herself without means to support herself. Thus, even if the risk of murder is removed, the threat to her life in the long run, even in the best of scenarios, would have been very real.

Herman notes that the first step in recovering from the traumatic experience is the regaining of safety in community. Mary's recovery from this particular trauma is therefore first felt in relationship with Elizabeth. In greeting her with joy, humility, and honor, Elizabeth creates a safe space for Mary to feel the joy of the new life within her, releasing all need for secondary plans of survival in the immediate future. However, even as the recovery begins, there is the parallel trauma knowing this news will likely end her future with Joseph. Whether or not she may find refuge with her cousin once the pregnancy becomes public, she will still be the mother of a fatherless child in a patriarchal society. Despite the risk of shame, violence, and shunning, Mary steps out of this safe space of Zechariah and Elizabeth's home, eventually announcing her situation to Joseph. At worst he may act with public violence, at best he may question her sanity. Mary defies all cultural and religious norms by telling her husband she is choosing to have a child that is not his. We are not told of Joseph's immediate reaction, only that his resolution is to divorce her quietly, with his ultimate decision to

---

21. Levine, "Gospel of Matthew," 471; Boys, "Patriarchal Judaism," 21–22.

remain as Mary's husband coming after divine intervention. In both these relationships, Mary's autonomous choice to abide by the will of God is affirmed as are the individual relationships which provide her with a place of safety.

However, as we know, recovery, as salvation, is an ongoing process. So too does the *after* of traumatic experience remain and evolve. In Mark 6:3, though Jesus' friend and neighbors in Nazareth do not acknowledge his relationship to the Father, they nonetheless identify him as Jesus, Son of Mary, indicating that paternity was in question. While Jesus was raised as the son of Joseph, the Gospel indicates that the rumored scandalous origins of his birth by Mary have persisted. That Mary chose to bear Christ is in itself a choice to integrate the trauma of being the woman about whom others whisper into a state of blessing.

2. Threats against the child Jesus: Flight into Egypt and the prophecy of Simeon

The risk of severed personal relationships and harm in the domestic sphere is soon replaced with the threat of political violence. The flight to Egypt in Matthew and the prophecy of Simeon in Luke may seem contradictory when viewed from a historical-critical perspective. However, both contain within them a story of joyful welcome coupled with foreboding. The same visit of the magi which brings with it honor and gifts also brings the threat of death. Any restored sense of security Mary felt in relationship to her community after Joseph's recommitment to her is quickly severed. Reflection on her perspective leads to questions regarding whether or not she was able to say goodbye to their relatives and friends; whether she ever saw her parents again; how long was it before they knew what became of her, Joseph, and Jesus? Did some of her loved ones die before knowing she was safe? Did she feel guilt at having left? Did she and Joseph hear of what happened to innocent children after their flight (Matt 2:1–18)?

And yet, in the midst of trauma of having to flee for safety, likely scared of being seen or questioned by authorities, we can also imagine Mary being grounded in her relationship with Joseph, that his discernment and love for his chosen family ran so deep as to leave his community and the majority of his belongings to escape to a strange land in order to keep them safe. Within this trauma there is also further recovery. Mary's chosen identity as mother of Jesus is affirmed in her relationship to her husband. There is a place of safety in the love of their family in the midst of their profound vulnerability.

In Luke, the sense of foreboding also takes place amid an occasion of joy. Mary and Joseph bring their child to Jerusalem "to present him to the Lord" and offer sacrifice (Luke 2:22–24). At this occasion two prophets, Anna and Simeon, begin to praise God, prophesying concerning the child's future. Simeon's words, however, are also a warning to Mary specifically: "This child is destined for the falling and rising of many in Israel, and to be a sign that will be opposed so that the inner thoughts of many will be revealed—and a sword will pierce your own soul too" (Luke 2:34–35).

Unlike their flight to Egypt in Matthew's Gospel, the threat to Mary and Jesus in this passage in Luke is not an immediate one. However, Simeon's prophecy does not make room for Mary to flee. The implication is that she will not be able to keep her child safe as his very being is one opposed to the powers of the world. Her suffering and his are not only conjoined; they are inevitable. Luke's repeated emphasis on Mary's pondering and treasuring of such instances in her heart may lead us to imagine her worry at what these words could mean (Luke 2:19, 51). It may lead us to question whether Mary was ever able to rest in any sense of safety regarding the general well-being of her son; whether these words remained in her mind, resurfacing with every perceived hazard.

3. Losing Jesus

> When they did not find him, they returned to Jerusalem to search for him. After three days they found him in the temple, sitting among the teachers, listening to them and asking them questions. (Luke 2:45–47)

Elizabeth Johnson observes that, upon finding her son, Mary not only expresses relief, but rebukes him for causing she and Joseph to be in a state of *odynasthai*. While this is translated in English as *worry*, Johnson notes it is only used two other times in Luke/Acts: once to describe the agony of hell in the parable of the rich man and Lazarus, and again as the profound grief of the Ephesian church as Paul leaves them for the last time before his death.[22] While the child Jesus' three-day disappearance may be seen as foreshadowing, symbolic of his death and resurrection, this foreshadowing

---

22. Johnson, *Truly Our Sister*, 283–84.

is also done in relationship to his mother. We can imagine one Marian trauma bleeding into the next in this scenario, potentially arising as new questions in her mind. Is this what Simeon spoke of? Is this moment the spear piercing her heart? What trouble has befallen him that he should be missing? In the context of Roman occupation and Simeon's prophecy, has he been the victim of political violence? Is he being held captive? Victimized by a sexual predator?

The phrase after three days is pregnant with the torment of unknowing and the imagining of worse case scenarios. That she is apart from him further means she has no means of protecting him. She could make efforts to keep him safe when he was a baby at her breast. She could flee with him. She could keep him close. The unknowing and inability to act to keep him safe, apart from her search, even after he is found is a feeling which will likely remain with her. Her identity as a mother must be reevaluated. She can no longer guarantee his safety, nor can she fully understand the workings of his heart and mind. The implication in Jesus' response is that they do not know him well enough to know where he would be, though the answer to him is so obvious as to have remained unsaid until this moment. Despite his explanation at his behavior, she and Joseph remain in confusion. As an adolescent, who nonetheless remains obedient to them, he has his own will and may carry himself away from the protection of his household.

All caregivers of children may attest to the feeling of fear at their child being in any potential danger; the fear that grips a parent's heart when the baby begins coughing while eating solid food, when they hit their head, or even sleep a bit to soundly. Many parents have had the experience of losing sight of their child at the grocery store. Even when the child is found moments later, it may seem as if those moments are stretched and suspended in time. Our reaction is often a physical one. We are propelled forward, our vision becomes hawk like, we become a fury of action. One can imagine that these three days to Jesus' parents felt an eternity. Did Mary eat? Could she sleep? Did Joseph have to remind her to drink, to breathe?

The recovery from this trauma begins only with the knowledge of Christ's safety. Even though he is now twelve years old, he would remain, in his mother's eyes, an extension of her own heart. His well-being remains bound with hers. However, from this a new sense of relationship between the two emerges. Christ is no longer the babe to be protected. He is the young man who must be raised in Wisdom for Mary now knows, in a very guttural way, that she cannot shelter him, but must rather equip him while he remains in the safety of their home.

4. The Galilean crisis: Mark 3:20–34; Luke 4:14–30, 8:19–21

The third traumatic mystery is Mary's experience of the rejection of Jesus by members of their home community. While the instance of finding Jesus in the temple is a traumatic reminder that with an increase in Jesus' age comes a decrease in her power to protect him and understand his actions, the onset of his ministry further marks a change in their relationship as mother and son. Mary is no longer his kin/mother in the sense of her ability to instruct him and provide him with safety. Rather, Jesus asserts the beginning of a new definition of kinship within the reign of God. Mary's relationship to her son is not close simply because of her role as mother. Rather, this relationship exists as far as she serves the reign of God.

According to Luke Timothy Johnson, unlike in Mark, Luke's gospel, "avoids any implication that Jesus' family was hostile to him, or he toward them."[23] However, Elizabeth Johnson observes that in both accounts, Jesus' family is outside looking in.[24] In Mark, Jesus' family hears the community accusing him of being possessed by a demon, presumably trying to seize him before he can bring the ire of the community upon himself. In Luke, his words at the synagogue in Nazareth provoke the rage of their community. They chase him out of Nazareth, attempting to throw him off the edge of the mountain (Luke 4:29–30). While the motivation for rejection differs, both accounts involve discrediting and shame. In Luke 8, when Jesus hears his mother and brothers are attempting to reach him from outside the crowd he replies, "My mother and my brothers are those who hear the word of God and do it" (Luke 8:20–21). Jesus does not deny Mary as his mother but identifies any such kinship as one within the context of serving the reign of God, rather than blood.

Since being driven out of Galilee, Mary is now following her son, perhaps from a distance. The fear of having the community turn against her at the time of her pregnancy with Jesus has come true years on. She is the mother of a child who has grown to speak in a manner that elicits violent reactions from respected members of the community. Luke Timothy

23. Johnson, *Gospel of Luke*, 133.

24. Johnson, *Truly Our Sister*, 217–21.

Johnson notes that Simeon's prophecy is actualized in Luke 4.[25] For Mary, we can imagine that to have stayed in Nazareth would have been to reject her son's words. She would perhaps also be putting herself at risk of becoming a victim of the community's anger. Once again, Mary sees that she cannot protect Jesus. While his disappearance in Jerusalem was an imagined danger, the violent anger of her fellow Nazarenes is a concrete threat. Mary of Nazareth, keeper of the home where Jesus finds safety, may thus have been divorced from her home, following her son alongside her other children. Unlike in Nazareth, Mary is not central to Jesus' daily life. She is rather one of many followers, and not the focus of his ministry. She and her other children find themselves outside, negotiating with their new role as disciples. While they once defined their relationship to Jesus primarily by blood, it is now defined in service to the reign of God.

Mary's hope is now invested in this larger kinship group. Rather than protecting Christ from the violent reactions to his call, we can imagine recovery from the attempted murder of her child is sought in the forging of a new purpose and new bonds within this community of disciples who struggles to understand and work for the reign of God.

5. Witness to the passion of Jesus

Mothers do not nourish, instruct, comfort, and raise their children so that they can be killed. Elizabeth Johnson notes that the many images of the *pieta* in Christian art attest to the solidarity parents have felt with Mary throughout Christian history, especially when we consider that Scripture does not mention this scene of the mother holding her dead child. It is one that takes place in the imagination of the believer who asks questions of what goes unmentioned in passion narrative; mainly, Mary's agony. Mary lives through the realization of every parent's worst fear: that harm will come to her child despite every effort to preserve them from danger; that the child's death will be premature and violent; that the parent will outlive the child. While only John gives an account of Mary at the foot of the cross we are not given any indication as to the physical, emotional, and guttural response this evokes in her (John 19:25–27). Some biblical scholars attest that due to her absence in the Synoptics, and otherwise prevalent mention in Luke, Mary was unlikely an eyewitness to her son's torture and death.

---

25. Johnson, *Gospel of Luke*, 81.

In this view, her presence at the foot of the cross is symbolic rather of her prominent place in the Johannine community as church leader and mother.

However, to dismiss Mary's presence as ahistorical, or mere symbolism, may be considered an injustice to those parents who have found in her an unfortunate companion in the grief and anger involved in the loss of a child. If Mary was present, as she is in John, we can imagine that her choice to witness, to not turn away from the sight of her child in pain, was the ultimate act of love. For while powerless to keep him safe, she could scream, wail, cry out in anger, rush at the guards. When held back, she could at least accompany him. She could with her simple presence say, *Baby, I'm here. I am not going anywhere. I will stay with you. Mama's here.*

Judith Herman notes that it is common for men injured and dying in battle as well as for women who have been violently sexually assaulted to cry out to their mothers when met with the threat of annihilation.[26] While part of this horror is that their mother cannot hear them, or is unable to protect them, it is also evidence of a love that remains, and is grasped at when comfort is most needed. When George Floyd was murdered on the street in St. Paul, Minnesota, it took him eight minutes and forty-nine seconds to die. In his final moments he called out to his mother. Lonnae O'Neal writes, "To call out to his mother is to be known to his maker. The one who gave him to her. I watched the Floyd video, for us, the living. It's my sacred charge. I am a black mother."

Throughout Christian history mothers have heard pastors and theologians logically explain the theology of atonement; that Christ's death was necessary; that he came to die. Mary's witness, the presence of her love, and the cry that Jesus likely made for her stands against all imperial propaganda that would have us believe that the violent death of someone's child is necessary and desired by the Creator.[27] It is further a call to a love whose presence and witness transcends place and time. Floyd's mother died two years prior to his murder, and yet she was there in his cry.

Mary's witness at the cross in John further compels us to not look away, but to confront trauma head-on. It is an embodied witness, in which she is hearing the words of Christ on the cross. She is not disassociating but making the active choice to accompany. This is not to create in the faithful a sense of the right or wrong way to respond to a traumatic event. Rather, we may meditate on Mary providing a place of safe love for Jesus in this

---

26. Herman, *Trauma and Recovery*, 52.

27. O'Neal, "George Floyd's Mother."

moment of humiliation and violence. This may allow traumatized persons to feel their pain is seen and provides a method of embodied agency at a time when one is otherwise completely helpless by standing as witness in discipleship. So, while Floyd's mother could only comfort him in spirit, and onlookers had no power to physically stop the police officers from taking his life, they witnessed. They yelled out what the officers were doing. Darnella Frazier took video. They cried, screamed, and cursed. And as the trauma of witnessing this murder persists, they have the knowledge of their own strength in agency, having actively witnessed to the truth of the wounds, that they be seen.[28]

6. Holy Saturday

It may be argued that only Holy Saturday does justice to Mary's grief. With the resurrection comes the resurrected, glorified Christ who bears the signs of the crucifixion upon his spiritual body. There is the miracle of renewal, healing, and the transformation of the cave from tomb to a womb that cannot contain the life within it. However, only Holy Saturday respects the finality of Jesus' death. Only on Holy Saturday is his body fully contained within the tomb on the assumption that he is permanently sealed within it. We can imagine that the adrenaline of Friday has left behind an emotional pit of despair. Mary's child has died. She can no longer comfort him, cook for him, be angry with him, joke with him. His death is final.

Meditating upon this mystery evokes existential questions to which there is seemingly no answer, for it is in this middle space of speechlessness and a lack of easy answers that Holy Saturday dwells.[29] Shelly Rambo writes, "What does life mean in the moments when one leaves the graveyard, walks home, and crawls around and cannot see her way forward? Meaning is dead. Hope is dead. Love is dead."[30]

In the third mystery, where Mary and Joseph lose Jesus in Jerusalem, we asked whether she remembered to eat or drink. If she could sleep. Whether Joseph had to remind her to care for herself. The same questions

---

28. Treisman, "Darnella Frazier."

29. Shelly Rambo explores a trauma theology of remaining in which traumatized persons inhabit a middle space between the traumatic event and redemption. She juxtaposes the remaining of the event with Adrienne Von Speyr and Hans Urs von Balthasar's meditations on Holy Saturday. See Rambo, *Spirit and Trauma*.

30. Rambo, *Spirit and Trauma*, 73.

arise in this sixth mystery in addition to others that point to the sense of finality which would have come with Jesus' death. Was she numb? Did she lose consciousness? Could she only wail? No matter her physical and emotional state on Holy Saturday, Mary was forced to confront a world in which the days continued though her son was dead.

The questions of Holy Saturday persist through the seventh mystery, as even after the resurrection of Jesus there is a finality to the everyday aspects of Jesus' relationship to Mary as son. While Christ has risen to new life, there is still the death of her ability to guide and care for him as a parent in particular ways. In speaking of the trauma of stillbirth Linda Layne cites a poem by Marion Cohen which expresses the grief of knowing that even at the resurrection, when she is reunited with her baby girl, her daughter will have no need for the Carter's onesie she had saved for her.[31]

Nelba Marquez Green, founder of the Anna Grace Project, and mother of Anna Grace, a six-year-old killed in the Newtown massacre, advocates for an accompaniment of traumatized persons that witnesses to the truth of their pain. She argues that while attempts to redeem the horror which has taken place mask themselves as an effort to help traumatized persons, in actuality, they merely provide false answers, distancing themselves from the pain of the traumatized. Marquez Greene states, "Do not 'at least' my pain away." Believing their reunion will take place in heaven, she argues that even so, her daughter is still dead. Anna Grace cannot live an embodied life with her family in the present. Thus, the hope and life drawn from the Ana Grace Project does not provide a reason for Anna Grace's murder. It is still senseless and contrary to the will of God. Rather, by sitting in the middle space which acknowledges the abject horror of Ana Grace's death, Marquez Greene has found agency in proclaiming it as an injustice. In witnessing to the truth of the finality and meaninglessness of her daughter's death, Marquez Green can proclaim that it is antithetical to the God of Life, and thus make meaning in her creation of something new out of this traumatic event. As we will see with the seventh mystery, resurrection/new life requires this middle space.[32]

Thus, Mary's presence among the Christian community is predicated upon her witness to her son's murder as antithetical to the God of Life, and her experience that even while the resurrection brings new life, the scars of the crucifixion remain.

31. Layne, "'I Remember,'" 261.
32. Pisetzner, "What It's Like."

7. Remaining: Mourning through resurrection, Pentecost, and its aftermath

The last of the traditional sorrowful mysteries is the death of Jesus. While this is arguably the most moving of the seven, it assumes that Mary's grief ends at the cross, skipping over Holy Saturday, and is banished by the resurrection of her son on Sunday. Employing our theological imaginations along with what we know of Scripture and trauma studies, another narrative may be articulated. It is my hope that in prayerfully discussing these seven traumatic mysteries that greater justice may be given to Mary's experience of trauma both pre- and post-crucifixion.

It is tempting, in the face of the horror of the crucifixion of her son, to view Mary's previous traumas as simply sorrowful. However, as Serene Jones observes, traumatic events vary in both intensity and frequency. While one person with PTSD may suffer from the remaining of one violent attack, another may suffer from what Rambo describes as "repeated events of the low-intensity variety, like the constant threat of violence in some forms of domestic abuse or hostile workplace environments. In such instances the assault on the psyche is no less disabling than frontal attack; but because it never reaches an explosive level of violence we associate with traumatic harm, its corrosive effects are more likely to go unnoticed—and uninterrupted—for years."[33] The cross seems to eclipse Mary's previous traumas as it is the actualization of previously perceived threats. However, those threats to her child, and to her person, were nonetheless real, and more importantly keenly felt. We can imagine that the cross, rather than making such events as the flight into Egypt and the attempt on Jesus' life in Galilee less significant, heightens their significance, as they are now seen through the lens of his ministry's violent end. Mary may be looking back, seeing warning signs in a different light, perhaps even wishing she had done things differently. Simeon's prophecy makes horrible sense. She misses her confusion at his words.

In *The Blindfold's Eyes*, Dianna Ortiz, founder of TASSC International (Torture Abolition and Survivors Support Coalition International) and survivor of torture, discusses the unrelated trauma of her brother's murder. The threats on her life, her imprisonment, and torture do not eliminate her family's trauma at the loss of their son and brother. Rather, when Dianna first receives threats of murder and rape, one of the first things which comes

---

33. Rambo, *Spirit and Trauma*, 15.

to her mind is how to protect her family from fearing for her as they already lost her brother to violence. In captivity, she has a vision of being present for her family's grief, but it is unclear whether she is seeing their grief at her disappearance or the death of her brother. The events blur together.

In Catholic tradition Mary is called both "Cause of Our Joy," since God would become incarnate through her, and *Mater Dolorosa*, Mother of All Sorrows, the patroness of grief.[34] The early Christian community of which Mary remained a part was a traumatized community experiencing the continued threats of persecution and death. As Jesus' mother, we may imagine that the ordeal of watching her son die, unable to do anything but stand witness, remained with her for the rest of her life.[35] We can imagine that these psycho/spiritual wounds Mary bore would have been not unlike Jesus' visible physical wounds. If the marks of Christ's wounds were to remain as part of his resurrected body, we can imagine that Mary's internal wounding also remained. David Schnasa Jacobsen asserts that in resurrecting into new life Jesus' experience has not been erased, it is rather "taken up into the purposes of God. Revelation's final vision in chapters 21–22 includes the wiping away of tears in 21:4. Please note: there will be tears to be wiped away."[36] Thus, the resurrection and the promise of the reign of God does not erase the experience of suffering, but integrates it into new life and identity in Christ. By choosing to continue to live in community with the disciples, Mary the mother of Jesus chose to cultivate relationships with people whose actions would put them at risk of their own cross, whether it be a literal crucifixion, torture, imprisonment, or as was common among early Christian communities, disbanding and exile. After the death of her son, Mary lived in a community that was vulnerable to trauma.

Mary's presence with the disciples at Pentecost allows us to imagine that she might have been integrating the trauma of her experience of Jesus' death into a new purpose that allowed her to be in relationship with him in a new way despite his physical absence.[37] While she was formerly able to feel physical closeness and experience their relationship as mother and son in a tangible way, after the ascension and Pentecost, she would now feel his presence through the Holy Spirit, through the mutual care in relationship

34. Pelikan, *Jesus Through the Centuries*, 17–19, 125–36.

35. Rambo, *Spirit and Trauma*, 15.

36. Jacobsen, "Preaching," 413.

37. Herman, *Trauma and Recovery*, 207.

with his friends, and the mission of the early church.[38] However, according to Judith Herman, integration like this can only take place if grief has been given its due.[39] Furthermore, to cultivate a sense of reconnection to daily routines, personal worth, and purpose, grief must be honored as it inevitably resurfaces and evolves. Thus, Mary could only have found life after trauma by creating a space for her grief.

Despite physically appearing to the disciples and sharing meals with them numerous times prior to the ascension, Jesus cannot be present as a son to his mother in the same way he would have been prior to his death. Thus, while there is reassurance, meaning, and a new way of experiencing Christ through the Holy Spirit, there are still innumerable little deaths. We can imagine her ongoing grief at not being able to muss his hair when he says something cheeky, hear his laugh from another room, feel his embrace, his smell. Nor does Christ's resurrection erase the betrayal of his close friends, the violent public spectacle of his death, and the power taken from her as a mother who aches to console and protect her child. One can only imagine the layers of anger and grief. Even when new life is found after trauma, grief remains.

We may ask ourselves: Did she question the manner in which she and Joseph raised him, that he chose a path that would inevitably lead to the cross? Was she angry at herself? At Jesus? At Peter? Did she cry in anger to God for having her pour her being into raising her son, only to have him die? Did she relive the horrors of standing witness to her son's death in nightmares? Prior to Pentecost, could she speak beyond the wails of mourning? How long was it before she could eat again? Or sleep? In these ways, we can imagine Mary's grief being wide ranging: encompassing both the death of not being able to see him enjoy his favorite meal and the horror of his passion. We can also imagine that the *remaining* of this grief was heightened at particular times, such as when young followers of the Way were persecuted.[40] Once again, she would need space to grieve in order to continue finding new meaning in communion with the early Church.

In Catholic tradition, Mary the mother of Jesus is already a widow at the time of Jesus' passion. As a widow, and the mother of Jesus, she would have had a particular role within the early Christian community. Margaret MacDonald discusses the essential contributions of women to the identity

---

38. Acts 1:14.

39. Herman, *Trauma and Recovery*, 188.

40. Rambo, *Spirit and Trauma*. See also Acts 7–9.

of the nascent church through individual and communal acts of accompaniment. By the second century, widows had formed communities within their local *ekklesia*, taking it upon themselves to offer up the intentions of the community in prayer. We can thus imagine Mary taking part in one of the first groups of widows who were followers of the Way. As such widows were considered exemplary in their discipleship as they were often the first to respond to situations of death or persecution. Women more generally also brought food and a comforting presence to fellow Christians in prison.[41] Holding the trials, grief, and hope of the community as a Jewish woman, Mary and her sisters in Christ would also have engaged in prayers of lament, in which "there is a severity of affliction, a petitioner crying out or groaning for deliverance, and a God who hears and promises to deliver, even while he [*sic*] may delay in acting."[42] Thus, Mary the mother of Jesus would not only have experienced grief passively, as something which overtook her, but as a ministry. She and other widows would have actively chosen to express the grief of the community. Thus, lament is required for the individual and the community in order for new life to be found.

Herman notes that it is common for mourning and remembrance to be avoided as it can easily be viewed as a risk that we might fall into a pit of despair from which we might never climb out. However, she notes that while there is no predicting how long a period of mourning may last, particularly as grief is something which ebbs and flows, rather than starts and stops, it is necessary in integrating the loss into the *after* of the traumatic experience.[43] Being encouraged to mourn, to pause, to reflect, and to honor feelings of loss further allowed me to acknowledge that need in others. I too could begin to search for opportunities to meet someone else in their grief, making space for their own need to pause, to feel sorrow, to honor the mourning within their mourning. Like Mary the mother of Jesus, we find ourselves entrusting our grief to those around us who acknowledge its validity and persistence, while nursing the suffering and losses of others.

CONCLUSION

This paper has attempted to witness to the matrix of traumatic experience through the lens of the trauma-informed mysteries of Mary the mother of

41. MacDonald, "Religious Lives," 646.

42. Hassler, "Glimpses of Lament," 175.

43. Herman, *Trauma and Recovery*, 188.

Jesus. Like many women, we can imagine Mary's trauma being the aftermath of events which held both the threat of annihilation and the joy of new life. Her love for the baby in her womb, and the joy which the Spirit arouses in her occurs alongside threats of shame, ostracization, and death. The new life of her child is embraced as both prophecy and tangible threats elicit fear. The rapturous joy of the giving of the Spirit at Pentecost is felt amid the horrific memory of the crucifixion. Her own witness as a traumatized person may provide a space for traumatized persons to feel seen, particularly as her efforts at protecting her child and the trauma of his death are a witness against any claims on the necessity of human suffering. The conflicting emotions brought up throughout these mysteries may further attest to the middle space in which the persistence of traumatic experience, and the evolution of recovery throughout a person's lifetime is attested to, hinting at an eventual hope against hope that does not seek to elide the person's experience, but heals as an affirmation of it akin to Christ's wounds, postresurrection.

Mary's potential feelings of fear, anger, guilt, grief, and rage break through simplified religious formulas which do further violence to traumatized persons in their demand of forgiveness. It creates room for anger at God, doubt, wrestling, and even hopelessness to be considered sacred and necessary in an ongoing recovery. In its paradoxes, these trauma informed mysteries may even be taken a step further, such that one's discipleship is no longer held in conflict with such states and emotions but is one with it.

As such, in meditating upon these mysteries we may eventually proclaim the *Shalom* we were created for as being gloriously contrary to traumatic events that rupture persons' sense of selves in both their autonomy and relationships. We may work toward and proclaim an eschatological hope that does not erase traumatic experience but rises from it. Thus, while one's experience of having been hungry remains, they are filled. While one may have become victim of the proud, they also may speak of the lifting up of the humble. Thus, like Mary we might one day proclaim,

> *My soul glorifies the Lord*
> *and my spirit rejoices in God my Savior,*
> *for he has been mindful*
> *of the humble state of his servant.*
> *From now on all generations will call me blessed,*
> *for the Mighty One has done great things for me—*
> *holy is his name.*
> *His mercy extends to those who fear him,*

from generation to generation.
He has performed mighty deeds with his arm;
he has scattered those who are proud in their inmost thoughts.
He has brought down rulers from their thrones
but has lifted up the humble.
He has filled the hungry with good things
but has sent the rich away empty.
He has helped his servant Israel,
remembering to be merciful
to Abraham and his descendants forever,
just as he promised our ancestors.
(Luke 1:46–54)

BIBLIOGRAPHY

Agbasiere, Joseph Thérèse. "The Rosary: Its History and Relevance." *African Ecclesial Review* 30:4 (1988) 242–54.

Boys, M. C. "Patriarchal Judaism, Liberating Jesus: A Feminist Misrepresentation." *Union Seminary Quarterly Review* 56 (2003) 48–61.

Campbell, Jacquelyn, et al. "Pregnancy-Associated Deaths from Homicide, Suicide, and Drug Overdose: Review of Research and the Intersection with Intimate Partner Violence." *Journal of Women's Health* 30:2 (2021) 236–44.

Clark, Robin E., et al. "Pregnant and Homeless: How Unstable Housing Affects Maternal Health Outcomes." *Housing Matters*, Mar. 20, 2019. https://housingmatters.urban.org/research-summary/pregnant-and-homeless-how-unstable-housing-affects-maternal-health-outcomes.

"Domestic Violence and Pregnancy Fact Sheet." Washington, DC: National Coalition Against Domestic Violence. https://vawnet.org/sites/default/files/assets/files/2016-09/DVPregnancy.pdf.

Farley, Margaret. *Just Love: A Framework for Christian Sexual Ethics.* New York: Continuum, 2006.

Gebara, Ivone. *Out of the Depths: Women's Experience of Evil and Salvation.* Minneapolis: Fortress, 2002.

Goizueta, Roberto. *Caminemos con Jesus: Toward a Hispanic/Latino Theology of Accompaniment.* Maryknoll, NY: Orbis, 2010.

Green, Joel B. *The Gospel of Luke.* New International Commentary on the New Testament. Grand Rapids: Eerdmans, 1997.

Gutiérrez, Gustavo. *The God of Life.* Translated by Matthew J. O'Connell. Maryknoll, NY: Orbis, 1991.

Hassler, Andrew. "Glimpses of Lament: 2 Corinthians and the Presence of Lament in the New Testament." *Journal of Spiritual Formation and Soul Care* 9:2 (Fall 2016) 164–75.

Herman, Judith. *Trauma and Recovery: The Aftermath of Violence—From Domestic Abuse to Political Terror.* London: Little, Brown, 2015.

Jacobsen, David Schnasa. "Preaching as the Unfinished Task of Theology: Grief, Trauma, and Early Christian Texts in Homiletical Interpretation." *Theology Today* 70:4 (2014) 407–16.

Johnson, Elizabeth A. *Truly Our Sister: A Theology of Mary in the Communion of Saints.* New York: Continuum, 2009.

Johnson, Luke Timothy. *The Gospel of Luke.* Sacra Pagina. Collegeville, MN: Liturgical Press, 1991.

Katoppo, Marianne. "Asian Theology: An Asian Woman's Perspective." In *Asia's Struggle for Full Humanity: Towards a Relevant Theology; Papers from the Asian Theological Conference, January 1979,* edited by Virginia Fabella, 140–51. New York: Orbis, 1980.

Kelly, Elizabeth. "The Rosary as a Tool for Meditation." *Loyola Press* (blog), n.d. https://www.loyolapress.com/catholic-resources/prayer/personal-prayer-life/different-ways-to-pray/the-rosary-as-a-tool-for-meditation-by-liz-kelly/.

Layne, Linda L. "'I remember the day I shopped for your layette': Consumer Goods, Fetuses, and Feminism." *Fetal Subjects, Feminist Positions,* edited by Lynn M. Morgan and Meredith Wilson Michaels, 251–78. Philadelphia: University of Pennsylvania Press, 1999.

Levine, Amy-Jill. "Gospel of Matthew." In *Women's Bible Commentary*, edited Carol A. Newsom et al., 465–77. Louisville: Westminster John Knox, 2012.

MacDonald, Margaret. "The Religious Lives of Women in Early Christianity." In *Women's Biblical Commentary*, edited by Carol A. Newsom et al., 640–47. Louisville: Westminster John Knox, 2012.

Oakes, Kaya. *The Defiant Middle: How Women Claim Life's In-Betweens to Remake the World.* Minneapolis: Broadleaf, 2021.

O'Donnell, Karen. *Broken Bodies: The Eucharist, Mary and the Body in Trauma Theology.* London: SCM Press, 2018.

O'Neal, Lonnae. "George Floyd's Mother Was Not There, but He Used Her as a Sacred Invocation." *The Undefeated*, May 28, 2020. https://andscape.com/features/george-floyds-death-mother-was-not-there-but-he-used-her-as-a-sacred-invocation/.

Ortiz, Dianna. *The Blindfold's Eyes: My Journey from Torture to Truth.* Maryknoll, NY: Orbis, 2002.

Pelikan, Jaroslav. *Jesus Through the Centuries; Mary Through the Centuries.* New York: History Book Club, 2005.

Pisetzner, Amanda. "A Sandy Hook Mom Describes What It's Like Losing a Child to Gun Violence." *Vice News*, Dec. 13, 2017. https://www.vice.com/en/article/a-sandy-hook-mom-describes-what-its-like-losing-a-child-to-gun-violence/.

Rambo, Shelly. *Spirit and Trauma: A Theology of Remaining.* Louisville: Westminster John Knox, 2010.

Ribas, Mario. "Liberating Mary, Liberating the Poor." In *Liberation Theology and Sexuality*, edited by Marcella Althaus-Reid, 123–35. London: SCM Press, 2006.

Szyszkiewicz, Barb. "Pray the Rosary, Franciscan Style: A Crown of Prayers for Mary." *Catholic Digest* 83 (2019). https://www.catholicdigest.com/faith/prayer/pray-the-rosary-franciscan-style/.

Treisman, Rachel. "Darnella Frazier, Teen Who Filmed Floyd's Murder, Praised For Making Verdict Possible." *NPR*, Apr. 21, 2021. https://www.npr.org/sections/trial-over-killing-of-george-floyd/2021/04/21/989480867/darnella-frazier-teen-who-filmed-floyds-murder-praised-for-making-verdict-possib.

Viljoen, Anneka. "Theological Imagination as Hermeneutical Device: Exploring the Hermeneutical Contribution of an Imaginal Engagement with the Text." *HTS Theological Studies* 72:4/a3172 (2016). http://dx.doi.org/10.4102/hts.v72i4.3172.

A Trauma-Informed Christology

"Healing Happens 'After No Body Becomes Some Body'"

CHELLE STEARNS

I HAVE TAUGHT THEOLOGY for over a decade at an American graduate school that trains pastors and therapists at the intersection of theology and psychology. When I first started teaching there, I had no idea how this interdisciplinary intention would challenge some of the most basic ways I approach doctrine and my theological method.

In my first year, a student approached me and asked what difference the doctrine of "the resurrection of the dead" made to people who had been sex trafficked? She was about to complete an applied portion of her degree program by working directly with survivors, and she needed to know that the bodies of these women and children had real hope for today, not just in a far-off heaven. I was stopped in my tracks. Neither my seminary education nor my PhD had prepared me to respond to her question. In that moment, I could have given her a semblance of an answer, but it would have felt a bit trite. These particular bodies required a particular theological response, not a pat answer. During my theological studies I had often railed against anti-materialist Gnostic tendencies within the Christian tradition—agreeing with theologians like Trevor Hart that "matter matters!"[1]—but I had not included a thoroughgoing notion of the diverse experience of bodies in my theological inquiry. The practical question of how to address the traumatic experience of particular bodies in a doctrinal context caused me to realize that I had not really established a legitimate space for bodies at

1. See Hart, "Lecture 1: 'Clayey Lodging.'"

all within my theology. More importantly, I could not answer the practical reality of how to bring a theology of creation, hope, and reconciliation into the everyday lives of those who have been psychologically, physically, and sexually abused and terrorized. I needed new language and new tools to tell the story of Jesus.

Soon after this I started to study trauma theory. Trauma theory caused me to stop and reconsider how I integrated theological language into my view of the world, which then impacted how I listened to stories and how I made sense of the people and the bodies within those stories. Often the implicit missing details of a story, those fragments that get lost at the edge of narrative, can be more significant than the explicit plotline. Details are often lost in the wake of traumatic experience, which is why retelling can feel disjointed or rambling. Bearing witness to these disjointed stories of harm and trauma is vital to the process of healing embodied persons. As trauma theorist Peter Levine argues, "Traumatized people have their lives arrested until they are somehow able to process these intrusions, assimilate them, and then finally form coherent narratives that help put these memories to rest,"[2] thus setting them free to grow as people who inhabit complex embodied stories and memories. The more I read, the more I realized that trauma theorists, such as Levine, have sounded an alarm about the importance of comprehending the impact of traumatic experience and how it manifests and lingers in the body. To respond to this reality, I needed to add and cultivate a body-oriented and body-based approach to my theological system. Thus, a capacity to sit with words, stories, and bodies began to intertwine within my teaching.

To aid this shift in thinking, I found that trauma-informed theology that joined together the methodologies of constructive theology and trauma studies could often deconstruct a predominantly proposition or word-based theological approach, offering a multiplicity of new "language" and multidisciplinary terminology to expand my theological work. Moreover, I worked to keep my core theological commitments intact even as the picture began to shift and refocus. For example, while the character of Jesus remained a theologically well-defined person in my reading of the Bible, the bodies of other characters in the stories began to be more enfleshed in my imagination and "take up more room" in my analysis.[3] As a result, bodies became important sources in my theological knowing.

2. See Levine, *Trauma and Memory*, 8.

3. Shelly Rambo demonstrates this well in her analysis of the resurrection narrative

This essay focuses on that work by first exploring the body-oriented approach of trauma studies, incorporating a theology of the body of Jesus Christ, and then developing a trauma-informed Christology. Within this interdisciplinary frame, the physical body of Jesus becomes a location from which to reimagine how to do theology that takes bodies, healing, and redemption seriously. That is, if Jesus takes on all of humanity within his incarnate body, even traumatic experience to the point of death, then all of humanity (and all of creation, Rom 8 and Col 1) is being reconciled in and through the physical body of Jesus.

THE LANGUAGE OF THE BODY

Theological method often relies on word-centric systems of thinking. A rich tradition of attending to silence, referred to as negative or apophatic theology, also has a legitimate place in theological method,[4] but systematic and dogmatic theology tends to have a foundational confidence in rational assent to propositional statements. When one has experienced trauma, however, a different mode of theology is necessary. Trauma within the body activates a kind of disintegration of how one makes sense of the world and can even dislocate or fragment one's capacity for language, thus requiring alternative modes of understanding and meaning making. It is not surprising, then, that in the aftermath of trauma rational assent to particular "word-based" tenets of belief is not sufficient for the lived experience of faith. Instead, the embodied witness or enduring presence of other people becomes necessary for one's capacity to make sense of what has happened and is happening in the body while beginning the process of healing. "Witnessing" within one's theological work, then, cannot simply turn to "word-centered" proclamation, but should instead, as trauma theologian Shelly Rambo suggests, incorporate body-centered witness as a vital part of theological understanding.[5] To talk about the body within our specific theological method, however, we first must turn to how trauma

---

in the Gospel of John in "Biblical Witness in the Gospel of John," in *Spirit and Trauma*. She plays with the ideas of what is seen and unseen, what is known and not known, and what is elided or missed in the re-telling/re-living/re-interpreting of traumatic (death) and earth-shattering (resurrection) events.

4. See, for example, Williams, "Saying the Unsayable"; and Williams, "Negative Theology."

5. Rambo, *Spirit and Trauma*, 37. She also critiques an "imitation" or "sacrifice"/martyrdom model of witness.

works in the body, brain, and mind, especially in our ways of knowing and understanding the world.

Let's begin by defining what is meant by "trauma." In her book *Spirit and Trauma*, Rambo provides a workable definition of trauma. She differentiates between suffering and lingering post-traumatic stress: "Suffering is what, in time, can be integrated into one's understanding of the world," thus it is felt, has an impact on someone, yet is made sense of in the present. She continues, "Trauma is what is not integrated in time; it is the difference between a closed and an open wound. Trauma is an open wound."[6] "Open wounds" is Rambo's language for non-integrated, harmful experiences that we may not be consciously aware of or may not access consciously but that our bodies "know" and "remember" and "speak." In other words, our bodies hold memories and shape language in unique and distinct ways. Thus, a basic definition of trauma, for our purposes, is wounding experience that is unassimilated.

Rambo has a second definition of trauma that demonstrates how the effects of trauma in procedural memory (implicit emotional or bodily memory) can move from the individual body into more social and cultural bodily expressions and ramifications. Trauma, she argues, "is an event that continues, that persists in the present. Trauma is what does not go away. It persists in symptoms that live on in the body, in the intrusive fragments of memories that return. It persists in symptoms that live on in communities, in the layers of past violence that constitute present ways of relating."[7] Thus, even on the level of the communal or societal, the trauma that remains hidden or unacknowledged will remain and likely reemerge. Trauma leaves some form of mark, especially within the bodies of those affected.[8]

In his book *The Body Keeps the Score*, trauma theorist Bessel van der Kolk details the results of how trauma becomes lodged in one's body, or more accurately one's interconnected neurobiological body and mind. As he explains, in the wake of traumatic events—be they emotional or physical trauma, or both—the body and the brain change dramatically. He notes that brain scans show that Broca's area of the brain—which is correlated with speech and verbal processing—"goes dark" during traumatic experience;

6. Rambo, *Spirit and Trauma*, 7.

7. Rambo, *Spirit and Trauma*, 2.

8. Unfortunately, there is not space in this essay for a conversation about cultural and generational trauma. To explore this area of trauma studies, see Menakem, *My Grandmother's Hands*; Alexander et al., *Cultural Trauma and Collective Identity*; and the final chapter in Levine, *Trauma and Memory*.

whereas Brodmann area 19 of the brain—which catalogues images and visual stimuli—"lights up."[9] The impact of traumatic events on the bodies that experience them is thus an overstimulation of one's visual and emotional memory, with little or no language or verbal logic to make sense of one's experience. The technical term for this is *alexithymia*, which also refers to the loss of connection to one's emotions.[10] Memory stored in the brain is often disconnected from language and rationality but felt deeply in the "interoceptive pathways" within the body.[11] Hence, van der Kolk maintains, even if the parts of the brain more associated with "logic" or "reasoning" do not function with an experience of clear memory, the parts of the brain associated with embodied sensations and emotions continue to function with dysregulated reminders about events long after the trauma has passed.

Other trauma theorists, such as Peter Levine, Resmaa Menakem, and Pat Ogden, focus more on the workings of the "vagus nerve" as explained in "polyvagal theory." This theory explains that when current events or experiences trigger these past bodily memories, the amygdala—often referred to as "the alarm system of the brain"—responds directly to these bodily memories by sounding a kind of false alarm, causing the autonomic systems in the body to respond as if the traumatic experience is happening again, right now. The body's responses are sent into overdrive while language and reason shut down once again.[12] This is called a false negative, but it is a very real experience to the person caught in this bodily memory cycle. It is real because the person's body, brain, and senses send them back into the visceral experience of the original traumatic event.[13]

To one caught in these traumatic, embodied, often wordless memories, a solely word-based theology and practice of faith can feel disconnected to their experience and way of knowing. In the midst of this visceral experience, propositional statements and religious platitudes may have little purchase or accessible meaning. Meanwhile, Christian faith and church gatherings are often predominantly centered around word-based communication and proclamation (especially evangelical or Protestant expressions). Scripture is read, hymns are sung, and the word is preached.

---

9. van der Kolk, *Body Keeps the Score*, 44.

10. See van der Kolk, *Body Keeps the Score*, 100–101 and 249.

11. See van der Kolk, *Body Keeps the Score*, 151, 347.

12. For a brief, practical overview of this theory, see Wagner, "Polyvagal Theory in Practice." See also Porges, *Pocket Guide to the Polyvagal Theory*.

13. See Levine, *Waking the Tiger*.

The practice of doing theology is similar; first order questions are set out, books are read, theological commitments are argued, and the ramifications of those conclusions are discussed. In these contexts, there is not clear space to recognize or access the complex role of embodied experience in the expression of truth and memory; people may feel as if they are just disembodied heads and "minds" engaged in truth as an idea exchange and explication through mere written and verbal communication.

In trauma-informed practice and theology—in contrast—the body of traumatized persons becomes more central and is explicitly addressed.[14] Trauma activates a kind of perpetual shattering of meaning-making and knowing in the mind and body that requires a different level of engagement and a more holistic form of epistemic access and truth encounter. As Rambo noted after she interviewed pastors and church leaders in New Orleans impacted by the hurricane Katrina and the devastation caused by the storm, devastating trauma is similar to the hidden "undertow" in a river.[15] The traumatized person may "present well" and look like they've been "cleaned up" after the event, but the effects run deep and undetected. They remain under the surface, unseen and unnoticed by others, ready to pull the person back under, down into a swirl of pain-embodied memory that to others seems incommensurate with the events of the present moment. (This may be why well-meaning family members, friends, politicians, church leaders, etc. are often confused why the person or the community doesn't "just get over it" and "move on" from the experience.) Rambo contends that in this undertow, death and life are mixed, and death haunts life in the "after." As one church leader in New Orleans put it, "The Storm is gone, but the 'after the storm' is always here."[16]

If the procedural memory of the body holds the key to recognizing and engaging the undertow of trauma, and if church communities—as members of the body of Christ—are to be restorative spaces for those who have experienced trauma, then a categorical shift must happen.[17] Before we can respond theologically, or otherwise, to anyone effected by trauma, we must be willing to learn something about how "language" emerges from the body. Philosopher Mark Johnson, in his book *The Meaning of the Body*,

---

14. For an example of how this impacts those with disabilities, see Fulkerson, "Creative Christian Identity."

15. See Rambo, *Spirit and Trauma*, 14 and 128.

16. Rambo, *Spirit and Trauma*, 1 and 143, quoting Deacon Julius Lee.

17. For example, see Baldwin, *Trauma-Sensitive Theology*, especially the third chapter.

can help us categorize how making sense of things in and through the body happens.

Johnson's primary goal in *The Meaning of the Body* is to explore the aesthetics of human understanding through connecting body, word, and world in the process of knowing. Language, in Johnson's theory, is the result of bodily movement and engagement, whether verbal or non-verbal.[18] No language or meaning can exist without the movement of biological bodies. All persons require bodily ways of investigating the world. They also require "shared language" through which to understand the world, and that process involves consistently social embodied experiences.[19] We are not simply biological bodies, argues Johnson. Our bodies are also ecological (where we live and breathe), phenomenological (how our bodies move), social (referring to our families and our close social network), and cultural (the ways that we ethnically, racially, communally, etc. live and are known).[20] All persons concomitantly navigate their collective and experiential "bodies" to know or communicate anything, from our most basic human functioning to our most conceptual thinking.

Without the body, Johnson further maintains, there is no development of the mind or means of communication:

> These ways of learning the meaning of the world all involve the body—its perceptual capacities, motor functions, posture, expressions, and ability to experience emotions and desires. Such capacities are at once bodily, affective, and social. *They do not require language in any full-blown sense, and yet they are the very means for making meaning and for encountering anything that can be understood and made sense of* . . . when we grow up, we do not somehow magically cast off these modes of meaning-making; rather, these body based meaning structures underlie our conceptualization and reasoning, including even our most abstract modes of thought.[21]

For example, language development, in various forms, is highly correlated with physical care and touch in infancy.[22] Without touch and bodily

18. Johnson, *Meaning of the Body*, 266.

19. Johnson, *Meaning of the Body*, 266.

20. Johnson, *Meaning of the Body*, 275–77.

21. Johnson, *Meaning of the Body*, 36.

22. For an introduction to how love, emotion, early childhood nurturing, and the structure of the brain are connected in human development, see Lewis, et al., *General Theory of Love*.

interaction, a baby cannot learn to eat, much less to walk or speak.[23] Hence, be it preverbal, nonverbal, or highly abstract modes of thought, the body and its collected memory are the foundation for all modes of thinking and being, regardless of the ability of the body, brain, or the mind.

With this in mind, if we return to Bessel van der Kolk's *The Body Keeps the Score*, we can connect language and meaning with a trauma-informed understanding of body and the loss of bodily sense. He contends that those who suffer from Post-Traumatic Stress Disorder (PTSD) can experience dissociation from their body, *alexithymia*, and in the process disconnection from one's sense of self.[24] In other words, he explains, "trauma makes people feel like either *some body else*, or like *no body*."[25]

This kind of dissociation or disconnection makes simple tasks that link the body and the brain together, such as identifying everyday objects (e.g., a set of keys or a baseball) placed in the hand while one's eyes are closed (or in any situation, depending on the level of PTSD) impossible. The subject becomes closed off to her body and as a result the brain is unable to categorize and make sense of the various stimuli in the world. As van der Kolk argues, "When our senses become muffled, we no longer feel fully alive" because those with post-traumatic symptoms "often have trouble putting the picture together."[26] His assertion is this kind of trauma response cuts people off not only from their bodies but also from their basic humanity. In these moments of disconnection, the body demands we stop and listen to its needs.

The primary way to overcome trauma and "regain a sense of who you are,"[27] contends van der Kolk, is to "get back in touch with *your body*, with *your Self* . . . . The full story can be told only after those structures are repaired and after the groundwork has been laid: after no body becomes some body."[28] This crucial process of moving from "no body" to "some body"—returning to a sense of one's "Self" through the return to one's bodily senses

---

23. There have been numerous studies on how lack of touch, being held, and learning to move in early life leads to brain damage and the inability to develop language skills, especially in reference to institutionalized Romanian orphans from the 1980s. For an introduction to this, see "Episode 2: What Makes Me? Romanian Orphans."

24. See van der Kolk, *Body Keeps the Score*, 89–104 and 249.

25. van der Kolk, *Body Keeps the Score*, 249.

26. van der Kolk, *Body Keeps the Score*, 91.

27. van der Kolk, *Body Keeps the Score*, 249.

28. van der Kolk, *Body Keeps the Score*, 249.

and awareness—is essential to one's humanity and depends on being able to organize one's bodily memories into a coherent whole.[29]

Through his distinction between conscious and unconscious memory, Peter Levine adds to this emphasis on returning to one's bodily senses. Levine notes that emotional or bodily memory often remains at an unconscious, unattended level; if and when that memory manifests in our bodies, it is seldom consciously understood. Memories that are conscious or explicit are typically declarative or episodic. These are the facts or the warm and textured details of a narrative which are often immediately available, accessible, or self-evident. Sometimes these are even stories that have been repeated over and over, providing identity and meaning for a person, even if they are difficult, harmful, misinterpreted, or not entirely "true." In contrast, that which is least conscious or implicit is "procedural memory"[30] or emotional and bodily memory. These are the elements of a story that are felt or reside in the body but not always (or maybe never) acknowledged or even accessible to the person. Procedural memories sit beneath the surface of experience and understanding, often felt but unseen.[31]

Cathy Caruth, in following a Freudian trajectory, adds another layer of complexity to the process of connecting memory to the body. She argues that traumatic memory is marked by the "inherent forgetting"[32] of the traumatic experience, thus making it inaccessible to the conscious self. As one lives in "the after" or that which "remains" in the effects of traumatic experience, the experience remains unclaimed, forgotten, or "not fully perceived" while the event haunts the survivor. As she claims, sometimes "a history can be grasped only in the very inaccessibility of its occurrence."[33] Caruth recognizes how the unconscious self both shows and hides the history of trauma to survive and remain sane. To acknowledge that the event (or series of events) happened is unbearable, thus the full reality and impact remains inaccessible.[34] In the end, traumatic reality cannot be encountered "head on." One must approach or awaken the real indirectly.

---

29. van der Kolk, *Body Keeps the Score*, 249.

30. Levine, *Trauma and Memory*; especially chapter 3, "Procedural Memory."

31. Levine, *Trauma and Memory*, 17 and 26.

32. Caruth, *Unclaimed Experience*, 17–18.

33. Caruth, *Unclaimed Experience*, 17–18.

34. See her chapter on the dream of the "burning child" for more details: Caruth, "Traumatic Awakenings," in *Unclaimed Experience*, 91–111.

Because the trauma remains inaccessible and unassimilated, thinking back to Rambo's definition of trauma, *reenactment* of the harm and pain is often inescapable. Caruth refers to this as the "double wound," that trauma may be inaccessible for a season but will emerge eventually. In light of what we've discussed so far, Caruth's work bears witness to the unpredictability of how the body remembers. She uses the language of "wound" to bring attention to how body memory can emerge suddenly in a seemingly disconnected moment, through something that engages the emotional and bodily memory such as smell, music, a turn of phrase, etc. The "story of the wound . . . cries out" and in that moment the event itself is happening, reenacting, suddenly made "available" to the conscious mind.[35] When we are in the midst of living out the consequences or the ramifications of what has happened, *reality is too much to bear.* Human beings cannot take in the whole of the narrative. The double side to the wound means that one side protects us from the truth so that we might survive. The other side disorients us so that we might continue to seek out the truth (or reenact the "event").[36] The wound, until it is integrated into conscious process and memory, continues to cry out because all paths of healing must reclaim lost experience.

This reclamation occurs in the realm of confused senses, bodily disconnection, and unassimilated experience, yet this is the only way one can make sense of anything. When one lives in the "after," what was known and understood before must be relearned and restructured. The senses need to be opened anew, and fresh language acquired to connect to bodily memory. Depending on the kind and severity of the trauma, this can be a total reconstruction of knowing. Until some form of psychological integration occurs, the wound will continue to cry out.

One integral reason wounds remain unassimilated and continue to cry out is the lingering impact of shame. Shame is vital to any conversation involving trauma because it often hides reality and blocks direct access to the truth of one's experience. Moreover, shame becomes internalized and intertwined in one's being, making change or acknowledgment of harm and pain difficult or, at times, impossible. When shame and traumatic experience intermix, reality is discolored, and the imagination becomes disordered throughout one's life.

---

35. Caruth, *Unclaimed Experience*, 4.

36. "Trauma is not simply an effect of destruction but also, fundamentally, an enigma of survival." Caruth, *Unclaimed Experience*, 58.

Shame has multiple causes, but in children it is often the result of the critical gaze or voice of someone in authority. Stephen Pattison, in his book *Shame: Theory, Therapy, Theology*, discusses how the critical gaze of an adult, even a well-meaning parent, can reinforce internalized shame and then fragment and disorient the formation of self.[37] This impact can become catastrophic for those who have experienced sexual, physical, and/or emotional abuse, especially as children. This internalized shame can disorient and cause despondency, often becoming the organizing principles of one's life. This can leave a person without language or words around their experience. As Pattison argues, "Shame is . . . a state of linguistic and social exclusion and alienation" which leads to an overwhelming sense of despair, because "shame emerges when trust in other people and the self is shattered."[38]

Psychologist and trauma expert Dan Allender attributes much of this intertwined sense of shame, fragmentation, and distrust to how abusers groom or emotionally implicate children into their own abuse.[39] Abusers will often be the one person in a child's life who sees her beauty and desires. This acknowledgment and attunement to the child meets an inherent longing for emotional intimacy. Every child is hard wired for this kind of parental and affectionate bonding, and this connection is how the child grows, eats, gains language, and encounters the world from their earliest experiences.[40] For example, the hormone and neurotransmitter oxytocin "stimulates pleasure and reward centers and is the neurological basis for

---

37. See also Pattison, *Saving Face*.

38. Pattison, *Shame*, 74.

39. Much of this material comes from the class "Faith, Hope, and Love" that Dr. Allender and I taught together at The Seattle School of Theology & Psychology. See also Allender, *Healing the Wounded Heart*.

40. The hitch here, as Allender asserts, is that the abuser then takes this vulnerable and necessary period of brain development and social bonding and twists it to meet their own needs. The child, in many ways, becomes complicit and intertwined in their own abuse because some of their deepest needs and desires are being met in the relationship. Moreover, their development necessitates their interrelatedness to the one who gives them attention. This then creates a secret bond between the abuser and the abused, forging a life-long loyalty to the abuser. This loyalty disorients and turns the world upside-down for the child, even in adulthood. Trust and loyalty become the location of their most egregious harm. The rush of oxytocin in the body, which should produce feelings of safety and connection, are now distorted in the child, causing the person to feel extreme fear and danger instead of love.

social bonding, especially with the people closest to you."[41] The development of the brain in babies and young children is directly related to how they experience connection through hugs, snuggles, and touch, which is why internalized shame in childhood remains throughout one's life. When we think back to Johnson's connection between the body and the development of language, we can pay attention to how trauma and shame have the capacity to tinge and become intertwined in every form of language and meaning making.[42]

This spiral of shame is so powerful that it creates a kind of "divided self," often isolating a person throughout their entire lives, even if they are surrounded by loving and generative community. The person may be highly functioning in public, but they are disconnected from their capacity for intimacy, trust, faith, hope, and love. As Pattison argues, "Shame . . . produces a feeling of meaninglessness and hopelessness as the disoriented self drowns amidst its own confusion."[43] The lingering impact of the disoriented self in the wake of traumatic experience and internalized shame presents an intractable problem from a therapeutic perspective because trauma lodged in the body is never really "cured" but rather normalized into how one experiences the day-to-day. In this view of shame, the divided self becomes the standard from which to understand and evaluate the world.

"TRAUMA AS THE OPEN WOUND": RAMBO'S DEFINITION OF TRAUMA

If shame can create an unintegrated and divided self, then it would be helpful to return to Rambo's definition of trauma as "unintegrated experience." Trauma is a short-circuit in a healthy mind and body, but it does not have

---

41. Editorial, "More You Hug Your Kids."

42. Not all shame or harm functions the same way, however, in every body. This may begin to explain why it is that some people seem to have more "grit" or "resilience" in the aftermath of trauma while others are disoriented or dissociative in their daily life. It should be noted here that some extreme trauma responses are worked out through an overly competent and work-oriented life, so just because someone is successful and high functioning in society does not guarantee mental well-being or lack of traumatic experience. As van der Kolk remarks, "Most great instigators of social change have intimate personal knowledge of trauma . . . . Read the life history of any visionary, and you will find insights and passions that came from having dealt with devastation." van der Kolk, *Body Keeps the Score*, 356.

43. Pattison, *Shame*, 73.

to be the defining characteristic of any life. At the same time, the lingering impact of trauma remains, whether seen or unseen. In Rambo's words, "Trauma is what is not integrated in time; it is the difference between a closed and an open wound. Trauma is an open wound."[44] If we bring Caruth's language into this definition of trauma, trauma remains unclaimed and inaccessible to the conscious mind.

Rambo's theology is not attempting to articulate why there is suffering or evil in the world. Instead, she wants to understand what to do when one encounters death (literal or figurative) that shatters "all one knows about the world and all the familiar ways of operating within it."[45] From the depths of this experience, she claims that the entire topography of the Christian faith becomes a "mixed terrain" of life and death, truth and fiction, past and future, safety and danger.[46] What was once demarcated and clear is now utterly disordered and disjointed. As she asserts, "Trauma becomes not simply a detour on the map of faith but, rather, a significant reworking of the entire map."[47] In particular, Rambo argues that trauma shatters the framework of redemption, dislocating a person's ability to evaluate and understand "time, body, and word" with any ordered integrity.[48]

Rambo's methodology emerges from this claim. From early in *Spirit and Trauma*, she commits to pay special attention to the shattered edges of experience, testimony, and witness. If life and death are mixed or confused in the experience of trauma, then the best or most appropriate response would be to witness, in a presence or embodied way, what remains amid this mixed terrain.[49] Given that there is often an overly triumphalistic Christian emphasis on a linear conception of redemption—that life comes immediately from death—which leads to a "Jesus paid it all so just get over it" set of assumptions, the mixed terrain of unintegrated traumatic experience has little to no place in the pew on Sunday mornings, much less in Christian spirituality. Christian experience shaped by the pew makes it

---

44. Rambo, *Spirit and Trauma*, 7.

45. Rambo, *Spirit and Trauma*, 4: "Life takes on a fundamentally different definition, and the tentative and vulnerable quality of life in the aftermath means that it is life always mixed with death."

46. Rambo, *Spirit and Trauma*, 6.

47. Rambo, *Spirit and Trauma*, 9.

48. Rambo, *Spirit and Trauma*, 18.

49. Rambo, *Spirit and Trauma*, 10–11.

difficult to recognize, welcome, or attend to life in the body that accounts for one's experiential, unconscious memory, and traumatic wounding.

Nonetheless, Rambo insists, the wound of trauma demands an embodied witness to linger with that which remains in the aftermath of trauma. The persistent witness of the Spirit in the "middle space" of trauma thus becomes the hinge between the unpredictable relationship of life and death: "the middle Spirit provides a vision of God's presence in the abyss."[50] In this model, healing does not have a linear directionality but is, instead, situated in this middle place of embodied and enduring witness. Theologically speaking, redemption is both initiated and sensed in the very location of disintegration.

From a pastoral or theological perspective, Christian formation in this realm of trauma must be approached with creative and intuitive improvisation. Rather than jumping to quick fixes, pat answers, or hurried "spiritual" destinations, pastors, therapists, artists, and others need to learn to abide in this space of disorientation and become embodied witnesses to the complexity of traumatic experience, picking up the shattered fragments of memory and reorienting the senses to reconnect the embodied person to love. As Rambo argues, "The voice from the wound makes a demand: witness death and witness the possibility of life arising from it."[51] To linger close to the wound of trauma and shame is to maintain that life is not only possible but that it arises from the very location of disintegration. This is an inherently theological assertion, one which is profoundly held in embodied life of the Incarnate One, Jesus Christ, the implication of which we want to explore.

THE EMBODIED WITNESS OF JESUS CHRIST

Because Jesus Christ lived close to the wound of humanity, even to the point of death, he has become an embodied witness of moving through betrayal, the trauma of the cross, death, and back into resurrected life. Jesus not only reveals something of how God's love lingers in the body of those who are traumatized but reveals what it means to be a human being fully alive even as life and death intertwine. To investigate the implications of this, we will now turn to explore the theological ramifications of Jesus' embodied witness to both life and death.

50. Rambo, *Spirit and Trauma*, 113.
51. Rambo, *Spirit and Trauma*, 34.

To explore the embodied witness of Jesus is to first ask if the full humanity of Jesus is of any consequence to the Christian faith. Or if God takes the material world seriously enough for Jesus to become truly and fully human. The answer to these questions has the capacity to shift our perception of how to live out the Christian faith and how to interpret scripture. This is in many ways to start with the "who" of Jesus rather than the "how" or the "what."

As an example of this, Dietrich Bonhoeffer, in his collection of lectures *Christ the Center*, admonishes his students to consider Jesus Christ to be not only the center of one's theology but the center of the university, that is of all scholarship.[52] Then, if Jesus is the center, the first question should be about *who* he is, not *how* we are saved or reconciled or *what* faith is. For Bonhoeffer, "Only if I know who does the work can I have access to the work of Christ."[53] In this mode, to ask about the materiality of the body of Jesus is to ask the question of who this person is rather than ask how God could come to the world in a physical body. He then identifies Christ as the "Counter-Logos" to the "human logos." Bonhoeffer advocates encounter with this Jesus, an encounter that transforms. As he maintains, "When the Counter-Logos appears in history, no longer as an idea, but as 'Word' become flesh, there is no longer any possibility of assimilating him into the existing order of the human logos."[54] We are to be conformed to the Counter-Logos, rather than creating a Jesus in our own image. To use a musical metaphor, the "'Word' become flesh" has come to *re-tune* the universe so that the diversity of persons and things can play together in symphonic harmony. All of creation groans and longs for this harmonic unity to sound (Rom 8:19–23). I take this to mean that Jesus, as the Counter-Logos, takes on all of humanity to heal, transform, and liberate flesh that has become bound by harm, shame, suffering, and trauma. We can use the words "evil" and "sin" here instead, but we come to the same implications.[55] To encounter the *who* of Jesus is to be reconciled and re-formed to/by this Logos.

To borrow from some of the language above, in this way of thinking we are saved from our "disoriented selves" toward transformation and health, to a re-orientation within the love and grace of God. Theologian Kathryn Tanner compares this disorientation of the human condition

52. For the introduction of this idea, see Bonhoeffer, *Christ the Center*, 28–37.

53. Bonhoeffer, *Christ the Center*, 38.

54. Bonhoeffer, *Christ the Center*, 30.

55. See McFadyen, *Bound to Sin*.

to the aftereffects of an earthquake.[56] Sin and evil do not have just individualistic impacts; they are more like fallen stones, walls, and buildings that impact both individuals and whole societies. We are all found under the rubble. To be "saved" and "reconciled," we have to be pulled from the wreckage and then put back together. Our "memory" of God's love and grace is disordered. Healing then is an opening of human hearts and minds to God's Logos of love and grace. This process of reconciling, or re-tuning the world, is a complicated, long, and often chaotic undertaking.

To push Tanner's metaphor, Jesus becomes *in-carne*—in the flesh—to not only be with us in the rubble—in our broken existence—but to find new ways to pull us from the wreckage of our shame and unintegrated traumas so that we might know what it means to live in the light. Early Christian images of Jesus as the great physician resonate here; since solidarity under the rubble brings no ultimate relief, Jesus our physician can find us deep in the debris, dig us out, bring us to safety, and then attend to our particular wounds. Though suffering remains, God is liberating and healing in the midst of all that feels overwhelming and entrenched. Hope, then, is not just "pie in the sky" deception but a deep and abiding witness to God's enduring love and presence.

This brings us back to van der Kolk's words that healing happens "after no body becomes some body."[57] When persons are broken and traumatized they lose touch with their humanity and of their bodily senses. To find their sense of self they have to move from this feeling of existing as "no body" to becoming "some body" once more. If Christ is the great physician, then van der Kolk's idea connects significantly with our understanding of God's self-emptying—*kenotic*—embodied love so beautifully described in Paul's articulation of the Christic hymn found in Philippians 2. This early creedal song names Jesus as the one who is the ultimate *Some body* whose identity is deeply embedded as God (Phil 2:6), revealing a God who does not grasp after power because his power is revealed through a subversive embrace of vulnerability.[58] In this embrace of vulnerability, Jesus becomes the ultimate

---

56. Tanner, *Christ the Key*, 69.

57. van der Kolk, *Body Keeps the Score*, 249.

58. See Coakley, "*Kenosis* and Subversion." Primary for Coakley is the holding together of the vulnerability of human life with the power of divinity, that in Christ we have a category in which to talk about the shape of the relationship between humanity and divinity. Thus, Jesus reveals a God who establishes and maintains power through vulnerability. When I say that God is vulnerable, I mean that God, in the very act of creation, does not impose a coercive and absolute power over the creation. Instead, there

no body by taking the form of a servant (Phil 2:7), even to the point of death on the cross. In this creedal song, the enfleshed Jesus takes on all human experience and trauma and becomes one who is betrayed and crushed by those he came to love. Yet in his solidarity with humanity he is not overcome but is able to raise up all of humanity as he is raised from death into life. Thus, in his becoming no body he is revealed to be *the* Some body who can restore humanity to its embodied and reordered self.

Jesus' status as a no body traverses the depth of any trauma.[59] His body gets into the muck and mire of human experience with an interwovenness that is difficult to articulate and has too rarely been explored in systematic theology. By pushing into this Christological "withness," we follow Gregory of Nazianzus's idea that we find our redemption in our unity with the body and life of Jesus because Jesus is the "leaven in the lump"—or the yeast in the bread—raising and hallowing all of humanity through his own rising from the dead. This resonates with another of Gregory's ideas, "For that which He has not assumed He has not healed; but that which is united to His Godhead is also saved."[60] These ideas connect because both claim the necessity of the full humanity of Jesus, that his act of emptying his divinity held a crucial paradox of his being. He would always be God because by nature he is God and, in this identity, can remain fully God as he becomes fully human—two "natures" in one person.[61] He did not merely "appear" human—as in the heresy of *docetism*—by simply putting on a human costume rather than becoming human. He also did not retain a "Divine mind" in his human form—as in *Apollinarianism*, the particular heresy that Nazianzus refutes as he claims that Christ assumes all of humanity. By taking

---

is space for the created order to rebel against and reject God. God is not some monolithic tyrant who demands our love and loyalty but a God who draws near and provides what is necessary for relationship and reconciliation.

59. The argument here refers to Jesus taking on the fullness of human experience, rather than him taking on every kind of human experience or trauma for redemption to be possible. Feminist, womanist, and mujerista theologians, for example, have wondered if a male savior can save women, though to engage this important question with the depth required is beyond the scope of this short essay. For a few examples see Ruether, "Christology and Feminism"; and do Vale, "Can a Male Savior Save Women?"

60. Gregory Nazianzus, "To Cledonius the Priest Against Apollinarius," loc. 123 of 1469.

61. Jeremy Begbie uses the construction of the major chord and the distinct relationality of musical space to demonstrate how the divine and the human can exist simultaneously in one space and remain distinct with each nature retaining integrity of being. Begbie asserts that within his concept of aural space, in contrast to "visual" space, "a different way of thinking about space is possible." Begbie, "Through Music," 145.

on the whole of human life and experience, humanity is healed. In all of this, Jesus Christ reveals not only what it means to be truly human but what it means to be truly God.[62]

The ramifications of this understanding of participation in Christ move at least two directions when we think about traumatic experience. First, we participate in the body of Jesus, for he has gone before us into the darkness of traumatic human experience and death, and has not been overwhelmed or overcome by it. The one who is Lord of all of creation has made a way forward toward the possibility of life, even if we cannot see where the path leads or ends. Second, Jesus participates with humanity on the long path of traumatic disorientation in the body and mind, embracing the full scope of human bewilderment and dissociation. Pain and fragmentation require a reimagined set of terminology and language for our theology of how trauma impacts individuals and communities. The path of Jesus through human experience bears witness to the process of allowing the horrors of life enough space to be acknowledged, felt, and interwoven into human experience. This then become a place of reconciliation, life, and the presence of the Holy Spirit's "weary trickle of love"[63] as we navigate, in solidarity with Jesus, such treacherous landscapes of the soul. Through the Spirit, love remains, love lingers, and this is a great mystery of life in Christ.

CONCLUSION

As I conclude, I want to lay out a few concerns that make some of this theological inquiry precarious. First, jumping too quickly to Jesus as a blanket solution to all harm and suffering can feel slightly out of touch or even trite with regard to the ongoing and unpredictable nature of trauma in the body.

---

62. See Fee, "New Testament and Kenosis Christology," 40; and Fee, *Paul's Letter to the Philippians*, 206–8.

63. This insight into Hans Urs von Balthasar comes from Shelly Rambo. "Between death and life, the Spirit's witness can be described in two movements: tracking the undertow and sensing life. These movements of Spirit attend to suffering that remains long after an event is over. They also witness to forms of life that appear tenuous and fragile. . . . Balthasar and Speyr patterned Christian life in terms of Christ's death; to witness meant to imitate Christ in his sufferings. But they also told another story, one that did not, in the end, register in the formal theology. They narrated a witness to the between—to the disorientation of discerning divine presence in hell and to the weary trickle of love trying to make its way toward life. The shape of life, in the Spirit, is precisely this work—the work of testifying to the oozing of love into the space of life and of discerning life where it is not." Rambo, *Spirit and Trauma*, 160; referencing Balthasar, *Heart of the World*, 152.

I often think of this as the "Sunday School answer" of Christology in that the answer to most questions is "Jesus." The problem is this answer is akin to bringing a small band aid to a war zone. Something more substantial is necessary along with a more knowledgeable and nuanced approach to the healing of wounds. Second, a turn to naming Jesus's solidarity with us in our suffering can have the felt experience of being met in one's sorrow and confusion. Among my students this has often been named as a focus on Holy Saturday rather than Good Friday or Resurrection Sunday, or the necessary space for lament to be embodied, walked, and sounded. Two concerns arise here. The first is that lament, the naming of sorrow and wrong, should never be unto itself, or exist on its own. Lament should always lead us somewhere generative, even if it takes a lifetime to get there. The second is that we should not name Jesus as the one who is in full solidarity with us in death and trauma without a theology that points to how God dynamically and creatively addresses and reconciles "all the death-dealing forces and the social injustices that often trivialize the lives of many."[64] The work of God in this model of "solidarity only" can sometimes feel empowering yet ultimately impotent. Embodied witness that does not overcome death and trauma does not address a practical faith of resurrection in the most broken places of our hearts and lives.

When I think about the question from my student, so many years ago, wondering if the doctrine of the resurrection of the dead has any consequences for working with traumatized bodies today, I realize that it is the body of Jesus that holds the key. I have found new language and new tools to not only tell the story of Jesus but to retell the story of humanity, unafraid to name trauma, shame, and harm. In his physical body, Jesus embraces and takes on the fullness of human life, and through his body all bodies are being brought to life, even if the process is long and slow. As Jesus descends into the darkness of human trauma and experience, the Holy Spirit lingers to remind us that even in the utter darkness light pierces through the abyss and shows the way. This reconciling dance of Son and Spirit brings delight to the Father, as all things are reconciled through and in the body of Jesus. I am overwhelmed by the delight of God in this, rather than the theologies of anger or impatience that I have sometimes encountered. Instead, a trauma-informed Christology has to be defined by God's delight, not in the disorganized self or disordered imagination, never that, but in being shown

---

64. Dube, "Talitha Cum Hermeneutics of Liberation," 145.

and accompanied on the long and winding path home to goodness, beauty, and the possibility of being truly loved.

BIBLIOGRAPHY

Alexander, Jeffrey C., et al. *Cultural Trauma and Collective Identity*. Oakland: University of California Press, 2004.

Allender, Dan. *Healing the Wounded Heart: The Heartache of Sexual Abuse and the Hope of Transformation*. Grand Rapids: Baker, 2017.

Baldwin, Jennifer. *Trauma-Sensitive Theology: Thinking Theologically in the Era of Trauma*. Eugene, OR: Cascade, 2018.

Balthasar, Hans Urs von. *Heart of the World*. Translated by Erasmo S. Leiva. San Francisco: Ignatius, 1979.

Begbie, Jeremy. "Through Music: Sound Mix." In *Beholding the Glory: Incarnation Through the Arts*, edited by Jeremy Begbie, 138–54. Grand Rapids: Baker Academic, 2001.

Bonhoeffer, Dietrich. *Christ the Center*. Translated by Edwin H. Robertson. San Francisco: Harper San Francisco, 1978.

Caruth, Cathy. *Unclaimed Experience: Trauma, Narrative, and History*. Baltimore, MD: Johns Hopkins University Press, 1996.

Coakley, Sarah. "*Kenosis* and Subversion: On the Repression of 'Vulnerability' in Christian Feminist Writing." In *Powers and Submissions: Spirituality, Philosophy, and Gender*, 3–39. Oxford: Blackwell, 2002.

do Vale, Fellipe. "Can a Male Savior Save Women? The Metaphysics of Gender and Christ's Ability to Save." *Philosophia Christi* 21:2 (2019) 309–24.

Dube, Musa W. "Talitha Cum Hermeneutics of Liberation: Some African Women's Ways of Reading the Bible." In *The Bible and The Hermeneutics of Liberation*, edited by F. Botta and Pablo R. Andiñach, 133–45. Atlanta: Society of Biblical Literature, 2009.

Eagleman, David. "Episode 2: What Makes Me? Romanian Orphans." PBS, *The Brain with David Eagleman*, aired Oct. 21, 2015. https://youtu.be/Jg-qwWZUoe4.

Editorial. "New Study: The More You Hug Your Kids, the More Their Brains Develop." *DailyHealthPost*, May 5, 2019. https://dailyhealthpost.com/hug-baby-brain-development/?utm_source=link&fbclid=IwAR3gDaxFz2GtEX66UwNzMSh23a YsQFeoMCZy5xJ9NcujEEBSoUoiIDokNqw.

Fee, Gordon. "The New Testament and Kenosis Christology." In *Exploring Kenotic Christology: The Self-Emptying God*, edited by C. Stephen Evans, 25–44. Vancouver, BC: Regent College Publishing, 2006.

———. *Paul's Letter to the Philippians*. Grand Rapids: Eerdmans, 1995.

Fulkerson, Mary McClintock. "Creative Christian Identity: Christianity and Culture Reconsidered." In *The Gift of Theology: The Contribution of Kathryn Tanner*, edited by Rosemary P. Carbine and Hilda P. Koster, 161–73. Minneapolis: Fortress, 2015.

Gregory of Nazianzus. "To Cledonius the Priest Against Apollinarius." In *Collected Writings*, loc. 72–194 of 1469. Fig-Books.com, 2012. Kindle.

Hart, Trevor. "Lecture 1: 'Clayey Lodging': Being Human and Why Matter Matters." "Taking Flesh: Christology, Embodiment, and the Arts," New College Lectures, University of New South Wales, May 12–14, 2015. https://newcollege.unsw.edu.

au/academic-program/new-college-lectures/history-publications/taking-flesh-christology-embodiment-and-the-arts.html.

Johnson, Mark. *The Meaning of the Body: Aesthetics of Human Understanding*. Chicago: University of Chicago Press, 2007.

Levine, Peter. *Trauma and Memory*. Berkeley, CA: North Atlantic, 2015.

———. *Waking the Tiger: Healing Trauma*. Berkeley, CA: North Atlantic, 1997.

Lewis, Thomas, et al. *A General Theory of Love*. New York: Vintage, 2001.

McFadyen, Alistair. *Bound to Sin: Abuse, Holocaust, and the Christian Doctrine of Sin*. Cambridge: Cambridge University Press, 2000.

Menakem, Resmaa. *My Grandmother's Hands: Racialized Trauma and the Pathway to Mending Our Hearts and Bodies*. Las Vegas: Central Recovery, 2017.

Pattison, Stephen. *Saving Face: Enfacement, Shame, Theology*. Farnham, UK: Ashgate, 2013.

———. *Shame: Theory, Therapy, Theology*. Cambridge: Cambridge University Press, 2000.

Porges, Stephen. *The Pocket Guide to the Polyvagal Theory: The Transformative Power of Feeling Safe*. New York: Norton, 2017.

Rambo, Shelly. *Spirit and Trauma: A Theology of Remaining*. Louisville, KY: Westminster John Knox, 2010.

Ruether, Rosemary. "Christology and Feminism: Can a Male Savior Save Women?" In *Christology and Cultural Criticism*, 45–56. Eugene, OR: Wipf & Stock, 2001.

Tanner, Kathryn. *Christ the Key*. Cambridge: Cambridge University Press, 2010.

Wagner, Dee. "Polyvagal Theory in Practice." *Counseling Today*, June 27, 2016. https://ct.counseling.org/2016/06/polyvagal-theory-practice/#.

Williams, Rowan. "Negative Theology: Some Misunderstandings." *Modern Theology* 40:1 (Jan. 2024) 243–55.

———. "Saying the Unsayable: Where Silence Happens." In *The Edge of Words: God and the Habits of Language*, 156–85. London: Bloomsbury, 2014.

van der Kolk, Bessel A. *The Body Keeps the Score: Brain, Mind, and Body in the Healing of Trauma*. London: Penguin, 2014.

Conclusion

West of New Jerusalem

Preston McDaniel Hill

TIME DOES NOT HEAL all wounds. The blunt fact of trauma is that the echoes of overwhelming violence may reverberate throughout the bodies, minds, and communities of humanity until kingdom come. For survivors of trauma, this is not an entirely hopeless fact; it is an incredibly relieving balm because it recognizes with dignified witness the unspeakable depths of their pain:

> Too often we believe that when physical healing occurs, mental healing naturally follows, and that with time, all wounds heal. Such is not always the case, however. Violence often cuts so deep into our minds that surface healings cover it over and, hidden away, allow it to expand. The balmlike work of theology and of religion is to uncover and mend such wounds.[1]

In the aftermath of suffering that shatters, some of us will learn to walk again. But we may always walk with a limp. The challenge for theology and the church is to witness to this limping and to welcome it not as a threat to our identity but as a profound symbol of our common life together in brokenness, where Christ meets us. Our goal is never to exhaustively sew up all wounds: the inscrutable mystery and hope of healing comes when Christ comes again. Our goal is to hold space for Christ's healing, to embrace one another in our brokenness, to look the wound of trauma straight in the face, and to laugh with boldness and tears. For we know it is not time that

---

1. Jones, *Trauma and Grace*, 2.

heals our wounds: it is the One who comes in the fullness of time. Until New Jerusalem comes, we are wandering east of Eden.

The essays in this volume have borne witness to a unique suffering that persists, that haunts, that remains. As theologians we have attempted to delicately gather around the site of trauma, to behold the enigma of suffering that languishes and returns. We have not tried exclusively to resource recovery in trauma with the tools of theology or pastoral care (though hopefully that occurs as needed). Neither have we tried to reinterpret our Christian tradition according to an abstracted schema of trauma theory unmoored from concrete suffering. Ours has been a more delicate task: to obey the imperative of wounds that continually cry for witness. Trauma is the wound that festers and grows until it is heard. As theologians, we have attempted to think through the story of Christ with ears open to the testimony of traumatic suffering.

Witnessing to trauma presents a challenge for considering the relationship between death and life in the story of Christ. It is sometimes assumed that death and life are in an immovable opposition to one another. Traumatic suffering complicates this soteriological polarity because it plainly shows that death and life, though opposed, can often coexist in an agonizing dissonance for those who have suffered overwhelming violence. For survivors of trauma, death remains in life.

What might be involved in the task of approaching the dissonance of trauma as death-in-life? On the one hand it is obvious that the opposition between death and life can not and should not be dissolved, as if it were possible to make death and life naturally compatible with one another. If this were the case, trauma would not be suffering, but merely a unique instance of the permeation of agreeable counterparts. The stories of survivors quickly show that this is not the case. Trauma is traumatic because the dissonance between death and life is unbearable. As death inhabits life it agitates living. The two forces grate against one another. Clearly there is opposition.

On the other hand, the phenomenon of dissociation as the central pathogenic mechanism of traumatic stress impedes the assumption that death and life exist in an opposition that precludes the phenomenon of their coexistence.[2] Survivors dissociate because they perceive death invading life with overwhelming force. Dissociation is the recognition of death's haunting coexistence in the midst of life and a subsequent turning away from that

---

2. Van der Kolk and Fisler, "Dissociation."

death because it does not fit with life. The dissonance is unbearable. Dissociation is the mind's attempt to make life win out over death in the wake of the recognition that death and life have become co-incidental. Clearly there is coexistence.

The very dissonance of traumatic suffering testifies to both the agonizing opposition and tenuous intermingling of death and life in extreme stress. But the healing of trauma also testifies to the relationship between death and life. In dissociation, the more one tries to destroy memories of death's harm by turning away from them toward life, the more death will haunt life.[3] This is a tragic irony. Pressing into the opposition does not cause life to be relieved of death: it causes death to abound. Dissociating from traumatic memory agitates traumatic memory. What was once adaptive for survival is now counterproductive for recovery. Ironically, the complexity of healing calls not for an encouragement of the dissociative beating down by life against death, but an acceptance of death's presence. The healing process involves a profound acceptance of the opposition between the two, and an en-largening of one's capacity to hold the ambivalence of death-in-life. The alleviation of death-haunting-life is neither a dissolving of the opposition, nor a defeat by one of the two oppositional energies. Traumatic stress is alleviated only when it is mourned; the irony is that life pours most profoundly through the survivor when the presence of death in life is recognized and transformed as a pathway to more life than could ever be expected, a life that death did not originally intend or anticipate. Life and death are opposed, but death exists in the midst of life, and only loses its haunting force when life accepts it, in which case death becomes the means of a new kind of living. Simply put, there remains death-in-life; there can also emerge life-from-death.

The irony of death-in-life and life-from-death does not escape Christology. Indeed, it is both possible and promising for Christian theology to perceive in the figure of Christ a robust redemption that is colored with the texture of this curious dynamic between death and life. Christ redeemed humanity from the curse by becoming a curse (Gal 3:13). Christ trampled down death by submitting himself to it (Heb 2:14). It appears that God neither accepted death as natural nor avoided death as a threat, but incorporated it into the humanity he assumed in order that by his submission

---

3. Herman, *Trauma and Recovery*, 47, 89. Herman relays the irony in terms of "constriction" which designates the narrowing, numbing, and dissociative consciousness of traumatic survival which, while initially adaptive, eventually deteriorates personhood.

to it he might do much more than oppose it with his life. As Alan Lewis has said, "God is the one who knows how to die and knows that in accepting death there is life, and life only through accepting death."[4] By his willing submission to our death, Christ made death itself a site of new life, so that we may find his blessing in our darkest domains. Von Balthasar memorably called this breathtaking path into life through death *Karsamstagzauber*, or "the magic of Holy Saturday." Holy Saturday is the day of a divine reception of human death in order that, somehow, Sunday might break forth with life from and through that very death. The love of Christ poured out on the Friday cross exceeds itself into a weary trickling that finds its way through Saturday death and hell to an inexplicable and entirely unanticipated turn toward Sunday resurrection life:

> Could this be the residue of the Son's love which, poured out to the last when every vessel cracked and the old world perished, is now making a path for itself to the Father through the glooms of nought? Or, in spite of it all, is this love trickling on in impotence, unconsciously, laboriously, towards a new creation that does not yet even exist, a creation which is still to be lifted up and given shape?[5]

Shelly Rambo identifies this text from von Balthasar as emblematic of trauma's theological testimony to death persisting throughout life. Trauma, the open wound, remains as a tenuous form of death haunting life. These wounds cry for theological witness.[6] And beyond a witness to their remainder, they cry for a testimony to the possibility of life emerging within them.

This volume has attempted to extend a theological witness of trauma into soteriological relief. Trauma not only witnesses to death that persists in life: trauma witnesses to death that finds relief by its transformation in life. Death's remainder is no threat to the promise of the gospel: death is free to persist because Christ has made it possible for the death that remains to become a surviving, trickling site of new life. Christ is a basic figure in Christian theology that gives expression to a redemption that corresponds to this rich and promising relationship between death and life. As the

---

4. Lewis, *Between Cross and Resurrection*, 255. Lewis is collecting the thought of Eberhard Jüngel who states that "God's life does not exclude death but includes it. . . . Love carries death within itself . . . absolutely weak. . . . And yet it is so strong . . . in favor of life" (*God as the Mystery*, 220, 325–26).

5. Von Balthasar, *Heart of the World*, 45.

6. Rambo, *Spirit and Trauma*.

unambiguous self-disclosure of God, Jesus Christ is the divine promise that God himself has pierced into the heart of our most unspeakable suffering in order that, by his union with us in all of our overwhelming terror, he may absorb its blow, sap its force, and finally enrich us with all of his own life and peace.

However, believing this promise will never imply that we belittle the reality of suffering. If life emerges from the site of death, then the persistence of death must be acknowledged as the remaining reservoir from which life inexplicably proceeds. When life comes from (not despite) death, death must be affirmed. Paradoxically, it is often in the impossible moments of torturous affliction that grace reveals itself most pointedly. It was in the Bethlehem manger of an outcast refugee woman that Christ was born, bringing God's own self into loving union with humanity. It was in the gore of a Roman cross that Christ redeemed humanity from the bondage of the sinners and the alienation of the sinned against. It was from the heavy hand of death's tomb that Christ rose in newness of life. Time and time again, divine grace is revealed in darkness. Until New Jerusalem comes, and God is all in all, Christ reveals the love of God *not despite* our brokenness but *in and through it*. The story of Christ demonstrates a grace that is expansive enough to hold the not-yet-healed. In fact, it might just be the case that persistent wounds have the capacity bear greater witness to God's glory than any miraculous or instantaneous healing.

One of the implications of the story of Christ's redeeming person and work in the midst of traumatic suffering is that Christians can be liberated out of assuming that healing and wounding are always opposites. Survivors do not necessarily recover *from* trauma or heal *from* their wounds: they recover *for* them and heal *toward* them. For those who haven't severely suffered this may be hard concept to grasp. Trauma is inconvenient and elusive because it persists. The wound often remains, even in healing:

> When trouble takes the form of violating assault, it knocks everything off kilter, making the future a problem because the present is a problem. Painfully, this trouble is not something from which we ever fully recover. The damage it causes is real and often permanent—even if, in the short term, we find ways to manage the fallout.[7]

The permanence of suffering in our east-of-Eden world keeps us from naive optimism or sanguine tales of straightforward recovery. However, this does

---

7. Jones, *Trauma and Grace*, 165.

not mean nihilistic despair for the Christian either. Neither does it imply a masochistic thirst for an increase of death: after all, it is death's opposite, life itself, which emerges in rebellion against the death that sought to displace it. Life's emergence from death is the affirmation of death but never the approval of death. This is precisely the archetypal dynamic and once-for-all sacrifice that Christ has enacted on behalf of all humanity, a reception of our death, and in suffering it away a transformation of it into resurrection life so that all wounds now have the possibility to bear beauty and glory, not in approval of trauma harm, but in affirmation of its severity and hope in its healing.

When viewed through a cruciform matrix, death's persistence is life's potential. The recognition of this unanticipated dynamic between death and life allows one to simultaneously bear witness to the reality of complex and persistent suffering while holding hope for the promise of cosmic redemption that only the return of the crucified Christ can finally bring. Looking forward to New Jerusalem takes wounds that remain seriously, allowing for the sacred space of their stories, and thereby anticipates an unfathomable healing that could only possibly transpire when God sums up all things in himself. Until then, our life is lived east of Eden. Living east of Eden and west of New Jerusalem means looking complex suffering in the face, recognizing persistent pain, and hoping for healing by affirming these pains, not ignoring them:

> It is to be awakened—to mourn and to wonder. And to stand courageously on the promise that grace is sturdy enough to hold it all—you, and me, and every broken, trauma-ridden soul that wanders through our history. To us all, love comes . . .[8]

For many around the world, the Love that comes to the trauma of our humanity has a name and a human face: Jesus Christ, the love of God incarnate. The imperative of Christian theologians and their spiritual communities is to join Jesus as he comes to be what only he can to the trauma and terror of our world.

BIBLIOGRAPHY

Herman, Judith. *Trauma and Recovery: The Aftermath of Violence—From Domestic Abuse to Political Terror*. New York: Basic, 1992.

8. Jones, *Trauma and Grace*, 165.

Jones, Serene. *Trauma and Grace: Theology in a Ruptured World.* Louisville: Westminster John Knox, 2009.

Jüngel, Eberhard. *God as the Mystery of the World: On the Foundation of the Theology of the Crucified One in the Dispute Between Theism and Atheism.* Translated by D. L. Guder. Edinburgh: T&T Clark, 1983.

Lewis, Alan E. *Between Cross and Resurrection: A Theology of Holy Saturday.* Grand Rapids: Eerdmans, 2001.

Rambo, Shelly. *Spirit and Trauma: A Theology of Remaining.* Louisville: Westminster John Knox, 2010.

van der Kolk, Bessel, and Rita Fisler. "Dissociation and the Fragmentary Nature of Traumatic Memories: Overview and Exploratory Study." *Journal of Traumatic Stress* 8:4 (1995) 505–25.

von Balthasar, Hans Urs. *Heart of the World.* Translated by Erasmo Leiva. San Francisco: Ignatius, 1979.

www.ingramcontent.com/pod-product-compliance
Lightning Source LLC
Chambersburg PA
CBHW030824270326
41928CB00007B/885